PS   Shapiro, Adrian M.
3525
.A1772 Carson McCullers

CARSON McCULLERS

GARLAND REFERENCE LIBRARY
OF THE HUMANITIES
(VOL. 142)

CARSON McCULLERS
*A Descriptive Listing
and Annotated Bibliography of Criticism*

Adrian M. Shapiro
Jackson R. Bryer
Kathleen Field

GARLAND PUBLISHING, INC. • NEW YORK & LONDON
1980

Library of Congress Cataloging in Publication Data

Shapiro, Adrian M
  Carson McCullers: a descriptive listing and
annotated bibliography of criticism.

  (Garland reference library of the humanities ;
v. 142)
  Includes index.
  1. McCullers, Carson Smith, 1917–1967—
Bibliography. I. Bryer, Jackson R., joint author.
II. Field, Kathleen, 1951–   joint author.
Z8532.23.S48 [PS3525.A1772]   016.813'52
ISBN 0-8240-9534-0   79-7909

Printed on acid-free, 250-year-life paper
Manufactured in the United States of America

CONTENTS

Prefatory Note   vii

Part I: Works by Carson McCullers

Acknowledgments   3
Format, Terms, and Method   5
A.   Separate Publications   7
B.   Contributions to Books and Pamphlets   77
BB.   Contributions to Books and Pamphlets (Reprints)   83
C.   First Publication in Magazines and Newspapers   95
D.   Miscellanea
      1.   Adaptations of Carson McCullers' Works   105
      2.   Recordings   106
      3.   English-Language Foreign Editions of Carson
         McCullers' Works   107

Part II: Works about Carson McCullers

Acknowledgments   111
E.   Books and Sections of Books   113
F.   Periodical Articles   137
G.   Reviews of Books by Carson McCullers   179
      1.   *The Heart Is a Lonely Hunter*   181
      2.   *Reflections in a Golden Eye*   188
      3.   *The Member of the Wedding* (Novel)   194
      4.   *The Member of the Wedding* (Play)   204
      5.   *The Ballad of the Sad Café*   205
      6.   *The Square Root of Wonderful*   216
      7.   *Clock Without Hands*   218
      8.   *Sweet as a Pickle and Clean as a Pig*   233
      9.   *The Mortgaged Heart*   235

H. Reviews of Carson McCullers' Plays in
Performance 245
1. *The Member of the Wedding* 247
2. *The Square Root of Wonderful* 255
I. Dissertations 261
J. Foreign-Language Material 267

Index 277

PREFATORY NOTE

This book is the first attempt to present a full and scholarly bibliography of writings by and about Carson McCullers. It is divided into two major sections. The first, a descriptive listing of Mrs. McCullers' works, was prepared by Adrian M. Shapiro and represents the only complete gathering of all relevant publication information about the various printings and editions of her works in English. As such, it goes well beyond the previous highly selective and preliminary checklists available to scholars and students.

The second major section, an annotated bibliography of writings about Mrs. McCullers, has been compiled by Jackson R. Bryer and Kathleen Field. It supplements both the three earlier, unannotated listings in *Bulletin of Bibliography*, by Stanley Stewart (F226), Robert S. Phillips (F177), and William T. Stanley (F225), as well as the more recent annotated checklist prepared by Robert F. Kiernan for G.K. Hall's Reference Guide series (E69). It does so chiefly by adding many local newspaper pieces about Mrs. McCullers and her work—mainly reviews of her books, but also some interviews and a few news stories and editorials. These are drawn chiefly from collections at the Humanities Research Center, University of Texas, Austin; the Library and Museum of the Performing Arts at Lincoln Center, The New York Public Library; the Bradley Memorial Library, Columbus, Georgia; and the files of Houghton Mifflin, her publisher.

The inclusion of these additional newspaper items serves several purposes. Most obviously, it provides a much more complete picture of the critical attention which Mrs. McCullers and her fiction have received, especially during her lifetime. Her books were reviewed widely by local reviewers throughout the United States from the very start of her career. Unlike many modern novelists, she did not serve a long apprenticeship writing stories or publishing her early books with obscure publishers. Aside from one story, her first publication, at age 22, was *The Heart Is a Lonely Hunter*, brought out with considerable fanfare and publicity by Houghton Mifflin in the spring of 1940.

As this bibliography makes clear, Carson McCullers became a literary celebrity and *wunderkind* almost literally overnight. *Heart* received lavish praise from such established members of the literati as Richard Wright (G48), Clifton Fadiman (G9), Robert Littell (G22), and May Sarton (G37); but it also was noticed appreciatively by such important local critics as Fanny Butcher of the Chicago *Daily Tribune* (G2), Frank Daniel of the Atlanta *Journal* (G8), Lewis Gannett of the New York *Herald Tribune* (G12), Albert Goldstein of the New Orleans *Times-Picayune and States* (G15), Harry Hansen of the New York *World-Telegram* (G16), Fred G. Hyde of the Philadelphia *Inquirer* (G17), and Cara Green Russell of the Norfolk *Virginian-Pilot* (G35). Significantly, McCullers was praised by commentators from all regions of the country throughout her career; and another purpose served by the inclusion of the additional newspaper notices is to suggest that she was far more than a regional writer born in Georgia and fostered by the Southern literary establishment. As the second half of this bibliography makes clear, her works were praised on their first appearance by critics from all areas of the United States; when she died, editorials were printed in newspapers from New York to California. To be sure, she was always particularly revered and loved by Southern critics. They interviewed her, heaped praise on her fiction, and mourned her death. Predictably, the newspapers in her hometown of Columbus, Georgia, followed her activities closely long after she moved North. Some of these articles are valuable for the biographical information they contain, some just for the local regional response to her fiction which they contain.

We have also included a number of reviews of British editions of Mrs. McCullers' works. These again show the extent to which her writings were appreciated beyond the boundaries of her native land; they also document the responses of a reading public whose interests went beyond the local color appeal that her fiction had for readers in the American South. Thus, it is in the spirit of suggesting both the breadth of Mrs. McCullers' reception geographically and the wide variety of the nature of those responses—and how they vary perhaps just because of geography—that we offer these additional local newspaper items. Some are indisputably ephemeral; others present important new insights and viewpoints. All, however, are important in expanding our perceptions of the critical reception of an important modern American writer.

Part I
Works by Carson McCullers

ACKNOWLEDGMENTS

In compiling my part of this bibliography, I have enjoyed the aid of many persons, and take this opportunity to express my gratitude. I owe special thanks to J. Albert Robbins, Indiana University, under whose guidance I began this project and who never lost interest or ceased to be of help. I am also very grateful to Erika Wilson and Ellen Dunlap at the University of Texas Humanities Research Center; and to David Harris at Houghton Mifflin Co., who showed more than a normal amount of patience and complied with my many requests. The British Library Reference Division also generously assisted, as did Matthew J. Bruccoli at the University of South Carolina, who vetted an early draft.

For digging back into their files to answer my queries I thank the following people: Laurie Callahan, New Directions Publishing Co.; Fern B. Nelson, Samuel French, Inc.; Nicholas Benton, Time-Life Books; Jeanne Sheriff, Jonathan Cape, Ltd.; A.R. Beal, Heinemann Educational Books; Norman S. Berg, Berg Publishing Co.; Janet Mundy, Barrie and Jenkins, Ltd.; and Audrey Wood, formerly of the Liebling-Wood Agency.

Thanks also to Virginia Spencer Carr, whose biography of McCullers proved very helpful; to Paul Myers, Curator of the Theatre Collection at the New York Public Library, Lincoln Center; to William R. Cagle at the Lilly Library; and to Miss Floria V. Lasky, Co-Executrix of the Carson McCullers estate.

ADRIAN M. SHAPIRO
Houston, Texas
June 1980

FORMAT

Section A lists chronologically and describes all separate publications (books and plays) by McCullers. All first printings of first American editions and first English editions are described fully, and all subsequent printings of all editions are also described. The numbering code for Section A indicates the edition and printing for each entry. Thus for *Reflections in a Golden Eye*, A2.1.b indicates that it is the second book published by McCullers, and that the entry describes the first edition (1), second printing (b). No states or issues were found.

Section B lists chronologically the first appearance of McCullers material in books and pamphlets by other authors. (Subsequent appearances of these works are listed in *Supplement BB*.) Items that were previously unpublished are so designated. Only first printings of these books are described.

Section C lists chronologically the first publication in magazines and newspapers of McCullers material. Each entry is designated according to genre.

Section D includes miscellanea of three types: 1. Adaptations of McCullers' works, 2. Recordings of McCullers, 3. English-language foreign editions of McCullers' works.

TERMS AND METHODS

Edition: All the copies of a book printed from a single setting of type--including all reprintings from standing type, from plates, or by photo-offset processes.

Printing: All the copies of a book printed at one time (without removing the type or plates from the press).

Binding variants are described according to the grain patterns illustrated in Jacob Blanck, ed., *The Bibliography of American Literature* (New Haven: Yale University Press, 1955-). Color specifications are taken from the ISCC-NBS (Inter-Society Color Council--National Bureau of Standards)

Centroid Color Charts, as suggested by Tanselle.[1] No attempt
has been made to assign priority for binding variants.

Dust jackets for Section A entries have been described in
detail for whatever additional information they may provide.
Unless otherwise instructed, the reader may assume that the
spines of dust jackets or bindings are printed horizontally;
when vertically-printed spines are stipulated, they read from
top to bottom. The term *perfect binding* refers to a glued
binding such as that used on large telephone books and many
paper-covered books.

The state of the book's edges is described according to
Gaskell's definitions:

> *Cut* is used when the three edges have been cut smooth
> by a plough or guillotine.

> *Uncut* refers to leaves which have not been cut by the
> binder.

> *Unopened* should not be confused with uncut. It re-
> lates to the bolts (i.e., the folds) of the leaves
> and signifies that they are intact. To read an un-
> opened book it is necessary to slit the bolts with a
> paper knife.

> *Trimmed* refers to a book having a cut top-edge but
> with the leaves at the tail and fore-edge only lightly
> trimmed so as to remove the largest projections but
> leaving a generally rough and uneven appearance.[2]

Locations are given by the National Union Catalogue sym-
bols--with these exceptions:

AMS	Collection of Adrian M. Shapiro
BL	The British Library
HRC	Humanities Research Center, The University of Texas at Austin
Lilly	Lilly Library, Indiana University
TxHU–DC	The University of Houston Downtown Campus
TxHU–CLC	The University of Houston at Clear Lake City

---

[1]G. Thomas Tanselle, "A System of Color Identification
for Bibliographical Description," *Studies in Bibliography*, 20
(1967), 203-234.

[2]Philip Gaskell, *A New Introduction to Bibliography*
(New York: Oxford University Press, 1972), p. 237.

SECTION A

SEPARATE PUBLICATIONS

This section lists chronologically and describes all books, plays, and separate publications by McCullers. All first printings of first American editions and first English editions are described fully, and subsequent printings and editions are also described.

A1   THE HEART IS A LONELY HUNTER

A1.1.a
First American edition, first printing (1940)

The

HEART IS A

LONELY HUNTER

BY CARSON McCULLERS

1940

The Riverside Press
HOUGHTON MIFFLIN COMPANY · BOSTON

A1.1.a: 20.5 x 14 cm

```
COPYRIGHT, 1940, BY CARSON SMITH McCULLERS

ALL RIGHTS RESERVED INCLUDING THE RIGHT TO REPRODUCE
THIS BOOK OR PARTS THEREOF IN ANY FORM
```

The Riverside Press
CAMBRIDGE · MASSACHUSETTS
PRINTED IN THE U.S.A.

[i-iv] [1-3] 4-94 [95-97] 98-322 [323-326] 327-356; 180 leaves
[1-22]^8 [23]^4

Contents: p. i: title; p. ii: copyright; p. iii: 'TO | REEVES
McCULLERS | AND TO | MARGUERITE AND LAMAR SMITH'; p. iv:
blank; p. 1: 'PART I'; p. 2: blank; pp. 3-94: text; p. 95:
'PART II'; p. 96: blank; pp. 97-323: text; p. 324: blank;
p. 325: 'PART III'; p. 326: blank; pp. 327-356: text.

Typography and Paper: 15.9 (16.5) x 10.2 cm. Thirty-five
(occasionally thirty-six) lines per page. Running heads:
rectos, versos, 'THE HEART IS A LONELY HUNTER'. Wove paper.

Binding: Brown pink (33) buckram with dark flecks. Front red-
stamped: 'THE HEART | IS A | LONELY HUNTER | BY CARSON
McCULLERS'. Spine redstamped: 'THE HEART | IS A LONELY |
HUNTER | McCULLERS | HOUGHTON | MIFFLIN CO.'. White wove
endpapers of heavier stock than the text paper. Cut edges.

Dust jacket: Front and spine are printed in white script
shadowed in red against background of vertical green lines.
Front: 'The | Heart | is a | Lonely | Hunter | [red] *CARSON* |
McCULLERS'. Spine: 'The | Heart | is a | Lonely | Hunter |
[red] *McCULLERS* | [white] | *H.M. CO.*'. Back has photograph
of the author and three paragraphs about the novel. Front
flap has blurb for the novel with double rules at top and
bottom. Back flap has blurb for *Summer's Lease* by E. Arnot
Robertson, with double rules at top and bottom.

Publication: June 4, 1940. $2.50. Unknown number of copies
of the first printing. Copyright June 4, 1940. Copyright
#A140741.

Locations: Lilly, HRC, DLC

Note: The working title for this novel was "The Mute." An
outline of the work appears in A9 and B12.

The Heart is a Lonely Hunter

H.M.CO.

Carson McCullers

Author of
'THE HEART IS A LONELY
HUNTER'

*An editor, a critic, a publisher read this
novel in proof. Here is what they say:*

A strange and powerful book, standing quite apart from anything I can recall. The scene is a small Southern mill town; the central figure is a mute, a quiet, tolerant man to whom four people turn to express their individual hopes and beliefs. His very silence endows him in their eyes with a godlike quality; his human fallibilities are shut within his silence.

A perfectly magnificent piece of work; one of the best first novels I think I ever read. The author writes with an extraordinary intensity, so that those interested only in a good story will read and love it. But the implications of what she writes go way beyond a mere good story, deep into the loneliness of the individual human spirit. One thinks about it for days.

This week I have read 'The Heart is a Lonely Hunter' and I shall not recover soon. In years I have not read a book that touched me so deeply. I can't understand how a twenty-two-year-old girl can know so much of love and loneliness, and of the human need for understanding. It is a great story of friendship deeply done and felt in universal terms.

Dust jacket for A1.1.a

A1.1.b
Second printing: May 1940.

A1.1.c
Third printing: July 1940.

A1.1.d
Fourth printing: August 1940.

A1.1.e
Fifth printing: September 1941.

A1.2
First English edition (1943)

THE HEART IS A
LONELY HUNTER
By Carson McCullers

LONDON
THE CRESSET PRESS
1943

A1.2: 18.2 x 12.2 cm

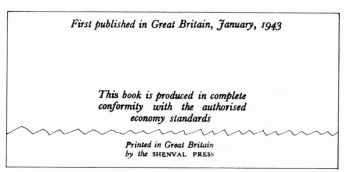

First published in Great Britain, January, 1943

This book is produced in complete
conformity with the authorised
economy standards

Printed in Great Britain
by the SHENVAL PRESS

[i-iv] [1] 2-308; 156 leaves

B-I^{16}, S-T^8, V^4, W^8

Contents: p. i: half title; p. ii: '*By the Same Author* |
REFLECTIONS IN A GOLDEN EYE'; p. iii: title; p. iv: copyright;
pp. 1-308: text.

Typography and Paper: 14.7 (15.1) x 9.7 cm. Thirty-eight
lines per page. Running heads: rectos, versos, 'THE HEART IS
A LONELY HUNTER'. Wove paper.

Binding: Medium greenish blue (173) B cloth. Front and back
covers blank. Spine goldstamped: 'THE | HEART | IS A |
LONELY | HUNTER | CARSON | McCULLERS | THE | CRESSET | PRESS'.
White wove endpapers of heavier stock than the text paper;
cut edges.

Dust jacket: Background is gray and orange. Front has multi-
colored geometric design descending from a sunburst and is
signed 'TISDALL'. Front is printed in gray, red, and blue
letters within white boxes: 'Carson McCullers | THE | HEART |
IS A | LONELY | HUNTER'. Spine is printed vertically, bottom
to top, in gray, red, blue, and white letters: 'THE HEART IS
A Carson | LONELY HUNTER McCULLERS'. Printed horizontally
in gray letters at bottom of spine: 'THE | CRESSET | PRESS'.
Flaps are white. Front flap is about the novel. Back flap
has wartime promotion for the BBC.

Publication: January 1943. 9s. 6d. Unknown number of copies.

Location: HRC

A1.3

Second American edition

The | HEART IS A | LONELY HUNTER | BY CARSON McCULLERS | THE
WORLD PUBLISHING COMPANY | CLEVELAND | [publisher's device] |
NEW YORK

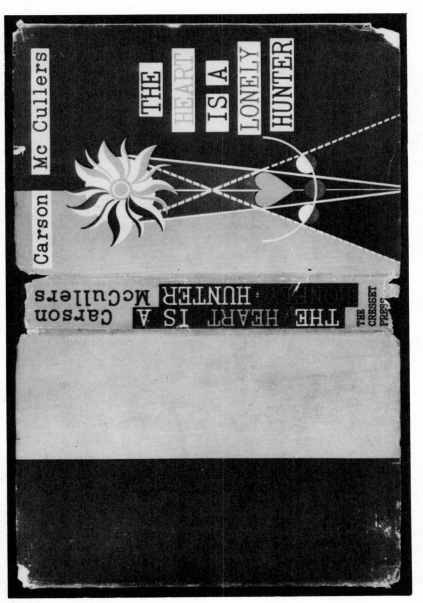

Dust jacket for A1.2

On copyright page: 'FORUM BOOKS EDITION | *First Printing May 1946*'.

Location: HRC

A1.4
Third American edition

The Heart Is A | Lonely Hunter | by Carson McCullers | [publisher's device] | PENGUIN BOOKS, INC. | NEW YORK

On copyright page: 'FIRST PENGUIN BOOKS EDITION, MAY, 1946'.

Location: HRC

A1.5
Fourth American edition

[title on facing pages] [verso] The Heart | is a | [rule composed of hash marks bent at right angles] | [publisher's device] BANTAM BOOKS | New York [recto] by Carson McCULLERS | LONELY HUNTER | [rule composed of hash marks bent at right angles]

On copyright page: 'Bantam Edition Published March, 1953'.

Location: HRC

Published as a Bantam Giant #A1091; reset in July 1961 as a Bantam Classic #SC102, in July 1964 as a Bantam Seventy-five #S2777, in October 1964 as a Bantam Ninety-five #N3431.

A1.6
Second English edition

THE HEART IS A | LONELY HUNTER | BY CARSON McCULLERS | LONDON: THE CRESSET PRESS

On copyright page: 'Reprinted in March 1953'.

Locations: HRC, MH

The third printing appears under a new publisher's imprint, Barrie & Jenkins.

A1.7
Third English edition

The | Heart is a | Lonely Hunter | by CARSON McCULLERS | [publisher's device] | LONDON 1954 | READERS UNION | THE CRESSET PRESS

On copyright page: *'This Readers Union edition was produced in 1954 for sale to its members only . . . This edition has been reset in 10 pt Pilgrim Type and printed by C. Tinling & Co Ltd at Prescot, Lancashire.'*

Location: HRC

A1.8
Fifth American edition

The Heart | Is a Lonely | Hunter | *Carson McCullers* | THE RIVERSIDE PRESS   CAMBRIDGE | HOUGHTON MIFFLIN COMPANY | BOSTON

Publication: September 15, 1961. $4.00.

Location: Houghton Mifflin

On the tenth and subsequent printings, the words "Riverside Press" were dropped from the title page and copyright page because the press ceased operation.

A1.9
Fourth English edition

The Heart is a Lonely Hunter | [rule] | CARSON McCULLERS | PENGUIN BOOKS

Publication: 1961, printed in Great Britain by C. Nicholls & Company Ltd.

Location: HRC

A2   REFLECTIONS IN A GOLDEN EYE

A2.1.a
First American edition, first printing (1941)

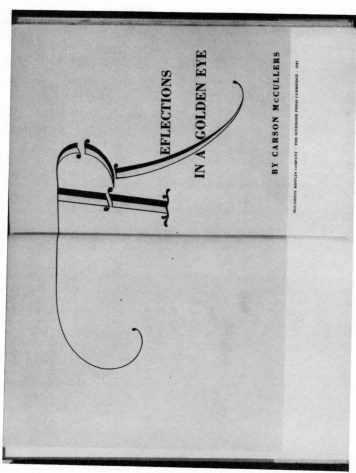

A2.1.a: 20.7 x 13.3 cm

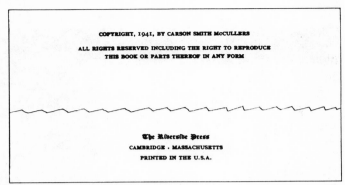

The Riverside Press
CAMBRIDGE · MASSACHUSETTS
PRINTED IN THE U.S.A.

[i-vi] 1-182 [183-186]; 96 leaves
[1]² [2-12]⁸ [13]⁶

Contents: p. i: half title; pp. ii-iii: title, on facing
pages [sweeping top serif of the letter R spills back onto
page ii; both leaves are of heavier stock than the other
leaves, and the facing title pages are overprinted in gray
yellow (90) (top 16.5 cm of each page)]; p. iv: 'Books by |
CARSON McCULLERS | THE HEART IS A LONELY HUNTER | REFLECTIONS
IN A GOLDEN EYE | [copyright]'; p. v: 'FOR | ANNEMARIE CLARAC-
SCHWARZENBACH'; p. vi: blank; pp. 1-183: text; pp. [184-186]:
blank.

Typography and Paper: 13.9 (15.1) x 8.5 cm. Twenty-five lines
per page. Running heads: rectos, versos, 'REFLECTIONS IN A
GOLDEN EYE'. Wove paper; pp. i-iv on heavy stock.

Binding: B cloth. Upper 16.5 cm of front, spine, and back is
light olive gray (112); lower portion is yellowish gray (93).
Front: '[on light olive gray background] REFLECTIONS [R is
calligraphic, drawn in yellow and shadowed in black] | IN A
GOLDEN EYE | [on yellowish gray background] BY CARSON
McCULLERS'. The serif of the R in "REFLECTIONS" extends
across spine and onto back cover. The spine is printed:
'[on light olive gray background] CARSON | McCULLERS | [rule,
composed by serif of the R from front cover] | REFLECTIONS |
IN A | GOLDEN | EYE | [on yellowish gray background] H.M. CO.'.
White wove endpapers of heavy stock. Cut edges.

Dust jacket: Black, unvarnished paper with white lettering.
Front: '*By the author of* | '*The Heart is a Lonely Hunter*' |
[a rectangle of cellophane 12 x 11.5 cm makes visible the
title printed on the front of the binding] | CARSON McCULLERS |
"... one of the most compelling, one of the most | uncanny
stories ever written in America."' Spine: 'CARSON |

By the author of
The Heart is a Lonely Hunter

REFLECTIONS

IN A GOLDEN EYE

CARSON McCULLERS

"...one of the most compelling, one of the most
uncanny stories ever written in America."

CARSON
McCULLERS

REFLECTIONS
IN A
GOLDEN
EYE

HOUGHTON
MIFFLIN CO.

The story proceeds from some
inner compulsion which is as un-
planned and as inevitable as life
itself. It is a story which *flows* in
every paragraph, flows with strange
and sinister twists and sudden
humorous flashes, but flows always
to its certain and incalculable end
...I find it utterly unlike anything
produced in our time... It is one
of the most compelling, one of the
most uncanny stories ever written
in America."

—Louis Untermeyer

Dust jacket for A2.1.a

McCULLERS | [rule] | REFLECTIONS | IN A | GOLDEN | EYE |
HOUGHTON | MIFFLIN CO.'. Back cover quotes Louis Untermeyer.
Front flap lists price. Back flap is blank.

Publication: February 14, 1941. $2.00. Unknown number of
copies of the first printing. Copyright February 14, 1941.
Copyright #A150440.

Locations: Lilly, HRC, MH, DLC

Note 1: Prior to its publication, this novella bore the working title of *Army Post*.

Note 2: The publication of *Reflections in a Golden Eye* was
preceded by its appearance in the October and November 1940
issues of *Harper's Bazaar* (C4).

Note 3: *Reflections* had an advance sale of 7,000 copies.

A2.1.b
Second printing: Same as first printing without date on title
page.

Dust jacket: Printed same as the original without the cellophane square.

Location: MH

A2.2
First English edition (1942)

REFLECTIONS
IN A GOLDEN EYE

By Carson McCullers

LONDON
CRESSET PRESS
1942

A2.2: 18.7 x 12.3 cm

> *First published May 1942*
>
> *This book is published in complete*
> *conformity with the authorized*
> *economy standards*
>
> *Printed in Great Britain*
> *by the* SHENVAL PRESS

[1-6] 7-121 [122]; 61 leaves

A-G^8, H^4(H$_4$ + I)

Contents: p. 1: half title; p. 2: blank; p. 3: title; p. 4:
copyright; p. 5: 'FOR | ANNEMARIE CLARAC-SCHWARZENBACH';
p. 6: blank; pp. 7-121: text; p. 122: blank.

Typography and Paper: 13.9 (15.1) x 8.9 cm. Thirty-three
lines per page. Running heads: rectos, versos, 'REFLECTIONS
IN A GOLDEN EYE'. Wove paper.

Binding: Red B cloth. Front and back are blank. Spine goldstamped reading vertically: 'REFLECTIONS IN A GOLDEN EYE ·
Carson McCullers · Cresset Press'. White wove endpapers; cut
edges.

Dust jacket: Front: '[white letters against red background]
REFLECTIONS | IN A GOLDEN EYE | [red letters against white
background] CARSON McCULLERS'. Spine: '[black letters against
red and white background] [reading vertically] REFLECTIONS IN
A GOLDEN EYE [five-pointed star] | CARSON McCULLERS [five-
pointed star] | [horizontally] Cresset | Press'. Back has
advertisements within a red and white frame for *The Three
Blossoms of Chang-An* and *Upon This Rock*. Front flap includes
the statement: 'This is Miss McCullers' first book to be
published in this country.' Back flap has drawing of a tower
extending from a globe, and four paragraphs promoting Radio
Free London.

Publication: May 1942. 6s. Unknown number of copies.

Locations: Lilly, HRC

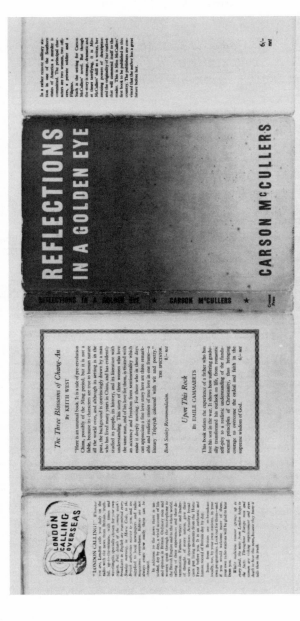

Dust jacket for A2.2

A2.3
Second American edition

[the whole within a frame, looped at each corner] Reflections
in a | Golden Eye | [bold face] CARSON McCULLERS | *Introduction
by Tennessee Williams* | THE NEW CLASSICS SERIES

On copyright page: 'THIS NEW CLASSICS SERIES EDITION IS
PUBLISHED | BY ARRANGEMENT WITH HOUGHTON MIFFLIN COM- | PANY
AND WAS FIRST RELEASED IN JANUARY, 1950 | MANUFACTURED IN THE
UNITED STATES | BY THE VAIL-BALLOU PRESS, INC., BINGHAMTON,
N.Y.'

Publication: February 18, 1950. $1.50.   5,000 copies of this
edition.

Locations: Lilly, HRC, DLC

Note: Although the copyright page notes that this edition was
first released in January 1950, the true date according to
the publisher is February 18.   This edition, augmented with
an introduction, was printed from the original plates.

A2.4
Third American edition

REFLECTIONS IN A | [hollow letters] GOLDEN EYE | [bull's-eye
device] | by Carson McCullers | [publisher's device] | BANTAM
BOOKS   New York

On copyright page: 'Bantam Edition Published September, 1950'.

Published as a Bantam Book #821; reset [October 1953?] as a
Bantam Book #1156, in March 1958 as a Bantam Book #A1763, in
February 1961 as a Bantam Classic #FC100, in July 1966 as a
Bantam Book #N5375.

Location: HRC

A2.5
Second English edition

REFLECTIONS | IN A GOLDEN EYE | By | CARSON McCULLERS |
LONDON | THE CRESSET PRESS | MCMLVIII

On copyright page: '*Reprinted April 1958*'.

Location: Houghton Mifflin

A2.6
Fourth American edition

Reflections | in a | Golden Eye | *Carson McCullers* | THE
RIVERSIDE PRESS   CAMBRIDGE | HOUGHTON MIFFLIN COMPANY | BOSTON

Publication: September 15, 1961. $3.00.

Locations: HRC, Houghton Mifflin

A3   THE MEMBER OF THE WEDDING

A3.1.a
First American edition, first printing (1946)

The

MEMBER

OF THE WEDDING

Carson McCullers

1 9 4 6

HOUGHTON MIFFLIN COMPANY BOSTON
The Riverside Press Cambridge

A3.1.a: 20.5 x 14 cm

[i–vi] [1–2] 3–55 [56–58] 59–168 [169–170] 171–195 [196–198];
102 leaves

[1–12]^8 [13]^6

Contents: p. i: half title; p. ii: '[within frame composed of
24 vertical yellow rules] BOOKS BY CARSON McCULLERS | *The
Heart Is A Lonely Hunter* | *Reflections In A Golden Eye* | *The
Member of the Wedding*'; p. iii: title; p. iv: copyright; p. v:
'*For Elizabeth Ames*'; p. vi: blank; p. 1: '*PART ONE*'; p. 2:
blank; pp. 3–55: text; p. 56: blank; p. 57: '*PART TWO*'; p. 58:
blank; pp. 59–168: text; p. 169: '*PART THREE*'; p. 170: blank;
pp. 171–195: text; pp. 196–198: blank.

Typography and Paper: 15.6 (16.2) x 9.8 cm.   Thirty-two lines
per page.   Running heads: rectos, versos, 'THE MEMBER OF THE
WEDDING'.   Wove paper.

Binding: Strong yellow (84) B cloth.   Front blackstamped:
'*The* | MEMBER | *OF THE WEDDING*'.   Spine blackstamped: '*THE* |
MEMBER | *OF THE* | WEDDING | [device of a tilted bell] |
McCullers | HOVGHTON | MIFFLIN CO.'.   Back is blank.   White
wove endpapers of heavier stock than text paper.   Top- and
bottom-edges cut; fore-edge trimmed.

Dust jacket: Front and spine have background composed of
orange, green, and olive splotches blended together.   Front

Dust jacket for A3.1.a

has stream of five-pointed stars extending from top to bottom
and is printed: 'The | Member | OF THE | Wedding | *Carson
McCullers*'. Spine is printed vertically: 'The Member of the
Wedding • *McCullers* H.M.Co.'. Back has photograph of the
author credited to Louise Dahl-Wolfe, and a paragraph on Mc-
Cullers' career. Front flap has three paragraphs about the
novella. Back flap has three paragraphs promoting *Reflections
in a Golden Eye.*

Publication: March 19, 1946. $2.50. Unknown number of copies
of the first printing. Copyright March 19, 1946. Copyright
#A2008.

Locations: Lilly, HRC, DLC

Note: Originally titled *The Bride of My Brother*, this novella
underwent almost seven different versions before the final
version was completed at the Yaddo Artists' colony in Saratoga
Springs during the summer of 1945.

A3.1.b
Second printing: March 1946. Title page is same as A3.1.a
without date.

Location: InU

A3.2
First English edition (1946)

THE

MEMBER

OF THE WEDDING

Carson McCullers

London
THE CRESSET PRESS
Mcmxlvi

A3.2: 18.6 x 12 cm

> *First published in Great Britain Mcmxlvi*
> *by the Cresset Press Ltd., 11 Fitzroy Square, London, W.1*
> *printed by the Western Printing Services Ltd., Bristol*
>
> ∿∿∿∿∿∿∿∿∿∿∿∿∿∿
>
> *This book is produced in complete conformity with the*
> *authorised economy standards*

[1-6] 7-183 [184]; 92 leaves

[1]^8, MW B - MW L^8, MW M^4

Contents: p. 1: half title; p. 2: 'By the Same Author | THE
HEART IS A LONELY HUNTER | REFLECTIONS IN A GOLDEN EYE'; p. 3:
title; p. 4: copyright; p. 5: 'FOR ELIZABETH AMES'; p. 6:
blank; pp. 7-183: text; p. 184: blank.

Typography and Paper: 14.9 (15.3) x 9.4 cm. Thirty-five
lines per page. No running heads. Wove paper.

Binding: Medium reddish orange (37) B cloth. Front goldstamped: 'THE MEMBER OF THE WEDDING'. Spine goldstamped:
'THE | MEMBER | OF THE | WEDDING | Carson | McCullers | Cresset |
Press'. Back is blank. White wove endpapers; cut edges.

Dust jacket: White and yellow letters against gray background.
Front: 'Carson Mc Cullers | The | Member | of the | Wedding'.
Spine reads vertically: 'Carson Mc Cullers the Member of the
Wedding | [horizontally] Cresset | Press'. Back has paragraph
on *The Twins* by Bernard Glemser. Front flap is about the
novella and lists price. Back flap is blank.

Publication: 1946. 7s. 6d. Unknown number of copies of the
only printing.

Location: HRC

A3.3
Second American edition

The | MEMBER | of the | WEDDING | by CARSON McCULLERS |
BANTAM BOOKS [publisher's device] New York

On copyright page: 'Bantam Edition Published November, 1950'.

Location: HRC

Carson McCullers

The Member of the Wedding

Carson McCullers *The Member of the Wedding* Cresset Press

THE TWINS

by

BERNARD GLEMSER

THIS is a story of conflict and loyalties within a tightly-knit family, of brothers and sisters who are rebellious and determined to lead their own lives, and are yet bound to each other by an unusually deep affection. The principal characters are the eldest brother, Paul, a quiet, sober young man who suddenly leaves his lovely Irish wife in tragic circumstances in order to go and live in Paris as an artist; his sister, Felice, who considered her desires and ambitions to be unique in the family, and her lover, Arturo; the strange woman, Marta, who is Paul's protector in Paris; and the twins, Lucy and Ivan, who were like a couple of mischievous puppies when they were born, but whose growth is stormy because they were born spiritually "married" to each other—the boy restless and intro-spective, dependent upon her as the very source of his life, the girl tender and light-hearted, continually forced by her long for him to sacrifice her own happiness. Drawn together by the profoundest love and understanding, it is nevertheless imperative for these two to separate from each other; and it is achieved eventually through Marta, painfully and dramatically.

9/6 net

CRESSET PRESS
11 FITZROY SQUARE, LONDON, W.1

Dust jacket for A3.2

Published as a Bantam Book #622; reset in March 1958 as a
Bantam Book #A1761; redesigned title pages in May 1962 (Bantam Classic #FC139), in March 1964 (Bantam Sixty #H2840), and
in August 1966 (Bantam Pathfinder #SP6565).

A3.4.a
Second English edition, first printing

THE MEMBER | OF THE WEDDING | By CARSON McCULLERS | LONDON |
THE CRESSET PRESS | MCMLVIII

Publication: April 1958. 9s. 6d.

Locations: HRC, Houghton Mifflin

A3.4.b
Second printing. London: Barrie & Jenkins, 1971. Offset
from the first printing with a redesigned title page.

A3.5
Third American edition

The Member | of the | Wedding | *Carson McCullers* | THE
RIVERSIDE PRESS CAMBRIDGE | HOUGHTON MIFFLIN COMPANY | BOSTON

Publication: September 15, 1961. $3.50.

Location: HRC

Note: On the spine of the binding, the publisher is spelled:
'HOVGHTON | MIFFLIN CO.'.

A3.6
Time Reading Program Special Edition (Fourth American edition)

[title on facing pages] CARSON McCULLERS | [green] The Member
of the Wedding | [black] *With a New Introduction* | *by Oliver
Evans* | *TIME Reading Program Special Edition* | [publisher's
device] | TIME INCORPORATED · NEW YORK

Publication: December 1965. 95,000 copies of this edition.

Location: HRC

A3.7
Third English edition. London: Heinemann, 1967. Not seen.

Publication: 7s. 7,600 copies of the first printing.

Note: The following information was received from the publisher
in a letter dated February 3, 1977: "... sales have increased

rapidly over the last two years, partly because the book was prescribed for an examination in South Africa. Our New Windmill Series is designed to produce very reasonably priced hardback editions which are sold (at educational discounts) to schools for class and individual reading." There were 4,980 copies of the second printing (1972), 6,000 copies of the third printing (1975), and 12,000 copies of the fourth printing (1975).

A4   THE MEMBER OF THE WEDDING, A PLAY

A4.1.a
Only edition, first printing (1951)

The
MEMBER
of the
WEDDING

A PLAY BY
CARSON McCULLERS

A NEW DIRECTIONS BOOK

A4.1.a: 20.3 x 13.5 cm

[i-xii] 1-118; 65 leaves

$[1]^{17}$ ($[1]_1$ + 1 inserted leaf), $[2-4]^{16}$

Contents: p. i: half title; p. ii: '[rule of vertical hash
marks] | By CARSON McCULLERS | The Heart Is a Lonely Hunter |
Reflections in a Golden Eye | The Member of the Wedding
(Novel) | The Ballad of the Sad Café | [rule of vertical hash
marks]'; p. iii: blank; p. iv: photograph of 'THE SETTING BY
LESTER POLAKOV FOR THE BROADWAY PRODUCTION'; p. v: title;
p. vi: copyright; p. vii: 'TO | REEVES McCULLERS'; p. viii:
cast of characters; p. ix: summary of acts; p. x: production
note and list of actors; p. xi: 'ACT ONE'; p. xii: blank;
pp. 1-118: text.

Typography and Paper: 15.5 (16.9) x 9.3 cm. Thirty-five lines
per page. Running heads: rectos, versos, act designations.
Wove paper.

Binding: Medium reddish brown (43) B cloth. Front and back
are blank. Spine brownstamped vertically: 'THE MEMBER OF THE
WEDDING'. White wove endpapers. Top- and tail-edges cut;
fore-edge lightly trimmed.

Dust jacket: Brown letters on yellow background. Front:
[calligraphic letters] 'THE MEMBER | OF THE WEDDING |

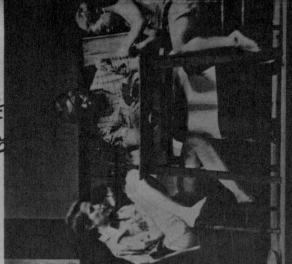

THE MEMBER OF THE WEDDING

THE MEMBER OF THE WEDDING   CARSON MC CULLERS

A PLAY BY CARSON McCULLERS

CARSON McCULLERS

(continued from front flap)

who does not stoop to the expected stencils and who sees people with her own eyes rather than through borrowed spectacles. Common speech becomes uncommon in Mrs. McCullers's usage of it. The girl Frankie, the Negro cook, and the young boy, are as vividly drawn as any characters to have come out of the contemporary theatre."

Carson McCullers was born in 1917 in Columbus, Georgia, where she spent her childhood. Later she took courses at Columbia and New York University, her first publication being a short story in Story in 1936. Her first novel, The Heart is a Lonely Hunter, appeared in 1940 and immediately won her recognition as one of the finest prose writers of her generation. Reflections in a Golden Eye (now in New Directions' New Classics Series) appeared in 1941 and the novel of The Member of The Wedding in 1946. Houghton Mifflin will soon publish an omnibus volume of all Mrs. McCullers' novels and stories, entitled The Ballad of The Sad Café.

Dust jacket for A4.1.a

[photograph of a scene from the play] | [yellow] A PLAY BY
CARSON McCULLERS'. Spine reads vertically: 'THE MEMBER OF
THE WEDDING CARSON MC CULLERS'. Back cover has photograph
of the author followed by a promotional blurb for the play
continued from the front flap, followed by a rule and a biographical paragraph about the author. Front flap identifies
the play as the 'WINNER OF THE DONALDSON AWARD AND THE | NEW
YORK DRAMA CRITICS' PRIZE FOR THE BEST | AMERICAN PLAY OF THE
1950 SEASON', and begins blurb for the play. Back flap is
about *Reflections in a Golden Eye*.

Publication: April 18, 1951. $2.75. 8,000 copies of this
printing. Copyright April 9, 1951. Copyright #DP717.

Locations: Lilly, HRC, DLC, MH

Note 1: This adaptation of McCullers' novella was begun with
Tennessee Williams in Nantucket during the summer of 1946.
A series of illnesses delayed the completion of the play, which
opened in Philadelphia for a pre-Broadway run on December 22,
1949; and at New York's Empire Theatre on January 5, 1950.

Note 2: Noted in binding variant of very deep red (14) B
cloth, with a blackstamped spine (HRC).

A4.1.b
Second printing (Fireside Theatre)

Differs from first printing in the following manner:
(1) P. ii is blank.
(2) The last two lines of p. iv are deleted ["New Directions
    Books are published ..."].
(3) Binding is gray reddish brown (46) B cloth; letters on
    spine are goldstamped.
(4) Rear flap of dust jacket does not mention New Directions
    Books; instead there is a paragraph concerning the Fire-
    side Theatre.

Locations: HRC, TxHU-DC

Note: Priority, if any, of first and second printings not
determined. Possibly published simultaneously.

A4.1.c
Third printing

Differs from first printing in the following manner:
(1) The word "Novel" on p. ii is italicized.
(2) P. iv [photograph of setting] is deleted.
(3) "BY THE COUNTRY LIFE PRESS, LONG ISLAND" is deleted from
    the copyright page.

(4) Binding is deep reddish orange (36) B cloth. Spine is
blackstamped in letters larger than those of first printing; the words "CARSON MC CULLERS" are added to the spine.
(5) All edges are trimmed.

Location: TxHU-CLC

A4.1.d
Fourth Printing

[rule of vertical hash marks] | The | MEMBER | of the |
WEDDING | A PLAY BY | CARSON McCULLERS | [publisher's device] |
A NEW DIRECTIONS PAPERBOOK | [rule of vertical hash marks]

Publication: December 3, 1963. As of February 18, 1977, 43,000
copies had been printed.

A5 THE BALLAD OF THE SAD CAFÉ: THE NOVELS AND
STORIES OF CARSON McCULLERS

A5.1.a
First American edition, first printing (1951)

The Ballad
of the
Sad Café

THE NOVELS AND STORIES OF

Carson McCullers

THE RIVERSIDE PRESS CAMBRIDGE
HOUGHTON MIFFLIN COMPANY
BOSTON
1951

A5.1.a: 20.3 x 13.6 cm

[i-vi] [1-3] 4-66 [67-69] 70-82 [83-85] 86-90 [91-93] 94-101
[102-105] 106-114 [115-117] 118-127 [128-131] 132-139 [140-
145] 146-236 [237-239] 240-465 [466-469] 470-498 [499-502]
503-514 [515-516] 517-540 [541-542] 543-567 [568-570] 571-594
[595-599] 600-651 [652-655] 656-764 [765-766] 767-791 [792-
794]; 400 leaves

[1-25]¹⁶

Contents: p. i: half title; p. ii: blank; p. iii: title; p. iv:
copyright; p. v: contents; p. vi: blank; pp. 1-791: text; pp.
792-794: blank.

Stories and novel(las): The Ballad of the Sad Café, "Wunderkind," "The Jockey," "Madame Zilensky and the King of Finland," "The Sojourner," "A Domestic Dilemma," "A Tree. A
Rock. A Cloud.," *The Heart Is a Lonely Hunter, Reflections
in a Golden Eye, The Member of the Wedding.*

Typography and Paper: The Heart Is a Lonely Hunter: 15.9
(16.5) x 10.2 cm; thirty-five lines per page. *The Member of
the Wedding*: 15.6 (16.2) x 9.8 cm; thirty-two lines per page.
All others: 16.5 (17.1) x 10.2 cm; thirty-six lines per page.
Running heads: rectos, versos, story titles. Wove paper.

Binding: Medium orange (53) B cloth. Front is lettered in
cover cloth within red rectangle: 'THE BALLAD | *of* | THE SAD
CAFÉ'. Spine is decorated in red and lettered in cover cloth

The Ballad of the Sad Café

The Ballad of the Sad Café

Including also:
The Heart is a Lonely Hunter
Reflections in a Golden Eye
The Member of the Wedding

Carson McCullers

Houghton Mifflin Co.

McCullers

THE HEART IS A LONELY HUNTER

"Here is a new voice speaking about new American spiritual country."
— Clifton Fadiman in the *New Yorker*

REFLECTIONS IN A GOLDEN EYE

"It is as though William Faulkner saw to the bottom of matters which merely excite him, shed his stylistic faults, and wrote it all out with Tolstoyan lucidity. . . . The novel is a masterpiece. It is as mature and finished as Henry James's *Turn of the Screw*."
— *Time*

THE MEMBER OF THE WEDDING

"The tremendous feeling of the world lost: and meaning lost: of life recovered and meaning recovered: the merciful power of the young to forget, and that be healed of fractures, is one of the realest things about this fine book."
— Francis Downing in the *Commonweal*

THE BALLAD OF THE SAD CAFÉ

"It is Carson McCullers at her best, and McCullers at her best is writing of the very first order, and on the highest levels of style, feeling, and poetic symbolism."
— James Laughlin

MRS. McCULLERS' COLLECTED WORK

"Carson McCullers has a great poet's eye and mind and senses, together with a great prose writer's sense of construction and character. She is a transcendental writer. There can be no slightest doubt of that. I have not been so excited by any books as by these for years."
— Edith Sitwell

". . . I have found in her work, such intensity and nobility of spirit as we have not had in our prose writing since Herman Melville . . . . she should be reassured by the constantly more abundant evidence that the work she has already accomplished is not eclipsed by time but further illumined."
— Tennessee Williams

within red rectangle: 'THE | BALLAD | *of the* | SAD CAFÉ |
McCULLERS | [redstamped at lower edge of spine] H.M. CO.'.
Back is blank. White wove endpapers of heavier stock than
the text paper. Cut edges.

Dust jacket: Front and spine have black background with white
lettering. The front pictures a lighted lamp in the upper
left-hand corner and is printed: '[fancy] The | Ballad | of
the | Sad Café | *Including also* | The Heart is a Lonely
Hunter • | Reflections in a Golden Eye • | The Member of the
Wedding • | *and new short stories by* | Carson McCullers'.
Spine is printed vertically: '[fancy] The | Ballad of the Sad
Café | [horizontally] McCullers | Houghton | Mifflin Co.'.
Back has six quotations about McCullers' work. Front flap
gives summary of the author's career, which continues onto
the back flap.

Publication: May 24, 1951. $5.00. Unknown number of copies
of the first printing. Copyright May 10, 1951. Copyright
#A55636.

Locations: Lilly, HRC, MH, DLC

Note 1: With the exception of "A Domestic Dilemma," all works
in this omnibus volume had been published previously.

Note 2: *The Heart Is a Lonely Hunter* and *The Member of the
Wedding* were printed from the original plates. Everything
else was reset and the whole was printed at Haddon Craftsmen
with the Book Find Club printing (see A5.1.b).

Note 3: Four binding variants have been noted. Variant #1
consists of light orange (52) BF cloth (HRC). Variant #2
consists of medium blue (182) boards with cloth spine of
medium reddish brown (43) B cloth (Houghton Mifflin). Variant
#3 has no free endpaper at the rear of the text and the last
leaf (pp. 793-794) is pasted down to back board (Lilly).
Variant #4 consists of medium yellowish green (120) B cloth
(TxHU-CLC).

A5.1.b
Second printing (Book Find Club)

Same as first printing except date is deleted from title page.

Locations: DLC, Houghton Mifflin

Note: Priority, if any, of first and second printings not
determined. Manufacturing records suggest they were published
simultaneously.

A5.1.c
Third printing (Book Find Club): May 1952

A5.1.d
Fourth printing (Book Find Club): January 1953

A5.1.e
Fifth printing (Book Find Club): April 15, 1953. 3,500 copies

A5.1.f
Sixth printing (Book Find Club): June 1954

A5.1.g
Seventh printing (Houghton Mifflin): December 10, 1958.
1,500 copies. Differs from first printing in that date has
been deleted from title page and everything following
'PRINTED IN THE U.S.A.' has been deleted from copyright
page.

Location: HRC

A5.2.a
First English edition, first printing (1952)

The Ballad | of the | Sad Café | THE SHORTER NOVELS AND
STORIES | OF | Carson McCullers | LONDON | THE CRESSET PRESS |
MCMLII

[i-vi] [1-3] 4-66 [67-69] 70-82 [83-85] 86-90 [91-93] 94-101
[102-105] 106-114 [115-117] 118-127 [128-131] 132-139 [140-
144] 145-156 [157-158] 159-182 [183-184] 185-209 [210-212]
213-236 [237-241] 242-293 [294-297] 298-406 [407-409] 410-433
[434]; 220 leaves

19.6 x 12.4 cm: A^{12} (first and third leaves only signed, A
and A* respectively), $B-O^{16}$

Contents: p. i: half title; p. ii: blank [bears BL copyright
receipt stamp 10th July 1952]; p. iii: title; p. iv: copyright
[bears copyright receipt stamp]; p. v: contents; p. vi: blank
[bears copyright receipt stamp]; pp. 1-433: text; p. 434:
blank [bears copyright receipt stamp].

    Stories and novellas: Same as A5.1.a excluding *The Heart
Is a Lonely Hunter*.

Typography and Paper: Same as A5.1.a. Offset from American
first printing.

Binding: Medium red cloth. Front and back casing blank.
Spine lettered in imitation gold: 'THE | BALLAD | OF THE | SAD
CAFÉ | CARSON | McCULLERS | [lower edge of spine] CRESSET |
PRESS'.

Publication: July 21, 1952. Unknown number of copies of the first printing. Copyright July 10, 1952.

Location: BL

Note: This edition was not seen. Information was furnished by the British Library Reference Division.

A5.2.b
Second printing: September 1952.

A5.3
Second American edition

[title on facing pages] [verso] BANTAM BOOKS • NEW YORK [publisher's device]

[recto] [horizontally] SEVEN [vertically] by | CARSON McCULLERS

On copyright page: 'Published June, 1954 | FIRST EDITION | The Stories in this volume are reprinted from THE BAL- | LAD OF THE SAD CAFÉ'.

Location: HRC

Note: This collection does not contain *The Heart Is a Lonely Hunter*, *Reflections in a Golden Eye*, or *The Member of the Wedding*. Otherwise the contents are the same as that of the first edition.

A5.4
Third American edition: *The Ballad of the Sad Café and Other Stories*. New York: Bantam Books, March 1958. Not seen.

Reprinted in May 1962 as a Bantam Classic #FC138, in June/July 1964 as a Bantam Sixty #H2833, in July 1965 as a Bantam Seventy-five #S3066, in August 1969 as a Bantam Modern Classic, in October 1970 as a Bantam Pathfinder, in November 1971 as a Bantam Book #NM4216.

A5.5
Second English edition: *The Ballad of the Sad Café: The Shorter Novels and Stories of Carson McCullers*. London: Cresset Press, 1958. 9s. 6d. Not seen. Contents same as First English edition. Second printing bears imprint of new publisher (London: Barrie & Jenkins, 1971), offset from first printing with new title page.

A5.6
Fourth American edition

Collected | Short Stories | *and the novel* | The Ballad of | the Sad Café | *Carson McCullers* | THE RIVERSIDE PRESS CAMBRIDGE | HOUGHTON MIFFLIN COMPANY | BOSTON

On copyright page: 'COPYRIGHT, 1936, 1940, 1941, 1942, 1943, 1946, | 1950, 1951, 1955'.
    Stories: "The Ballad of the Sad Café," "Wunderkind," "The Jockey," "Madame Zilensky and the King of Finland," "The Sojourner," "A Domestic Dilemma," "A Tree. A Rock. A Cloud.," "The Haunted Boy."

Publication: September 15, 1961. $3.50. Unknown number of copies.

Locations: HRC, Houghton Mifflin

Note 1: There has been much confusion regarding this edition, which has customarily been identified by the date 1955. In fact, there was no 1955 edition. This misconception probably arose because 1955--the copyright date for "The Haunted Boy," the most recent story to be included in the new collection-- is also the last date to appear on the copyright page. In 1974 when the "Pre-1956 Imprints" of the *National Union Catalog* appeared, this edition was unfortunately included, thereby perpetuating the error. The correct date for this edition is 1961.

Note 2: After the first printing of this edition, the title page was cancelled and changed to *The Ballad of the Sad Café and Collected Short Stories*. Also, the dates "1940" and "1946" were dropped from the copyright page. The writings that correspond to these dates are *The Heart Is a Lonely Hunter* and *The Member of the Wedding*. These works do not appear in the collection, but their copyright dates were erroneously included in the first printing.

Note 3: There were four printings of this edition, the last one consisting of 1,500 copies, January 18, 1973. The letterpress plates were ordered destroyed on August 13, 1976, with the notation, "when reprinted CONVERT TO OFFSET."

A5.7
Third English edition

THE | SHORTER NOVELS | AND STORIES | OF | CARSON McCULLERS | [publisher's device] | BARRIE & JENKINS | LONDON

Publication: 1972, £2.75.

Locations: Lilly, HRC

Note: The title of this edition has been shortened from that of the First English edition, although the contents remain the same.

A6   THE SQUARE ROOT OF WONDERFUL

A6.1
First American edition (1958)

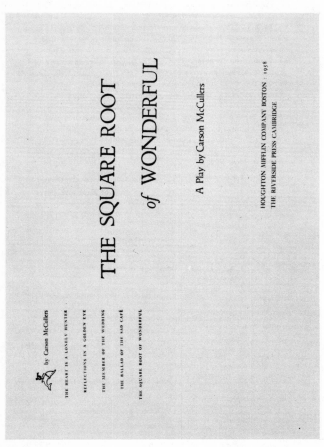

A6.1: Title on facing pages, each 21.3 x 13.9 cm

[i–vii] viii–x [xi–xiv] [1] 2–53 [54–55] 56–123 [124–125] 126–
159 [160–162]; 88 leaves

Perfect binding

Contents: p. i: half title; pp. ii–iii: title, on facing
pages, and list of other publications; p. iv: copyright; p. v:
note on first performance and cast; p. vi: blank; pp. vii–x:
'A Personal Preface' [signed 'Carson McCullers']; p. xi: cast
of characters and summary of acts; p. xii: blank; p. xiii: fly
title; p. xiv: blank; pp. 1–159: text; pp. 160–162: blank.

Typography and Paper: 15.5 (16.4) x 10.1 cm. Thirty-five
lines per page. Running heads: rectos, versos, act designations. Wove paper.

Binding: Blue gray (191) boards with gray cloth spine. Front
and back are blank. Spine is stamped: '[vertically] THE
SQUARE ROOT of WONDERFUL [vertical rule] *McCullers* [vertical
rule] HMCO'. Green laid endpapers. Cut edges; top-edge
tinted pale green.

Dust jacket: Front and spine have brown background. Front has
drawing of two lovers dressed in light blue among black bushes,

THE SQUARE ROOT OF WONDERFUL

BY CARSON McCULLERS

AUTHOR OF "THE MEMBER OF THE WEDDING"

McCULLERS • THE SQUARE ROOT OF WONDERFUL • H. H. Co.

CARSON McCULLERS

Photo by Werner H. Kuhn

Dust jacket for A6.1

and signed by [Robert] Galster. Front: '[yellow, calligraphic]
THE | SQUARE ROOT | OF | WONDERFUL | [drawing] | BY CARSON
McCULLERS | [white, roman] AUTHOR OF "THE MEMBER OF THE
WEDDING"'. Back has photograph of the author credited to
Werner H. Kuhn. The spine is printed vertically: 'McCullers •
[yellow] *THE SQUARE ROOT OF WONDERFUL* [black] • *H.M.Co.*'.
Front and back flaps are about McCullers' plays.

Publication: June 24, 1958. $3.00. Unknown number of copies
of this edition. Copyright June 2, 1958. Copyright #A342294.

Locations: Lilly, HRC, MH, DLC, Houghton Mifflin

A6.2.a
First English edition, first printing (1958)

[hollow letters] THE | SQUARE ROOT | OF WONDERFUL | [rule] |
[solid letters] A PLAY BY | CARSON McCULLERS | [rule] | London |
Cresset Press | 1958

[i-xii] [1] 2-159 [160]; 86 leaves

18.4 x 11.9 cm: [A]^8, B^8-K^8, L^6

Contents: p. i: half title; p. ii: '*By the same author*: |
THE HEART IS A LONELY HUNTER | REFLECTIONS IN A GOLDEN EYE |
THE MEMBER OF THE WEDDING | THE BALLAD OF THE SAD CAFE';
p. iii: title; p. iv: '*Copyright (©) 1958 by Carson McCullers.*
All applications for a license to perform | this play must be
made to the author's | agent, M.C.A. (England) Ltd., Story
Dept., | 130 Piccadilly, London, W.1. | No performance may
take place unless a | license has been obtained. | First
published in Great Britain | in 1958 by The Cresset Press,
11 Fitzroy | Square, London, W.1. Printed in | Great Britain
by Lowe & Brydon | (Printers) Ltd., London, N.W. 10.';
pp. v-viii: 'A Personal Preface' [signed 'Carson McCullers'];
p. ix: cast of characters and summary of acts; p. x: blank;
p. xi: fly title; p. xii: blank; pp. 1-159: text; p. 160:
blank.

Typography and Paper: 13.9 (14.3) x 9.1 cm. Thirty-five
lines per page. Running heads: rectos, versos, act designations. Wove paper.

Binding: Medium green (145) BD cloth. Front and back are
blank. Spine goldstamped: 'CARSON | McCULLERS | [vertically]
THE SQUARE ROOT OF WONDERFUL | [horizontally] CRESSET'. White
wove endpapers of different stock from the text paper. Cut
edges.

Dust jacket: Not seen.

Publication: 1958.   12s. 6d.   Unknown number of copies of the first printing.

Location: MH

A6.2.b
Second printing. London: Barrie & Jenkins, 1971.   Not seen.

A6.3.a
Second American edition, first printing

The Square Root | *of Wonderful* | A PLAY IN THREE ACTS | *by* *Carson* McCullers | [publisher's device] SAMUEL FRENCH, INC. | 25 WEST 45TH STREET   NEW YORK 36 | 7623 SUNSET BOULEVARD HOLLYWOOD 46 | LONDON   TORONTO

Publication: February 24, 1959. $1.00.   1,000 copies of the first printing.

Location: HRC

A6.3.b
Second printing. July 25, 1969. $2.00.   500 copies.   This printing may be distinguished from the first printing by an examination of the paper wrappers.   The front cover of the first printing lists the price, and the back cover has advertisements for *Janus* and *The Desk Set*.   The front cover of the second printing does not list the price, and its back cover has advertisements for *Poor Bitos* and *In White America*.

Location: AMS

A6.4
Third American edition

THE SQUARE ROOT | of WONDERFUL | A Play by Carson McCullers | NORMAN S. BERG, PUBLISHER | "SELLANRAA," DUNWOODY, GEORGIA | 1971

Publication: September 1971. $6.00.   1,000 copies.

Locations: InU, Houghton Mifflin

Note: Offset from first edition; advertised in *Books in Print* as the "library binding," although it is a handsome edition.

A7   CLOCK WITHOUT HANDS

A7.1.a
First American edition, first printing (1961)

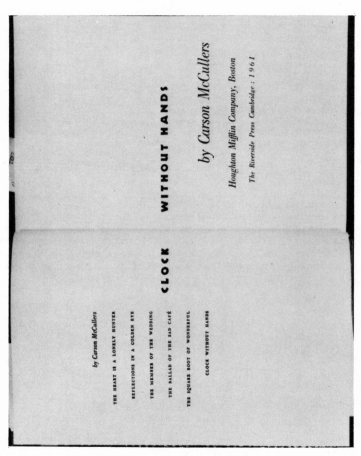

A7.1.a: 20.6 x 13.8 cm   Title on facing pages

[i-x] [1] 2-241 [242-246]; 128 leaves
$[1-8]^{16}$

Contents: pp. i-ii: blank; p. iii: half title; p. iv-v: title, on facing pages; p. vi: copyright; p. vii: '*for Mary E. Mercer, M.D.*'; p. viii: blank; p. ix: fly title; p. x: blank; pp. 1-241: text; pp. 242-246: blank.

Typography and Paper: 15.2 (15.8) x 10.2 cm. Thirty-three lines per page. Running heads: rectos, versos, 'CLOCK WITH-OUT HANDS'. Wove paper.

Binding: Deep reddish orange (36) B cloth. Front goldstamped within black circle: 'Clock | WITHOUT | Hands'. Back is blank. Spine goldstamped vertically: 'Clock WITHOUT Hands HOUGHTON MIFFLIN CO. | Carson McCullers'. Light olive brown endpapers. Trimmed edges; top-edge tinted yellow.

Dust jacket: Unvarnished black paper with dark gray yellow lettering. Front cover has circle cut out, and below is printed: 'A | NOVEL | BY Carson | McCullers'. Spine is printed in manner identical to that of binding. Back has photograph of McCullers credited to Louise Dahl-Wolfe; under-neath is printed "Carson McCullers." Flaps are about the novel and McCullers' career. Rear flap includes four passages about the author, beginning with Tennessee Williams and ending with V.S. Pritchett.

Publication: September 18, 1961. $4.00. 10,000 copies of
the first printing. Copyright June 12, 1961. Copyright
#A507644.

Locations: Lilly, HRC, MH, DLC, Houghton Mifflin

Note: The printing date for the sheets that made up this
printing was July 21, 1961.

A7.1.b
Second printing: September 7, 1961. 10,000 copies.

On copyright page: 'SECOND PRINTING'.

Locations: InU, HRC

A7.1.c
Third printing: September 13, 1961. 10,000 copies.

On copyright page: 'THIRD PRINTING'.

Location: InU

A7.1.d
Fourth printing: November 9, 1967. 1,300 copies from sheets
on hand.

On copyright page: 'FOURTH PRINTING'.

Locations: MBU, Houghton Mifflin

Note: Text and dies moved from Riverside Press to Wolff on
July 20, 1971. Voted out of print on November 15, 1971. All
components ordered destroyed on May 9, 1975.

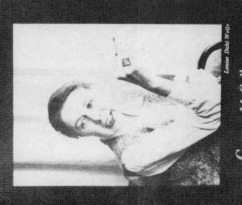

Clock without Hands Carson McCullers

HOUGHTON MIFFLIN CO.

Clock without Hands

A Novel by Carson McCullers

Carson McCullers

Louise Dahl-Wolfe

A7.2.a
Only English edition, first printing (1961)

CARSON McCULLERS

CLOCK WITHOUT HANDS

LONDON
THE CRESSET PRESS
1961

A7.2.a: 18.4 x 12 cm

> © 1961 by Carson McCullers
> Published in Great Britain by The Cresset Press
> 11 Fitzroy Square, London, W1
> First published in Great Britain in 1961
>
> Printed in Great Britain by the
> Shenval Press, London, Hertford and Harlow

[i-viii] 1-262 [263-264]; 136 leaves

[A]^{16}, B-F^{16}, G^{8}, H-I^{16}

Contents: pp. i-ii: blank; p. iii: half title; p. iv: 'BY THE
SAME AUTHOR: | Reflections in a Golden Eye | The Heart is a
Lonely Hunter | The Member of the Wedding | The Ballad of the
Sad Café | The Square Root of Wonderful (Play)'; p. v: title;
p. vi: copyright; p. vii: 'For | Mary E. Mercer, M.D.';
p. viii: blank; pp. 1-262: text; pp. 263-264: blank.

Typography and Paper: 14.1 (14.7) x 8.9 cm. Thirty-one lines
per page. No running heads. Laid paper.

Binding: Medium blue (182) BF cloth. Front and back are blank.
Spine is goldstamped: '[rule] | CLOCK | WITHOUT | HANDS |
CARSON | McCULLERS | [rule] | CRESSET'. White wove endpapers;
cut edges.

Dust jacket: White background. Front is printed with the
author's name in calligraphic letters of brown, red, and blue;
and the book title in black roman letters: CLOCK
'Carson | Mc WITHOUT | Cullers'.
HANDS

Back is printed with the author's name in same fashion, with
'ALSO BY' and book titles in black roman letters:

THE MEMBER OF THE WEDDING
'ALSO BY | Carson | Mc REFLECTIONS IN A GOLDEN EYE | Cullers'.
THE HEART IS A LONELY HUNTER
THE BALLAD OF THE SAD CAFÉ

Spine is printed in red, brown, and blue calligraphic letters:
'CARSON | Mc | CULLERS | Clock | without | Hands | CRESSET |
PRESS'. Front flap is about the novel and credits jacket
design to Hans Tisdall. Back flap is about McCullers (quotations from Graham Greene and V.S. Pritchett).

Publication: October 16, 1961.   16s. net.   Unknown number of copies of the first printing.

Locations: Lilly, HRC

A7.2.b
Second printing. London: Barrie & Jenkins, 1971.   Not seen. Offset from first printing with a new title page.

A7.3
Second American edition

CLOCK | WITHOUT | HANDS | [rule] CARSON McCULLERS | [Bantam Books publisher's device]

Originally published January 1963 as a Bantam Seventy-five #S2492; reprinted October 1967 as a Bantam Book #N3432.

Dust jacket for A7.2.a

A8   SWEET AS A PICKLE AND CLEAN AS A PIG

A8.1
Only American edition (1964)

A8.1: 20.6 x 13.5 cm

For Emily Altman and Dara Altman and Tony Lantz

[1-2] 3-31 [32]; 16 leaves

[1]^{16}

Contents: p. 1: title; p. 2: copyright; pp. 3-31: text; p. 32: blank.

Poems: "Sweet as a Pickle and Clean as a Pig," "How High is the Sky?," "I Sometimes Wonder," "Wednesday," "Song for a Sailor," "October Fair," "Trick or Treat," "Giraffe," "The Golden Egg Gobbler," "Olden Times," "Sport Williams," "Christmas Eve Rhyme," "Pandora's Box," "Slumber Party," "Favorite Eats," "The Unseen," "One World," "Astronaut," "Lands Afar," "A Rat and a Rainbow," "I am Old and Can Remember," "Kroochey, Kazoochey, Kaloochie, Kazeen."

Typography and Paper: 16.2 (17.5) x 9.7 (11.2) cm. Twenty-seven lines per page. No running heads. Wove paper.

Binding: Medium reddish orange (37) B cloth. Front has drawing from title page, greenstamped and measuring 7.1 x 9.5 cm. Back is blank. Spine is greenstamped vertically: '*Sweet as a Pickle and Clean as a Pig* McCULLERS HMCo'. Green wove pastedown and wrap around free endpapers; cut edges.

Dust jacket: Olive, red, and pink against white background. Front is divided into three rectangles. Upper rectangle contains drawing of a pickle. In center rectangle: '[black] CARSON McCULLERS | [white] *Sweet as a Pickle* | *and Clean as a Pig* | *Illustrated by Rolf Gérard*'. Lower rectangle contains drawing of a pig wearing a beret and holding a flower in its mouth. Spine is printed vertically: '[orange] *Sweet as a Pickle and Clean as a Pig* [two green fleurons] [black] *McCULLERS* [four orange fleurons] HMCo'. Back cover has drawing from title page. Front flap is about the book. Back flap has one paragraph each on the careers of McCullers and Gérard.

Publication: October 22, 1964. $2.75. 7,000 copies of the American edition, including 750 folded and gathered. Copyright September 15, 1964. Copyright #A717710.

Locations: Lilly, HRC, MBU

Note: All components ordered destroyed April 20, 1976.

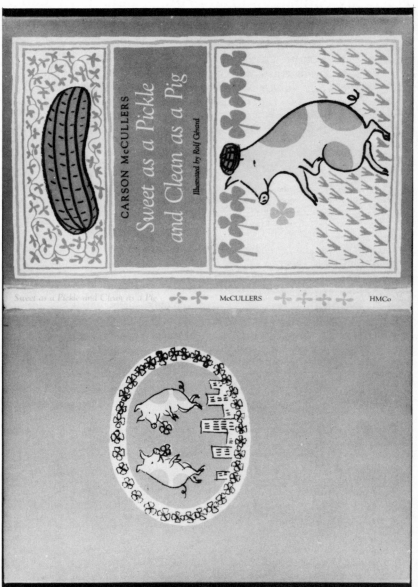

CARSON McCULLERS

*Sweet as a Pickle
and Clean as a Pig*

Illustrated by Rolf Gerard

Sweet as a Pickle and Clean as a Pig   McCULLERS   HMCo

Dust jacket for A8.1

A8.2
Only English edition (1965)

Sweet as a Pickle
and Clean as a Pig

CARSON McCULLERS

Illustrated by Rolf Gérard

JONATHAN CAPE
Thirty Bedford Square London

A8.2: 19.6 x 13.3 cm

For Emily Altman and Dara Altman and Tony Lantz

First published in Great Britain 1965
Text ©1964 by Carson McCullers

Illustrations ©1964 by Rolf Gérard

Printed in Great Britain by Fletcher & Son Ltd, Norwich
Bound by Richard Clay (The Chaucer Press) Ltd, Bungay, Suffolk

Offset from the American edition with the following differences:

Typography: 15.4 (16.8) x 9.1 (10.2) cm.

Binding: Vivid red (11) BF cloth. Front and back are blank.
Spine goldstamped vertically reading from bottom to top:
'[publisher's device, which reads horizontally] SWEET AS A
PICKLE AND CLEAN AS A PIG ~ CARSON McCULLERS'. White wove
paste-down and wrap around free endpapers. Cut edges.

Dust jacket: Pig illustrations are not spotted. Spine reads
bottom to top; Cape publisher's device replaces "HMCo." Front
and back flaps are printed with slightly altered versions of
those on American edition.

Publication: October 21, 1965. 12s. 6d. 4,000 copies of the
English edition.

Locations: Lilly, HRC

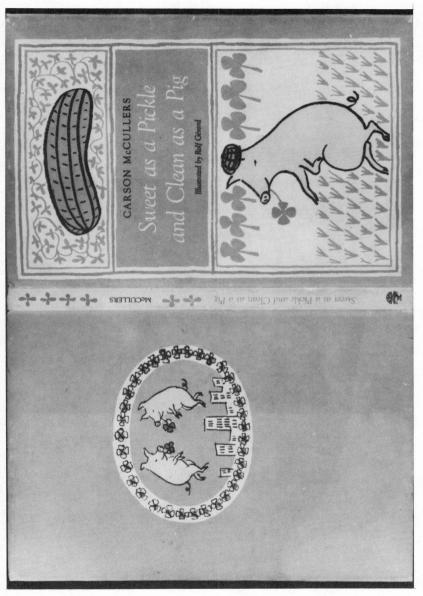

CARSON McCULLERS

Sweet as a Pickle
and Clean as a Pig

Illustrated by Rolf Gérard

Dust jacket for A8.2

A9.1
Only American edition (1971)

THE

MORTGAGED

HEART

CARSON McCULLERS

Edited by Margarita G. Smith

HOUGHTON MIFFLIN COMPANY
19 BOSTON 71

A9.1: 21.2 x 14.1 cm

Portions of this book were originally published as follows:
"The Russian Realists and Southern Literature" in *Decision*, copyright 1941 by Decision, Inc.; "The Flowering Dream" in *Esquire;* "The Haunted Boy," "How I Began To Write," "Our Heads Are Bowed," "Home for Christmas," "The Discovery of Christmas," "Who Has Seen the Wind?," "Art and Mr. Mahoney," "The Dual Angel," and "Stone Is Not Stone" in *Mademoiselle;* "A Hospital Christmas Eve" in *McCall's;* "Isak Dinesen: *Winter's Tales*" in *The New Republic;* "Correspondence" in *The New Yorker;* "Sucker" in *Saturday Evening Post;* "Isak Dinesen: In Praise of Radiance" in *Saturday Review;* "The Vision Shared" in *Theatre Arts*, copyright, 1950 by John D. MacArthur; "Loneliness — An American Malady" in *This Week*, copyright — 1949 — New York Herald-Tribune, Inc.; "Look Homeward Americans," "Night Watch Over Freedom," 'Brooklyn Is My Neighborhood," and "We Carried Our Banners — We Were Pacifists Too" in *Vogue;* "The Mortgaged Heart" and "When We Are Lost" in *Voices*, copyright 1952 by Harold Vinal. "Like That," "Instant of the Hour After," and "Breath from the Sky" appeared in *Redbook* in October 1971 as excerpts from this volume.
The outline for "The Mute" appeared in *The Ballad of Carson McCullers* by Oliver Evans, published in 1966 by Coward-McCann, copyright © 1965 by Peter Owen. The excerpt from an early, unpublished version of Tennessee Williams' Introduction to Carson McCullers' *Reflections in a Golden Eye* is published by permission of New Directions Publishing Corporation and Miss Audrey Wood, International Famous Agency, copyright © 1971 by Tennessee Williams. The editor is grateful to the estate of Sylvia Chatfield Bates for permission to reprint Miss Bates' comments. And to Random House, Inc. for permission to reprint the passage from *Out of Africa* by Isak Dinesen, copyright 1938 by Random House, Inc.

[i-vii] viii [ix] x [xi] xii-xix [xx] [1-3] 4-292 [293-300];
160 leaves

$[1-10]^{16}$

Contents: p. i: half title; p. ii: '*Books by Carson McCullers* |
The Heart Is a Lonely Hunter | Reflections in a Golden Eye |
The Member of the Wedding | The Ballad of the Sad Café | and
Collected Short Stories | The Square Root of Wonderful (*a
play*) | Clock Without Hands | Sweet as a Pickle and Clean as
a Pig | (*poetry for children*) | The Member of the Wedding
(*a play*)'; p. iii: title; p. iv: copyright; p. v: 'The dead
demand a double vision. A furthered zone, | Ghostly decision

of apportionment. For the dead can claim | The lover's senses,
the mortgaged heart. | --Carson McCullers, from "The |
Mortgaged Heart"'; p. vi: blank; pp. vii-viii: 'EDITOR'S
ACKNOWLEDGEMENTS'; pp. ix-x: 'CONTENTS'; pp. xi-xix:
'INTRODUCTION' [by Margarita G. Smith]; p. xx: blank; pp.
1-294: text; pp. 295-300: blank.

Stories: "Sucker," "Court in the West Eighties," "Poldi,"
"Breath from the Sky," "The Orphanage," "Instant of the Hour
After," "Like That," "Wunderkind," "The Aliens," "Untitled
Piece," "Author's Outline of 'The Mute' (*The Heart Is a Lonely
Hunter*)," "Correspondence," "Art and Mr. Mahoney," "The
Haunted Boy," "Who Has Seen the Wind?"

Essays and Articles: "Look Homeward Americans," "Night
Watch Over Freedom," "Brooklyn Is My Neighborhood," "We Carried
Our Banners--We Were Pacifists, Too," "Our Heads Are Bowed,"
"Home For Christmas," "A Hospital Christmas Eve," "How I
Began to Write," "The Russian Realists and Southern Litera-
ture," "Loneliness ... an American Malady," "The Vision
Shared," "Isak Dinesen: *Winter's Tales* (book review)," "Isak
Dinesen: In Praise of Radiance," "The Flowering Dream: Notes
on Writing."

Poetry: "The Mortgaged Heart," "When We Are Lost," "The
Dual Angel," "Stone Is Not Stone," "Saraband."

Typography and Paper: 15.6 (16.2) x 10.7 cm. Thirty-four
lines per page. Running heads: rectos, versos, 'THE MORTGAGED
HEART'. Wove paper.

Binding: Quarter binding of strong pink (2) unsized B cloth
on medium red (15) sized B cloth. Front goldstamped: 'THE
MORTGAGED HEART'; back cover is blank. Spine: '[goldstamped
within red rectangle] [ornament] | THE MORTGAGED HEART |
[three ornaments] | McCULLERS | [ornament] | [goldstamped
below red rectangle at lower edge of spine] HMCO'. Gray red
(19) laid endpapers of heavy stock; cut edges.

Dust jacket: Pink background with photograph of McCullers
wading in a stream on front cover. Above photograph is
printed: '[red] *Carson* | *McCullers* | [black] *The Mortgaged
Heart*'. Below photograph is printed: 'Edited by Margarita G.
Smith'. On the back is an excerpt from a *New York Times*
editorial, September 30, 1967, printed within a white frame.
Below frame is printed: 'Jacket photograph: Carson McCullers,
1938, by John Vincent Adams'. Spine is printed vertically:
'[red] *Carson*   [black] *The Mortgaged Heart* [horizontally,
        McCullers

Carson McCullers
The Mortgaged Heart

Edited by Margarita G. Smith

Carson McCullers
The Mortgaged Heart

HOUGHTON
MIFFLIN
COMPANY

A Lonely Hunter

Carson McCullers never rewrote the front pages to brand
them novels. Although she was concerned about the barbarism
of racism in her native South, her short stories and novels were
allegorical, yet crystalline. She dignified the individual, especially
life's losers.

The titles of her works — "The Heart Is a Lonely Hunter,"
"The Ballad of the Sad Café," "Clock Without Hands," "The
Member of the Wedding" — say much about her preoccupa-
tions. They do not reveal that for half her life she wrote in
physical pain as a result of illness and personal misfortune. Like
Faulkner, her stories transcended their regional Southern frame
because loneliness and frustration, love and grace are without
boundaries.

It is amazing that in this era of package deals in publishing,
when books are made, not born, Mrs. McCullers's works are
attaining universal recognition in films and plays. Her characters
are not larger than life and hardly heroic, yet they manage to
speak across generations in human and mystical tones. It is as
if the pathos of her own too-brief life could triumph, in the end,
over the countinghouses that dominate so much of the human
scene. Mrs. McCullers reflected the lonely heart with a golden
hand.

New York Times editorial, September 30, 1967
©1967 by The New York Times Company.
Reprinted by permission.

Jacket photograph: Carson McCullers, 1958, by John Vincent Adams

0491133

Dust Jacket for A9.1

red] HOUGHTON | MIFFLIN | COMPANY'. Front flap has blurb
for *The Mortgaged Heart*; back flap continues blurb and has
paragraph each about the author and the editor.

Publication: October 25, 1971. $7.95. Unknown number of
copies of the American edition. Copyright September 23,
1971. Copyright #A292076.

Locations: Lilly, HRC, MH, MBU, DLC, Houghton Mifflin.

Note: There was only one printing of this edition. The
letterpress plates and binder's dies were ordered destroyed
on August 25, 1976, with the notation: 'WHEN REPRINTING,
CONVERT TO OFFSET'.

A9.2
Only English edition (1972)

THE
MORTGAGED
HEART

CARSON McCULLERS

Edited by Margarita G. Smith

BARRIE & JENKINS
LONDON

A9.2: 17.7 x 12.7 cm

[i-vii] viii [ix] x [xi] xii-xix [xx] [1-3] 4-292 [293-300];
160 leaves

[A]^{16}, B^{32}-K^{32} (first and fifth leaves only signed, B and B*
respectively, etc.)

Contents: Same as A9.2 except: p. ii: '*Books by the same
author* | The Heart is a Lonely Hunter | Reflections in a

Carson McCullers
The Mortgaged Heart

Carson McCullers
The Mortgaged Heart

Edited by Margarita G. Smith

BARRIE & JENKINS

Dust Jacket for A9.2

Golden Eye | The Member of the Wedding | Clock without Hands';
p. iii: title; p. iv: copyright.

Typography and Paper: Same as A9.2. Offset from American
edition.

Binding: Black BF cloth. Spine goldstamped: '[vertically]
Carson McCullers | The Mortgaged Heart | [horizontally at the
base of spine] [publisher's device] | BARRIE | & | JENKINS'.
White wove endpapers of different stock from that of the text.
Cut edges.

Dust jacket: Front cover and spine are purplish blue. On
front cover: '[white] *Carson* | *McCullers* | [yellow] *The* |
Mortgaged | *Heart* | *Edited by Margarita G. Smith*'. Spine:
'[vertically] [white] *Carson McCullers* | [yellow] *The*
Mortgaged Heart | [horizontally at base of spine] [white]
[publisher's device] | BARRIE | & | JENKINS'. Back has photo-
graph of the author. Front flap has blurb for *The Mortgaged
Heart*. Back flap has list of McCullers' titles, and credits
jacket design to D.S. Ward; 1938 photograph is credited to
John Vincent Adams.

Publication: June 1972. £2.75 net. Unknown number of copies
of the English edition.

Location: HRC

CONTRIBUTIONS TO BOOKS AND PAMPHLETS

This section lists chronologically the first appearance of
McCullers material in books and pamphlets by other authors.
Items that were previously unpublished are so designated.
The first printings only of these books are described.

B1 O. HENRY MEMORIAL AWARD PRIZE STORIES
    1942
    O. HENRY MEMORIAL AWARD | PRIZE STORIES | OF | 1942 |
    [fancy rule] | SELECTED AND EDITED BY | HERSCHEL BRICKELL |
    ASSISTED BY MURIEL FULLER | [fancy rule] | [publisher's
    device] | DOUBLEDAY, DORAN AND COMPANY, INC. | Garden City
    1942 New York

    "The Jockey," pp. 231-237. See A5, C12.

B2 O. HENRY MEMORIAL AWARD PRIZE STORIES
    1944
    Twenty-Fifth Anniversary Edition | O. HENRY MEMORIAL
    AWARD | PRIZE STORIES | OF | 1943 | [fancy rule] |
    SELECTED AND EDITED BY | HERSCHEL BRICKELL | ASSISTED BY |
    MURIEL FULLER | [fancy rule] | [publisher's device] |
    DOUBLEDAY, DORAN AND COMPANY INC. | Garden City 1944
    New York

    "A Tree. A Rock. A Cloud," pp. 223-231. See A5, C16.

B3 THE BEST AMERICAN SHORT STORIES
    1944
    [red, black] THE | Best | AMERICAN | SHORT STORIES | 1944 |
    [fancy rule] | *and The Yearbook of the American Short
    Story* | [rule] *Edited by* | MARTHA FOLEY | [publisher's
    device] [broken rule] | HOUGHTON MIFFLIN COMPANY · BOSTON |
    [gothic] The Riverside Press Cambridge

    "The Ballad of the Sad Café," pp. 205-264. See A5.

B4 TAKEN AT THE FLOOD
    1946
    [ornament] Taken at the Flood | [rule] | THE HUMAN DRAMA
    AS SEEN BY | MODERN AMERICAN NOVELISTS | [rule] | Collected
    and Arranged by | ANN WATKINS | [publisher's device] |
    Harper & Brothers Publishers | [rule] | NEW YORK AND LONDON

    "The Baby-Killer" [from *The Heart Is a Lonely Hunter*],
    pp. 275-290. See A1, A5.

B5   THE BURNS MANTLE BEST PLAYS OF 1949-1950
      1950
      [rule] | THE BURNS MANTLE | BEST PLAYS OF 1949-1950 |
      AND THE | YEAR BOOK OF THE DRAMA | IN AMERICA | EDITED BY |
      JOHN CHAPMAN | *With Illustrations* | [publisher's device] |
      DODD, MEAD AND COMPANY | NEW YORK [three horizontal
      dashes] 1950 | [rule]

      The Member of the Wedding, pp. 91-117. Condensed version.
      See A4, B7, C21. Previously unpublished.

B6   PRIZE STORIES OF 1951
      1951
      Prize | Stories | of | 1951 | [publisher's device] The |
      O. Henry Awards | SELECTED AND EDITED BY HERSCHEL BRICKELL |
      [DOUBLEDAY & COMPANY, INC., GARDEN CITY, NEW YORK, 1951]

      "The Sojourner," pp. 192-201. See A5, C31.

B7   BEST AMERICAN PLAYS
      1952
      Best American | PLAYS | THIRD SERIES - 1945-1951 | EDITED
      WITH AN INTRODUCTION BY | JOHN GASSNER | [two theatre
      masks] | CROWN PUBLISHERS, INC. | NEW YORK

      The Member of the Wedding, pp. 173-203. See A4, B5, C21.

B8   UNDERSTANDING FICTION
      1959
      [rectangular decoration] CLEANTH BROOKS | ROBERT PENN
      WARREN | Understanding FICTION | [rectangular decoration]
      SECOND EDITION | [publisher's device] | NEW YORK |
      Appleton-Century-Crofts, Inc.

      "A Domestic Dilemma," pp. 262-270. See A5, C33.

B9   40 BEST STORIES FROM MADEMOISELLE 1935-1960
      1960
      40 best stories from Mademoiselle 1935-1960 | EDITED BY
      CYRILLY ABELS AND MARGARITA G. SMITH | [rule] Harper &
      Brothers, Publishers New York

      Note: The title page actually extends across two pages,
      but has been transcribed as if it were one.

      "Who Has Seen the Wind?," pp. 234-255. See A9.

B10   MODERN SHORT STORIES: THE FICTION OF EXPERIENCE
      1962
      MODERN SHORT STORIES | M. X. LESSER | Central Connecticut
      State College | JOHN N. MORRIS | Columbia University |

Mc GRAW-HILL BOOK COMPANY, INC. | New York   San Francisco
Toronto   London 1962

"Wunderkind," pp. 230-241.   See A5, A9, C3.

B11   THE BEST AMERICAN SHORT STORIES
1964
[black, <u>red</u>] THE | <u>BEST</u> | AMERICAN SHORT STORIES | <u>1964</u> |
and the Yearbook of the American Short Story | EDITED BY |
MARTHA FOLEY and DAVID BURNETT | HOUGHTON MIFFLIN COMPANY |
[gothic] The Riverside Press   Cambridge | [roman] 1964

"Sucker," pp. 217-226.   See A9, C48.

B12   CARSON McCULLERS
1965
Carson McCullers | HER LIFE AND WORK | * * * | Oliver
Evans | [publisher's device] | PETER OWEN • LONDON

"Author's Outline of *The Mute*" [*The Heart Is a Lonely
Hunter*], pp. 195-215.   Also contains previously unpublished material from letters, manuscripts, and notes.

American edition: *The Ballad of Carson McCullers*.   New
York: Coward McCann, 1966.

B13   THE SHORT STORY: FICTION IN TRANSITION
1969
[rule] | THE SHORT STORY: | Fiction in Transition |
[rule] | *Edited by* | J. CHESLEY TAYLOR | WASHINGTON STATE
UNIVERSITY | Charles Scribner's Sons -- New York

"Madame Zilensky and the King of Finland," pp. 476-484.
See A4, C14.

B14   THE LONELY HUNTER
1975
The Lonely Hunter | A BIOGRAPHY | OF *Carson McCullers* |
[rule] | *By* VIRGINIA SPENCER CARR | 1975 | [rule]
DOUBLEDAY & COMPANY, INC. | GARDEN CITY, NEW YORK

Contains previously unpublished material from letters,
manuscripts, and notes.

SECTION BB

CONTRIBUTIONS TO BOOKS AND PAMPHLETS (Reprints)

This section contains McCullers material that was published subsequent to its first appearance in books and pamphlets by other authors. The entries are arranged in chronological order.

BB1   *"Vogue's" First Reader*. New York: Messner, 1942.

       Contains "Brooklyn Is My Neighborhood," pp. 70-73.

BB2   *I Wish I'd Written That: Selections Chosen by Favorite American Authors*. Ed. Eugene J. Woods. New York: McGraw-Hill, 1946.

       Contains *The Ballad of the Sad Café*, pp. 300-364.

BB3   *55 Short Stories from "The New Yorker": 1940 to 1950*. New York: Simon and Schuster, 1949.

       Contains "The Jockey," pp. 310-314.

BB4   *A Treasury of Brooklyn*. Ed. Mary Ellen and Mark Murphy and Ralph Foster Weld. New York: William Sloane, 1949.

       Contains "Brooklyn Is My Neighborhood," pp. 44-48.

BB5   *Fifty Great Short Stories*. Ed. Milton Crane. New York: Bantam, 1952.

       Contains "The Jockey," pp. 58-62.

BB6   *The Literature of the South*. Ed. Richard Croom Beatty, Floyd C. Watkins, Thomas Daniel Young, Randall Stewart. Chicago: Scott, Foresman, 1952.

       Contains excerpt from *Member*, pp. 928-943.

BB7   *A Pocket Book of Modern American Short Stories*. Ed. Philip Van Doren Stern. New York: Washington Square, 1953.

       Contains "A Tree. A Rock. A Cloud.," pp. 283-292.

BB8   *American Accent*. Ed. Elizabeth Abell. New York: Ballantine, 1954.

       Contains "A Domestic Dilemma," pp. 75-85.

K.

BB9   *Short Story Masterpieces.* Ed. Robert Penn Warren and
      Albert Erskine. New York: Dell, 1954.

      Contains "The Sojourner," pp. 336-346.

BB10 *Empire City.* Ed. Alexander Klein. New York: Rinehart,
      1955.

      Contains "Brooklyn Is My Neighborhood," pp. 157-160.

BB11 *Great Tales of City Dwellers.* Ed. Alex Austin. New
      York: Pyramid, 1955.

      Contains "A Tree. A Rock. A Cloud.," pp. 35-43.

BB12 *Best American Plays--Third Series--1945-1951.* New York:
      Crown, 1956.

      Contains *The Member of the Wedding,* pp. 175-203.

BB13 *A College Treasury.* Ed. Paul Jorgensen and Frederick B.
      Shroyer. New York: Charles Scribner's, 1956.

      Contains "The Sojourner," pp. 91-97.

BB14 *Critics' Choice: New York Drama Critics' Circle Prize
      Plays.* Ed. Jack Gaver. London: Arco, 1956.

      Contains *The Member of the Wedding,* pp. 416-445.

BB15 *Modern English Readings.* 7th Edition. Ed. Roger Sherman
      Loomis, Donald Lemen Clark, and John Harlan Middendorf.
      New York: Rinehart, 1956.

      Contains "The Jockey," pp. 679-683.

BB16 *Story and Structure.* Ed. Laurence Perrine. New York:
      Harcourt, Brace and World, 1959.

      Contains "A Domestic Dilemma," pp. 495-503.

BB17 *Famous American Plays of the 1940s.* Ed. Henry Hewes.
      New York: Dell, 1960.

      Contains *The Member of the Wedding,* pp. 371-447.

BB18 *The Scope of Fiction.* Ed. Cleanth Brooks and Robert
      Penn Warren. New York: Appleton-Century-Crofts, 1960.

      Contains "A Domestic Dilemma," pp. 212-220.

BB19 *The Short Story and the Reader.* Ed. Robert Stanton.
      New York: Holt, Rinehart and Winston, 1960.

      Contains "A Tree. A Rock. A Cloud.," pp. 216-223.

BB20 *Studies in the Short Story.* 2nd Edition. Ed. Adrian H.
      Jaffe and Virgil Scott. New York: Holt, Rinehart and
      Winston, 1960.

      Contains "A Tree. A Rock. A Cloud.," pp. 74-82.

BB21 *American Dramatic Literature: Ten Modern Plays in
      Historical Perspective.* Ed. Jordan Y. Miller. New
      York: McGraw-Hill, 1961.

      Contains *The Member of the Wedding*, pp. 429-461.

BB22 *Stories of Modern America.* Ed. Herbert Gold and David L.
      Stevenson. New York: St. Martin's Press, 1961.

      Contains "A Domestic Dilemma," pp. 194-203.

BB23 *Firsts of the Famous.* Ed. Whit Burnett. New York:
      Ballantine, 1962.

      Contains "Wunderkind," pp. 138-150.

BB24 *When Women Look at Men.* Ed. John A. Kouwenhoven and
      Janice Farrar Thaddeus. New York: Harper and Row, 1963.

      Contains "A Tree. A Rock. A Cloud.," pp. 325-332.

BB25 *The Modern Talent: An Anthology of Short Stories.* Ed.
      John Edward Hardy. New York: Holt, Rinehart and Winston,
      1964.

      Contains "The Sojourner," pp. 426-436.

BB26 *Reading Literature: Stories, Plays and Poems.* Ed. Joseph
      Satin. Boston: Houghton Mifflin, 1964.

      Contains "A Tree. A Rock. A Cloud.," pp. 491-498.

BB27 *Reading Prose Fiction.* Ed. Joseph Satin. Boston:
      Houghton Mifflin, 1964.

      Contains "A Tree. A Rock. A Cloud.," pp. 491-498.

BB28 *Best Modern Short Stories Selected from the "Saturday
      Evening Post."* New York: Curtis, 1965.

      Contains "Sucker," pp. 128-137.

BB29 *Fifty Great American Short Stories.* Ed. Milton Crane.
      New York: Bantam, 1965.

      Contains "Madame Zilensky and the King of Finland,"
      pp. 479-487.

BB30   *Great Short Stories of the World*.   Ed. Whit and Hallie
       Burnett.   London: Souvenir Press, 1965.

       Contains "Wunderkind," pp. 337-347.

BB31   *Prize Stories 1965: The O. Henry Awards*.   Ed. Richard
       Poirier and William Abrahams.   Garden City, N.Y.:
       Doubleday, 1965.

       Contains "Sucker," pp. 189-197.

BB32   *Short Story: A Thematic Anthology*.   Ed. Dorothy Parker
       and Frederick B. Shroyer.   New York: Charles Scribner's,
       1965.

       Contains "The Jockey," pp. 144-148.

BB33   *Story Jubilee*.   Ed. Whit and Hallie Burnett.   Garden
       City, N.Y.: Doubleday, 1965.

       Contains "Wunderkind," pp. 337-347.

BB34   *Studies in Fiction*.   Ed. Blaze O. Bonazza and Emil Roy.
       New York: Harper and Row, 1965.

       Contains "The Sojourner," pp. 189-197.

BB35   *Ten Modern American Short Stories*.   Ed. David A. Sohn.
       New York: Bantam, 1965.

       Contains "Sucker," pp. 88-98.

BB36   *The Burns Mantle Best Plays of 1949-50 and the Year
       Book of the Drama in America*.   Ed. John Chapman.   New
       York: Dodd, Mead, 1966.

       Contains *The Member of the Wedding*, pp. 91-117.

BB37   *The Sense of Fiction*.   Ed. Robert L. Welker and Herschel
       Gower.   Englewood Cliffs, N.J.: Prentice-Hall, 1966.

       Contains "A Tree. A Rock. A Cloud.," pp. 365-371.

BB38   *The Art of Fiction*.   Ed. R.F. Dietrich and Roger H.
       Sundell.   New York: Holt, Rinehart and Winston, 1967.

       Contains "A Tree. A Rock. A Cloud.," pp. 422-429.

BB39   *The Discovery of Fiction*.   Ed. Thomas E. Sanders.
       Glenview, Ill.: Scott, Foresman, 1967.

       Contains "A Tree. A Rock. A Cloud.," pp. 316-323.

BB40   *Eight Short Novels.*   Ed. Dean S. Flower.   Greenwich,
       Conn.: Fawcett World, 1967.

       Contains *The Ballad of the Sad Café*, pp. 455–511.

BB41   *The Human Commitment: An Anthology of Contemporary
       Short Fiction.*   Ed. Don Gold.   Philadelphia: Chilton,
       1967.

       Contains "Sucker," pp. 219–230.

BB42   *Patterns of Literature.*   Ed. Julian L. Maline and
       James Berkley.   Syracuse, N.Y.: L.W. Singer, 1967.

       Contains *The Member of the Wedding* (play), pp. 336–401.

BB43   *Point of Departure.*   Ed. Robert Gold.   New York: Dell,
       1967.

       Contains "Sucker," pp. 143–153.

BB44   *College English: The First Year.*   5th Edition.   Ed.
       Alton C. Morris, et al.   New York: Harcourt, Brace and
       World, 1968.

       Contains "A Tree. A Rock. A Cloud.," pp. 415–420.

BB45   *Imaginative Literature: Fiction, Drama, Poetry.*   Ed.
       Alton C. Morris, et al.   New York: Harcourt, Brace and
       World, 1968.

       Contains "A Tree. A Rock. A Cloud.," pp. 55–60.

BB46   *The Literature of the South.*   Revised Edition.   Ed.
       Thomas Daniel Young, Floyd Watkins, and Richard Croom
       Beatty.   Glenview, Ill.: Scott, Foresman, 1968.

       Contains "A Tree. A Rock. A Cloud.," pp. 908–914, and
       "Wunderkind," pp. 900–908.

BB47   *The Modern Tradition.*   Ed. Daniel F. Howard.   Boston:
       Little, Brown, 1968.

       Contains "The Jockey," pp. 446–450, and "The Sojourner,"
       pp. 438–445.

BB48   *Fiction: Form and Experience.*   Ed. William M. Jones.
       Lexington, Mass.: D.C. Heath, 1969.

       Contains "A Tree. A Rock. A Cloud.," pp. 88–94.

BB49   *50 Best Plays of the American Theatre.*   Ed. Clive
       Barnes and John Gassner.   New York: Crown, 1969.

       Contains *The Member of the Wedding*, pp. 473–503.

BB50   *Seven Contemporary Short Novels.*   Ed. Charles Clerc and
       Louis Leiter.   Glenview, Ill.: Scott, Foresman, 1969.

       Contains *The Ballad of the Sad Café*, pp. 319–380.

BB51   *Short Stories: An Anthology.*   Ed. N. Nathan.   Indiana-
       polis: Bobbs-Merrill, 1969.

       Contains "A Domestic Dilemma," pp. 23–32.

BB52   *Fifty Years of the American Short Story from the O.
       Henry Awards 1919–1970.*   Ed. William Abrahams.   Garden
       City, N.Y.: Doubleday, 1970.

       Contains "The Jockey," pp. 485–489.

BB53   *The Impact of Fiction.*   Ed. Herbert L. and Ada Lou
       Carson.   Menlo Park, Calif.: Cummings, 1970.

       Contains "The Sojourner," pp. 207–215.

BB54   *Insight & Outlook--A Collection of Short Stories.*   Ed.
       Murray Rockowitz.   New York: Globe, 1970.

       Contains "Sucker," pp. 4–16.

BB55   *The Loners: Short Stories About the Young and Alienated.*
       Ed. L.M. Schulman.   New York: Macmillan, 1970.

       Contains "A Tree. A Rock. A Cloud.," pp. 266–276.

BB56   *Impact: Short Stories for Pleasure.*   Ed. Donald L.
       Stansbury.   Englewood Cliffs, N.J.: Prentice-Hall, 1971.

       Contains "Sucker," pp. 156–166.

BB57   *Studies in the Short Story.*   Alternate Edition.   Ed.
       Virgil Scott.   New York: Holt, Rinehart and Winston,
       1971.

       Contains "The Sojourner," pp. 582–589.

BB58   *The Tunnel and the Light; Readings in Modern Fiction.*
       Comp. Robert Lambert.   Boston: Houghton Mifflin, 1971.

       Contains "A Tree. A Rock. A Cloud.," pp. 281–290.

BB59   *The World of the Short Story: Archetypes in Action.*
       Ed. Oliver Evans and Harry Finestone. New York: Alfred A.
       Knopf, 1971.

       Contains "A Tree. A Rock. A Cloud.," pp. 327-333.

BB60   *The Age of Anxiety: Modern American Stories.* Ed. C.
       Jeriel Howard and Richard F. Tracz. Boston: Allyn and
       Bacon, 1972.

       Contains "A Tree. A Rock. A Cloud.," pp. 239-245.

BB61   *Feminine Plural: Stories by Women About Growing Up.* Ed.
       Stephanie Spinner. New York: Macmillan, 1972.

       Contains "Wunderkind," pp. 1-18.

BB62   *Forms of Prose Fiction.* Ed. James L. Calderwood and
       Harold E. Toliver. Englewood Cliffs, N.J.: Prentice-
       Hall, 1972.

       Contains "A Tree. A Rock. A Cloud.," pp. 463-469.

BB63   *American Models--A Collection of Modern Stories.* Ed.
       James E. Miller, Jr., Robert Hayden, and Robert O'Neal.
       Glenview, Ill.: Scott, Foresman, 1973.

       Contains "Madame Zilensky and the King of Finland,"
       pp. 91-98.

BB64   *By and About Women.* Ed. Beth K. Schneiderman. New
       York: Harcourt Brace Jovanovich, 1973.

       Contains "Wunderkind," pp. 31-43.

BB65   *Four Models: A Rhetoric of Modern Fiction.* Ed. James M.
       Mellard. New York: Macmillan, 1973.

       Contains "The Jockey," pp. 454-457.

BB66   *Quartet: A Book of Stories, Plays, Poems, and Critical
       Essays.* 2nd Edition. Ed. Harold P. Simonson. New
       York: Harper and Row, 1973.

       Contains "A Tree. A Rock. A Cloud.," pp. 251-257.

BB67   *The Short Story Reader.* 3rd Edition. Ed. Saundra
       Gould Berkley. Indianapolis: Odyssey Press, 1973.

       Contains "A Tree. A Rock. A Cloud.," pp. 446-454.

BB68   *The Trouble Is: Stories of Social Dilemma.*   Ed. Sylvia
       Angus.   Encino, Calif.: Dickinson, 1973.

       Contains "The Sojourner," pp. 415-424.

BB69   *Studies in Short Fiction.*   2nd Edition.   Ed. Douglas A.
       Hughes.   New York: Holt, Rinehart and Winston, 1974.

       Contains *The Ballad of the Sad Café*, pp. 373-419.

BB70   *A Woman's Place.*   Ed. L.M. Schulman.   New York:
       Macmillan, 1974.

       Contains "A Domestic Dilemma," pp. 182-195.

BB71   *The First Time: Initial Sexual Experiences in Fiction.*
       Ed. Karl Broer and Charles Weingartner.   Indianapolis:
       Bobbs-Merrill, 1975.

       Contains "Picnic" excerpt from *Heart*, pp. 223-231.

BB72   *Four Elements: A Creative Approach to the Short Story.*
       Ed. Anna Sherrill and Paula Robertson-Rose.   New
       York: Holt, Rinehart and Winston, 1975.

       Contains "A Tree. A Rock. A Cloud.," pp. 132-139.

BB73   *Quest for Meaning: Modern Short Stories.*   Ed. Glenn O.
       Carey.   New York: D. MacKay, 1975.

       Contains "A Tree. A Rock. A Cloud.," pp. 170-178.

BB74   *29 Short Stories: An Introductory Anthology.*   Ed.
       Michael Timko.   New York: Alfred A. Knopf, 1975.

       Contains "The Sojourner," pp. 343-350.

BB75   *200 Years of Great American Short Stories.*   Ed. Martha
       Foley.   Boston: Houghton Mifflin, 1975.

       Contains *The Ballad of the Sad Café*, pp. 650-700.

BB76   *Women and Fiction.*   Ed. Susan Cahill.   New York: New
       American Library, 1975.

       Contains "Wunderkind," pp. 182-194.

BB77   *The Short Story: An Introduction.*   Ed. W. Stone et al.
       New York: McGraw-Hill, 1976.

       Contains "A Tree. A Rock. A Cloud.," pp. 431-437.

BB78 *Twelve Short Novels.* Ed. Ray J. Sherer. New York: Holt, Rinehart and Winston, 1976.

Contains *The Ballad of the Sad Café*, pp. 486-533.

BB79 *Fiction: The Narrative Art.* Ed. James W. Kirkland and Paul W. Dowell. Englewood Cliffs, N.J.: Prentice-Hall, 1977.

Contains "The Sojourner," pp. 401-406.

BB80 *The Heath Introduction to Fiction.* Ed. John L. Clayton. Lexington, Mass.: D.C. Heath, 1977.

Contains "A Tree. A Rock. A Cloud.," pp. 558-565.

BB81 *Autumn Light: Illuminations of Age.* Ed. L.M. Schulman. New York: Crowell, 1978.

Contains "The Sojourner," pp. 1-16.

BB82 *Fiction 100.* 2nd Edition. Comp. James H. Pickering. New York: Macmillan, 1978.

Contains "A Tree. A Rock. A Cloud.," pp. 625-629.

BB83 *The Norton Anthology of Short Fiction, Complete Edition.* Ed. R.V. Cassill. New York: Norton, 1978.

Contains "The Jockey," pp. 833-837.

BB84 *The Norton Anthology of Short Fiction, Shorter Edition.* Ed. R.V. Cassill. New York: Norton, 1978.

Contains "The Jockey," pp. 429-433.

BB85 *Stories of the Modern South.* Ed. Benjamin Forkner and Patrick Samway. New York: Bantam, 1978.

Contains "The Sojourner," pp. 233-242.

BB86 *Story to Anti-Story.* Ed. Mary Rohrberger. Boston: Houghton Mifflin, 1979.

Contains "A Tree. A Rock. A Cloud.," pp. 505-511.

SECTION C

FIRST PUBLICATION IN MAGAZINES AND NEWSPAPERS

This section lists chronologically the first appearance of
McCullers material in magazines and newspapers. Each entry
is identified by genre.

C1   "Highway Brings Women of West, South Georgia More Closely
      Together." Columbus (Ga.) *Ledger-Enquirer*, July 21,
      1935, p. 7.

      Article. Signed "Carson Smith."

C2   "Little Girls at Juniper Lake Write Letters on Experiences
      During Fresh Air Camp Outing." Columbus (Ga.) *Ledger-
      Enquirer*, July 28, 1935, p. 12.

      Article. Signed "Carson Smith."

C3   "Wunderkind." *Story*, 9 (December 1936), 61-73.

      Fiction. Signed "Carson Smith." See A5, A9, B10.

C4   "Reflections in a Golden Eye." *Harper's Bazaar*, 74
      [First Installment] (October 1940), 60-61, 131-143;
      [Second Installment] (November 1940), 56, 120-139.

      Fiction. See A2, A5.

C5   "Look Homeward Americans...." *Vogue*, 96 (December 1,
      1940), 74-75.

      Article. See A9.

C6   "Night Watch Over Freedom." *Vogue*, 97 (January 1, 1941),
      29.

      Article. See A9.

C7   "The Devil's Idlers." *Saturday Review*, 23 (March 15,
      1941), 15.

      Book review of *Commend the Devil* by Howard Coxe.

C8   "Brooklyn Is My Neighborhood." *Vogue*, 97 (March 1941),
      62-63, 138.

      Article. See A9.

C9   "Books I Remember." *Harper's Bazaar*, 75 (April 1941),
      82, 122, 125.

      Article.

C10   "We Carried Our Banners--We Were Pacifists Too." *Vogue*,
      97 (July 15, 1941), 42-43.

      Article. See A9.

C11   "The Russian Realists and Southern Literature." *Decision*,
      2 (July 1941), 15-19.

      Article. See A9.

C12   "The Jockey." *New Yorker*, 17 (August 23, 1941), 15-16.

      Fiction. See A5, B1.

C13   "The Twisted Trinity." *Decision*, 2 (November-December
      1941), 30.

      Verse. Early version of "Stone Is Not Stone." See A9,
      C42.

C14   "Madame Zilensky and the King of Finland." *New Yorker*,
      17 (December 20, 1941), 15-18.

      Fiction. See A5, B13.

C15   "Correspondence." *New Yorker*, 17 (February 7, 1942),
      36-39.

      Fiction. See A9.

C16   "A Tree. A Rock. A Cloud." *Harper's Bazaar*, 76 (November
      1942), 50, 96-99.

      Fiction. See A5, B2.

C17   "Love's Not Time's Fool." *Mademoiselle*, 16 (April 1943),
      95, 166-168.

      Article. Signed "By a War Wife."

C18   "Isak Dinesen: *Winter's Tales*." *New Republic*, 108
      (June 7, 1943), 768-769.

      Book review. See A9.

C19   "The Ballad of the Sad Café." *Harper's Bazaar*, 77
      (August 1943), 72-75, 140-161.

      Fiction. See A5, B3.

C20 "Our Heads Are Bowed." *Mademoiselle*, 22 (November 1945), 131, 229.

Article. See A9.

C21 "The Member of the Wedding." *Harper's Bazaar*, 80 (January 1946), 94-96, 101, 128-138, 144-148.

Fiction. Part I only. See A3, A5.

C22 [Letter to the Editor]. Columbus (Ga.) *Ledger-Enquirer*, February 28, 1948.

Protests the restriction that prevented blacks from using the Columbus Public Library.

C23 "Tennessee Williams." *Life*, 24 (March 8, 1948), 14.

Letter to the editor.

C24 "How I Began to Write." *Mademoiselle*, 27 (September 1948), 256-257.

Article. See A9.

C25 "27 Leading Writers Are Out for Truman." New York *Times*, October 27, 1948, p. 20.

Political statement. Signed by McCullers.

C26 "The Mortgaged Heart." *New Directions*, 10 (1948), 509.

Verse. First published version. See A9, C35.

C27 "When We Are Lost." *New Directions*, 10 (1948), 509.

Verse. First published version. See A9, C36.

C28 "Art and Mr. Mahoney." *Mademoiselle*, 28 (February 1949), 120, 184-186.

Fiction. See A9.

C29 "Loneliness ... An American Malady." *This Week Magazine*, New York *Herald Tribune*, December 19, 1949, pp. 18-19.

Article. See A9.

C30 "Home for Christmas." *Mademoiselle*, 30 (December 1949), 53, 129-132.

Article. See A9.

C31   "The Vision Shared." *Theatre Arts*, 34 (April 1950),
      23-30.

      Article. See A9.

C32   "The Sojourner." *Mademoiselle*, 31 (May 1950), 90, 160-
      166.

      Fiction. See A5, B6.

C33   "A Domestic Dilemma." New York *Post*, September 16, 1951,
      Magazine, pp. 10M-M11.

      Fiction. See A5.

C34   "The Dual Angel: A Meditation on Origin and Choice."
      Botteghe Oscure, 9 (1952), 213-218; also *Mademoiselle*,
      35 (July 1952), 54-55, 108.

      Verse. Includes "Incantation to Lucifer," "Hymen, O
      Hymen," "Love and the Rind of Time," "The Dual Angel,"
      and "Father, Upon Thy Image We Are Spanned." See A9.

C35   "The Mortgaged Heart." *Voices*, 149 (September-December
      1952), 12.

      Verse. Revised version. See A9, C26.

C36   "When We Are Lost." *Voices*, 149 (September-December
      1952), 12.

      Verse. Revised version. See A9, C27.

C37   "The Pestle." *Botteghe Oscure*, 11 (1953), 226-246; also
      Mademoiselle, 37 (July 1953), 44-45, 114-118.

      Fiction. First portion of *Clock Without Hands*. See A7.

C38   "The Discovery of Christmas." *Mademoiselle*, 38
      (December 1953), 54-55, 118-120.

      Article.

C39   "The Haunted Boy." *Botteghe Oscure*, 16 (1955), 264-278;
      also *Mademoiselle*, 42 (November 1955), 134-135, 152-159.

      Fiction. See A5.6, A9.

C40   "Who Has Seen the Wind?" *Mademoiselle*, 43 (September
      1956), 156-157, 174-188.

      Fiction. Reworking of early script of *The Square Root
      of Wonderful*. See A6, B9.

C41   "Mick." *Literary Cavalcade*, 10 (February 1957), 16-22, 32.

Excerpt from *The Heart Is a Lonely Hunter*.

C42   "Stone Is Not Stone." *Mademoiselle*, 45 (July 1957), 43.

Verse. Revised version of "The Twisted Trinity." See A9, C13.

C43   "'Quarrels and Cussing'--Playwright Tells of Pangs." Philadelphia *Inquirer*, October 13, 1957, Amusements and the Arts Section, pp. 1, 5.

Article. Discusses *The Square Root of Wonderful*. See A6.

C44   "The Flowering Dream: Notes on Writing." *Esquire*, 52 (December 1959), 162-164.

Article. See A9.

C45   "Author's Note." *New York Times Book Review*, June 11, 1961, p. 4.

Article. Discusses *Clock Without Hands*. See A7.

C46   "To Bear the Truth Alone." *Harper's Bazaar*, 94 (July 1961), 42-43, 93-99.

Fiction. Chapter three of *Clock Without Hands*. See A7.

C47   "A Child's View of Christmas." *Redbook*, 118 (December 1961), 31-34, 99-100.

Article. See A9.

C48   "The Dark Brilliance of Edward Albee." *Harper's Bazaar*, 97 (January 1963), 98-99.

Article.

C49   "Isak Dinesen: In Praise of Radiance." *Saturday Review*, 46 (March 16, 1963), 29, 83.

Article. See A9.

C50   "Sucker." *Saturday Evening Post*, 236 (September 28, 1963), 69-71.

Fiction. See A9, B10.

C51   "Sweet as a Pickle and Clean as a Pig." *Redbook*, 124
      (December 1964), 49-56.

      Verse. See A8.

C52   "The March." *Redbook*, 138 (March 1967), 69, 114-123.

      Fiction. The last short story published before McCullers'
      death. This was the first of a trilogy about black peo-
      ple. The other two stories, "The Man Upstairs" and "Hush
      Little Baby," remain unpublished.

C53   "A Hospital Christmas Eve." *McCall's*, 95 (December
      1967), 96-97.

      Article. See A9.

C54   "Like That." *Redbook*, 137 (October 1971), 91, 166-170.

      Fiction. See A9.

C55   "Breath from the Sky." *Redbook*, 137 (October 1971), 92,
      228-233.

      Fiction. See A9.

C56   "Instant of the Hour After." *Redbook*, 137 (October 1971),
      93, 194-196.

      Fiction. See A9.

SECTION D

MISCELLANEA

1. Adaptations of McCullers' Works
     Film, Television, Theatre, Music

2. Recordings of McCullers' Voice

3. English-Language Foreign Editions of McCullers' Works

ADAPTATIONS OF CARSON McCULLERS' WORKS

Film

D1   *The Member of the Wedding.* Screenplay by Edward and Edna Anhalt. Hollywood: Columbia Pictures Corporation, 1952. Directed by Fred Zinnemann.

D2   *The Heart Is a Lonely Hunter.* Screenplay by Thomas C. Ryan. New York: Brownstone Productions, Inc., 1967. Directed by Robert Ellis Miller.

D3   *Reflections in a Golden Eye.* Screenplay by Chapman Mortimer and Gladys Hill. Hollywood: Warner Bros.--Seven Arts International Ltd., 1967. Directed by John Huston.

Television

D4   "The Invisible Wall." Adapted by McCullers from her short story "The Sojourner" and broadcast on CBS, "Omnibus," December 27, 1953.

D5   "The Sojourner." Adapted by McCullers and broadcast on NBC, May 25, 1964.

Theatre

D6   *The Member of the Wedding.* Adapted by McCullers from her novella. (See A6.)

D7   *The Ballad of the Sad Café*
Title page: THE PLAY | THE BALLAD | OF THE | SAD CAFÉ | CARSON | McCULLERS' | NOVELLA | ADAPTED TO | THE STAGE BY | EDWARD ALBEE [1963]

Published jointly by Houghton Mifflin and Atheneum
Publishers in hardback and paperback printings respectively, which are identical except for the bindings. The
play opened at the Martin Beck Theatre in New York,
October 30, 1963, directed by Alan Schneider.

Musical Adaptations

D8   "The Twisted Trinity." Song. Words by McCullers from
her poem; music by David Diamond. Published as part of
sheet music titled *7 Songs By David Diamond*. Philadelphia: Elkan-Vogel [1946].

Location: HRC.

D9   *F. Jasmine Addams*. Unpublished musical adapted from
McCullers' play *The Member of the Wedding*. Written and
directed by Theodore Mann. Produced off-Broadway in
May 1971.

Location: HRC.

D10   [*The Member of the Wedding*]. Musical based on McCullers'
play by the same title. Written by McCullers and Mary
Rodgers during 1966-1967, this remains uncompleted.

Location: HRC

2. RECORDINGS

D11   "Carson McCullers Reads from *The Member of the Wedding*
and Other Works." MGM Records (E3619 ARC), 12" Long
Play. Other works are *The Heart Is a Lonely Hunter*,
The Ballad of the Sad Café, and three poems: "Select
Your Sorrows If you Can," "There Was A Time When Stone
Was Stone," and "When We Are Lost What Image Tells."
May 1958.

Note: "Select Your Sorrows If you Can" appears in *The
Mortgaged Heart* (A9) under the title "Saraband." Four
lines of the poem were inadvertently omitted from the
phonograph recording when McCullers recited it from
memory. "There Was A Time When Stone Was Stone" is a
revised version of "The Twisted Trinity" (C13) and
appears in *The Mortgaged Heart* under the title "Stone Is
Not Stone." "When We Are Lost What Image Tells" was

originally titled "When We Are Lost" when it first appeared in *New Directions* magazine (C27). It appears under the shortened title but in somewhat different form in *Voices* (C36) and *The Mortgaged Heart*.

D12   "The Place of Drama in the Religious and Spiritual Life of America." McCullers' discussion on the CBS television program "Lamp Unto My Feet," August 19, 1958.

          3.   ENGLISH-LANGUAGE FOREIGN EDITIONS
                OF McCULLERS' WORKS

D13   *The Zephyr Book of American Prose*
      1945
      THE ZEPHYR BOOK OF | AMERICAN PROSE | *Edited by Ebba Dalin* | Introduction by | *Ebba Dalin* | [publisher's device] | The Continental Book Company AB | STOCKHOLM/ LONDON

      On copyright page: 'Copyright 1945 by The Continental Book Company AB, Stockholm | This edition must not be introduced into the British Empire or the U.S.A. | Printed by Albert Bonniers Boktryckeri, Stockholm'

      Contains "Captain Penderton's Ride" [from *Reflections in a Golden Eye*], pp. 343-348.

D14   *Reflections in a Golden Eye*
      1947
      REFLECTIONS | IN A GOLDEN EYE | *By* | *Carson McCullers* | [Zephyr Books publisher's device] | The Continental Book Company AB | STOCKHOLM/LONDON

D15   *The Ballad of the Sad Café*
      1968
      [fancy] Nan'un-do's Contemporary Library | [rule] | CARSON McCULLERS | THE BALLAD OF | THE SAD CAFÉ | (Complete and Unabridged) | *Edited with Notes* | *by* | Masaji Onoe | [publisher's device] | TOKYO | NAN'UN-DO

      English text; Introduction and notes in Japanese and English.

Part II
Works about Carson McCullers

ACKNOWLEDGMENTS

Our portion of this bibliography could not have been completed had we not enjoyed the assistance of numerous persons,
many of whom must remain specifically unacknowledged because
they are librarians throughout the United States and Great
Britain who responded anonymously to our requests for information. But there are others to be thanked individually. At
the University of Maryland, we enjoyed the complete coopera-
tion of the staff of the McKeldin Library; and our work was
greatly aided by a summer grant from the University's General
Research Board. In addition, Joanne Giza, Jane DeMouy, and
Ruth M. Alvarez provided invaluable research assistance.
Elsewhere, Ellen Dunlap and David Farmer made our short visit
to the University of Texas Humanities Research Center into an
extremely fruitful and pleasant experience. Joyce Hartman
was equally cheerful and helpful in putting at our disposal
Houghton Mifflin's files of reviews of Mrs. McCullers' books;
and Jeanne Hollis, Reference Librarian of the Bradley Memorial
Library in Columbus, Georgia, thoughtfully provided Xerox
copies of their entire newspaper clipping collection on Mrs.
McCullers.

                                        JACKSON R. BRYER
                                        KATHLEEN FIELD
                                        College Park, Md.
                                        August 1979

SECTION E

BOOKS AND SECTIONS OF BOOKS

This section lists alphabetically all books containing significant mention of McCullers. Titles of books entirely about
McCullers are given in all capital letters. For previously
published essays which are reprinted in books, annotations
are provided only for each item's original appearance, unless
it has been substantially revised for reprinting. Entries by
the same author are listed alphabetically by title. Little
effort has been made to locate all reprintings of individual
essays and reviews; we may well have overlooked some of these.
For book chapters of a general sort with a few pages on
McCullers, we have listed the page numbers for the full chapter first and then, in brackets, the pages on McCullers.
Specifically excluded from this section are biographical and
bibliographical listings for McCullers in standard reference
works--such as Leary's *Articles on American Literature*--and
all but a very few of the headnotes on McCullers which precede
anthologization of her work. Items which could not be verified are indicated by an asterisk (*).

E1 Abels, Cyrilly, and Margarita G. Smith, eds. *40 Best Stories from "Mademoiselle"--1935-1960*. New York: Harper, 1960. P. 234.

Biographical note and brief comment on short story "Who Has Seen the Wind?" selected for this collection because it "probes into human tragedy with the brooding and poetic concern with time passing."

E2 Aldridge, John W. *In Search of Heresy--American Literature in an Age of Conformity*. Port Washington, N.Y.: Kennikat Press, 1967. Pp. 16, 19, 39, 117, 144-147.

Discussions of the use of the Southern locale in *Heart* and *Member* and how it serves to give the fiction and its characters a location in space.

E3 Allen, Walter. *The Modern Novel in Britain and the United States*. New York: E.P. Dutton, 1964. Pp. 132-137.

McCullers is called, "Faulkner apart, the most remarkable novelist the South has produced." *Heart*, *Reflections*, *Member*, *Ballad*, and *Clock* are examined briefly.

E4 Angoff, Allan, ed. *American Writing Today--Its Independence and Vigor*. New York: New York University Press, 1957. Pp. 57, 75, 183, 190, 206, 217.

Brief references to McCullers, along with other Southern writers who "make excellent use of the life of the region." *Ballad* is praised for "the permanent truths of the human condition [that] are given in a rich context of folk superstition, folk humor, folk pathos."

E5 Auchincloss, Louis. "Carson McCullers." In his *Pioneers and Caretakers--A Study of 9 American Women Novelists*. Minneapolis: University of Minnesota Press, 1965. Pp. 161-169.

Discussions of plots and themes in *Heart*, *Reflections*, *Member*, *Ballad*, and *Clock*. McCullers' use of horror and

her handling of race relations, childhood, and the search
for love are stressed.

E6   Block, Maxine, ed. *Current Biography--Who's News and
       Why--1940.* New York: H.W. Wilson, 1940. Pp. 535-536.

       Discussion of style, symbolism, and theme in *Heart.* Also
       includes several lengthy quotations from McCullers.

E7   Bluefarb, Sam. "Jake Blount: Escape as Dead End." In
       his *The Escape Motif in the American Novel: Mark Twain
       to Richard Wright.* Columbus: Ohio State University
       Press, 1972. Pp. 114-132.

       Jake Blount is seen as an "escaper" who is alienated
       from everyone, "an outcast even among outcasts." He
       differs from other escapers in literature in that his
       escapes do not take him anywhere; they do not "bring
       about in him any spiritual regeneration.... they are
       the chronic condition of his life."

E8   Bonin, Jane F. *Prize-Winning American Drama: A Biblio-
       graphical and Descriptive Guide.* Metuchen, N.J.: Scare-
       crow Press, 1973. Pp. 108-110.

       A synopsis of *Member,* with a brief account of its popular
       and critical reception.

E9   Boyle, Kay. "'I Wish I Had Written *The Ballad of the
       Sad Café* by Carson McCullers.'" In Eugene J. Woods, ed.
       *I Wish I'd Written That--Selections Chosen by Favorite
       American Authors.* New York: McGraw-Hill, 1946. Pp. 300-
       301.

       Admiration for "the bold objective approach--graced with
       reverence and humility as it is ... the ruthlessness
       and fearless self-imposed experience of severing herself
       of all that would have made the story applicable and
       identifiable with self." Praises also the language in
       Ballad, its ability to transcend its location and time,
       and the presence in it of "the very simplest and there-
       fore the very greatest human emotions."

E10   Bradbury, John M. *Renaissance in the South--A Critical
       History of the Literature, 1920-1960.* Chapel Hill:
       University of North Carolina Press, 1963. Pp. 16, 107,
       110-112, 129, 142, 189, 196, 197.

       Examination of the need that the characters in *Heart,
       Reflections, Member,* and *Ballad* have for love and human
       communication and their failure to achieve acceptance.

E11 Brickell, Herschel. "Introduction." In his ed. *Prize Stories of 1951--The O. Henry Awards*. Garden City, N.Y.: Doubleday, 1951. Pp. vii-xxvi [xv].

Explanation that the inclusion in *Prize Stories* of "The Sojourner" was controversial. Nancy Hale felt that the story was written "in a sort of slick, popular vein not characteristic of her [McCullers] at all," while Brickell disagreed.

E12 Brooks, Cleanth, and Robert Penn Warren. "Interpretation [of "A Domestic Dilemma"]." In their ed. *Understanding Fiction*. 2nd Edition. New York: Appleton-Century-Crofts, 1959. Pp. 270-271.

The story is seen as centering on "Martin's intensity and delicacy of shifting emotions, and the complexity of his love for his wife."

E13 Brustein, Robert. "The Playwright as Impersonator." In his *Seasons of Discontent: Dramatic Opinions 1959-1965*. New York: Simon and Schuster, 1965. Pp. 155-158.

Reprinting of Brustein's review of Edward Albee's adaptation of *Ballad* (*New Republic*, 149 [November 16, 1963], 28-29). "If the author wants to talk ... about unnatural love, then I suggest he find a less quavering voice than that of Carson McCullers; but if unnatural love is all he wants to talk about, then I suppose any voice will do. At that level of sound, all voices fade into one shrill chorus of self-pitying squeaks."

E14 Bryant, Jerry H. *The Open Decision: The Contemporary American Novel and Its Intellectual Background*. New York: Free Press, 1970. Pp. 35, 245-249, 282.

Examination of McCullers' handling of the theme of the adolescent's transition to adulthood in *Member*. Central conflict is seen as Frankie's feeling that she lacks unity with the world, and her feeling that she is an unlikeable person who will never be accepted by society. McCullers' solution is not to have Frankie overcome her lack, but instead to share that condition with others through love.

E15 Calisher, Hortense. *Herself*. New York: Arbor House, 1972. P. 363.

McCullers mentioned briefly as a woman who used her profession to fend off the female experience.

E16   Cargill, Oscar. *Intellectual America--Ideas on the
      March*. New York: Macmillan, 1941. Pp. 396-397.

      McCullers is placed in a group of writers who use
      primitivism in their works. *Heart* proves "that one
      can be both tough and feminine."

E17   Carr, Virginia Spencer. THE LONELY HUNTER--A BIOGRAPHY
      OF CARSON McCULLERS. Garden City, N.Y.: Doubleday, 1975.

      Detailed biography which covers the full range of Mc-
      Cullers' life and draws heavily on interviews with
      friends and colleagues, unpublished correspondence, and
      published sources. Includes very little literary criti-
      cism, but summarizes reviewers' responses to McCullers'
      works.

E18   Carson, Herbert L., and Ada Lou Carson. *The Impact of
      Fiction--An Anthology of Short Stories--Study Guide and
      Supplement*. Menlo Park, Calif.: Cummings, 1970. P. 207.

      "'The Sojourner' combines several of Mrs. McCullers'
      favorite subjects--children, music and the passage of
      time. A sense of sadness and waste is suffused through-
      out the story. This effect is achieved by the author's
      precise diction and meticulous selection of details."

E19   Chapman, John, ed. *The Burns Mantle Best Plays of 1949-
      1950 and the Year Book of the Drama in America*. New
      York: Dodd, Mead, 1950. Pp. 9, 27, 28-29, 91-92, 347-
      348, 366, 390.

      Scattered references to *Member*.

E20   Clurman, Harold. "The American Playwrights--Carson
      McCullers." In his *Lies Like Truth--Theatre Reviews and
      Essays*. New York: Macmillan, 1958. Pp. 62-64.

      Essay on *Member* reprinted from New York *Herald Tribune*,
      January 29, 1950, Sec. 5, p. 3. See F44.

E21   ———. "The Kind of Theatre We Have." In Dorothy and
      Joseph Samachson, eds. *Let's Meet the Theatre*. New
      York: Abelard-Schuman, 1954. Pp. 73-79 [77-78].

      In discussing problems of getting new types of plays
      produced, Clurman mentions the example of *Member*.

E22   ———. *On Directing*. New York: Macmillan, 1972. Pp.
      17-19, 49, 122, 136-139, 189-196.

Passing mention of problems that came up in original production of *Member*. Also, reprint (pp. 189-196) of Clurman's "Some Preliminary Notes for *The Member of the
Wedding*" from *Directing the Play*, edited by Toby Cole
and Helen Krich Chinoy. See E23.

E23   ———. "Some Preliminary Notes for *The Member of the
Wedding*." In Toby Cole and Helen Krich Chinoy, eds.
Directing the Play--A Sourcebook of Stagecraft. Indiana-
polis: Bobbs-Merrill, 1953. Pp. 311-320 [311-319].

Clurman's personal notes made in November-December 1949,
during the "formative period of production" of *Member*.
Includes his thoughts on what the audience is to enjoy,
the style the production ought to have, his interpretation of the play's main action ("to get 'connected'") and
of the major characters. Reprinted in Clurman's *On
Directing*. See E22.

E24   Cook, Albert. *The Meaning of Fiction*. Detroit: Wayne
State University Press, 1960. P. 123.

Brief discussion of "A Domestic Dilemma."

E25   Cook, Richard M. CARSON McCULLERS. Modern Literature
Monographs. New York: Frederick Ungar, 1975.

Brief study which includes a biographical sketch; individual chapters explicating *Heart*, *Member*, *Ballad*, and
Clock; and an assessment of McCullers' career, focusing
on theme.

E26   Cook, Sylvia Jenkins. *From Tobacco Road to Route 66--
The Southern Poor White in Fiction*. Chapel Hill: University of North Carolina Press, 1976. Pp. 156-158.

Brief consideration of *Heart* as novel in which hope for
"saving or radicalizing" the poor whites in the South is
viewed very pessimistically.

*E27   Cowie, Alexander. *American Writers Today*. Stockholm:
Radiotjanst, 1956. Pp. 127-128.

E28   Cowley, Malcolm. "American Novels Since the War." In
Robert Richman, ed. *The Arts at Mid-Century*. New York:
Horizon Press, 1954. Pp. 243-250 [249].

Brief mention of *Member* reprinted from Cowley's *The
Literary Situation*. See E29.

E29   ——————. *The Literary Situation*. New York: Viking Press,
       1954. Pp. 47, 69, 94.

       Brief scattered mention of *Member*.

E30   D[asher], T[homas] E., and A[drian] S[hapiro]. "Carson
       McCullers 1917-1967." In *First Printings of American
       Authors--Contributions Toward Descriptive Checklists*.
       Volume 2. Detroit: Gale, 1978. Pp. 251-252.

       Bibliographical descriptions of several McCullers titles
       and facsimiles of title pages.

E31   Davidson, Marshall B., and the editors of *American
       Heritage*. *The "American Heritage" History of the Writer's
       America*. New York: American Heritage, 1973. P. 384.

       Brief mention of McCullers' theme of "spiritual
       isolation."

E32   De Beauvoir, Simone. *The Second Sex*. Tr. by H.M.
       Parshley. New York: Alfred A. Knopf, 1953. Pp. 300,
       305-306.

       Brief discussion of Frankie's encounter with sex and her
       pre-adolescent discontent with herself.

E33   Dusenbury, Winifred L. "An Unhappy Family." In her
       The Theme of Loneliness in Modern American Drama.
       Gainesville: University of Florida Press, 1960. Pp. 57-
       85 [58-67].

       Analysis of techniques used in *Member* to show Frankie's
       loneliness and isolation from her family and society.
       These include: unplanned action, irrelevant conversa-
       tion, and characters' misunderstanding each other.

E34   Edmonds, Dale. CARSON McCULLERS. Southern Writers
       Series, No. 6. Austin, Texas: Steck-Vaughn, 1969.

       Brief biographical chapter, followed by discussions of
       each novel and the two plays, as well as passing mention
       of selected short stories, poetry, and essays. Emphasis
       is on the Southernness of McCullers' writing.

E35   Eisinger, Chester E. "The New Fiction--Carson McCullers
       and the Failure of Dialogue." In his *Fiction of the
       Forties*. Chicago: University of Chicago Press, 1963.
       Pp. 243-258. See also pp. 16, 236, 237, 259, 283, 380.

Discussion of the failure of dialogue in *Heart, Reflections, Member,* and *Ballad*. McCullers, who makes use of the "gothic spirit," is "governed by the aesthetics of the primitive" and "her overview is antirealistic." Her characters, whose capacities for love are crippled, are doomed to "inevitable failure" in their attempts to communicate and are condemned to "eternal loneliness."

E36   Evans, Oliver. CARSON McCULLERS—HER LIFE AND WORK. London: Peter Owen, 1965; THE BALLAD OF CARSON McCULLERS, A BIOGRAPHY. New York: Coward-McCann, 1966.

Critical biography, with emphasis on the relation between McCullers' life and her work. Includes explications of the fiction and quotations from reviews and articles.

E37   ————. "The Theme of Spiritual Isolation in Carson McCullers." In Louis D. Rubin, Jr., and Robert D. Jacobs, eds. *South: Modern Southern Literature in Its Cultural Setting*. Garden City, N.Y.: Doubleday Dolphin, 1961. Pp. 333-348.

Essay reprinted from *New World Writing*, 1 (April 1952), 297-310. See F71.

E38   Falk, Signi L. *Tennessee Williams*. New York: Twayne, 1961. Pp. 24-25, 27, and passim.

Brief comparisons of McCullers' work with Williams'.

E39   Felheim, Marvin. "Eudora Welty and Carson McCullers." In Harry T. Moore, ed. *Contemporary American Novelists*. Carbondale: Southern Illinois University Press, 1964. Pp. 41-53 [48-53].

Concentrates on McCullers' view of loneliness and love, her use of the grotesque, her literary form (especially openings of her longer fiction), and her use of music and time.

E40   Fiedler, Leslie A. *An End to Innocence—Essays on Culture and Politics*. Boston: Beacon Press, 1952. Pp. 149, 202-203.

McCullers' work described as about "the impossibility of reciprocal love, the sadness of a world in which growing up means only learning that isolation is the fate of everyone of us." Frankie and Berenice's relationship is called "a female homosexual romance."

E41   ———. *Love and Death in the American Novel.* New York:
       Criterion Books, 1960. Pp. 126, 325, 449-451, 453.

       Passing comment on McCullers' use of homosexuality in
       Heart and *Member.*

       French, Warren. See E70.

E42   Gassner, John, ed. *Best American Plays--Third Series--*
       1945-1951. New York: Crown, 1956. P. 174.

       Brief mention and defense of *Member* even though it is not
       "a well-made play."

E43   ———. *Directions in Modern Theatre and Drama.* New
       York: Holt, Rinehart and Winston, 1965. Pp. 85-86.

       Brief comments on *Member.* Reprinted from *Form and Idea*
       in Modern Theatre. See E44.

E44   ———. *Form and Idea in Modern Theatre.* New York:
       Dryden, 1956. P. 85.

       Brief comments on *Member.* Reprinted in *Directions in*
       Modern Theatre and Drama. See E43.

E45   ———. "Introduction to Dover Edition." In William
       Archer. *Play-Making--A Manual of Craftsmanship.* New
       York: Dover, 1960. Pp. v-xxxi [xx-xxii].

       Brief mention of the lack of "standard" playwriting
       techniques in *Member.*

E46   ———. "New American Playwrights: Williams, Miller and
       Others." In Richard Kostelanetz, ed. *On Contemporary*
       Literature. New York: Avon Books, 1964. Pp. 48-63
       [61-62].

       Material reprinted in abridged form from *The Theatre in*
       Our Times. See E47.

E47   ———. *The Theatre in Our Times.* New York: Crown,
       1954. Pp. 78, 353, 514.

       Comments on *Member.* Reprinted in *On Contemporary*
       Literature. See E46.

E48   Gloster, Hugh M. *Negro Voices in American Fiction.*
       Chapel Hill: University of North Carolina Press, 1948.
       P. 205.

       Very brief comment on *Heart.*

E49 Gold, Herbert, and David L. Stevenson. [Comment on "A
     Domestic Dilemma"]. In their ed. *Stories of Modern
     America*. New York: St. Martin's Press, 1961. Pp. 194,
     203.

     Concerns the statement that the story makes about
     marriage.

E50 Gossett, Louise Y. "Dispossessed Love: Carson McCullers."
     In her *Violence in Recent Southern Fiction*. Durham, N.C.:
     Duke University Press, 1965. Pp. 159-177.

     Discussion of the nature of violence in McCullers' works.
     It is "private" rather than "public." She makes "vivid
     the violence of the psychological and physiological ill-
     nesses that result from thwarted or abnormal love."
     Works discussed include *Heart*, *Member*, *Reflections*,
     Ballad, *Clock*, "A Domestic Dilemma," "A Tree. A Rock. A
     Cloud.," "Madame Zilensky and the King of Finland," and
     "The Haunted Boy."

E51 Graver, Lawrence. CARSON McCULLERS. University of
     Minnesota Pamphlets on American Writers, No. 84. Minnea-
     polis: University of Minnesota Press, 1969.

     Biographical sketch and lengthy analyses of symbolism,
     imagery, character portrayal, and style in *Heart*,
     Reflections, *Member*, *Ballad*, and *Clock*. No discussions
     of the plays or stories. Reprinted in *American Writers--
     A Collection of Literary Biographies*. See E52.

E52 ————. "Carson McCullers--1917-1967." In Leonard
     Unger, ed. *American Writers--A Collection of Literary
     Biographies*. Volume 2. New York: Charles Scribner's,
     1974. Pp. 585-608.

     Reprinting of Graver's Minnesota Pamphlet. See E51.

E53 Gray, James. *On Second Thought*. Minneapolis: University
     of Minnesota Press, 1946. P. 254.

     Brief criticism of the "pretensions and absurdities" of
     Heart and *Reflections* and praise for the "thoroughly
     honest and quite unmannered" *Member*.

E54 Gray, Richard. "Moods and Absences: Carson McCullers."
     In his *The Literature of Memory--Modern Writers of the
     American South*. Baltimore: Johns Hopkins University
     Press, 1977. Pp. 265-273.

     View of McCullers as a transitional figure in the Southern
     tradition. In her fiction, she externalizes "her own

state" of "'loneliness'" or loss and tries, "through the
medium of the South, to anatomize human nature, to chart,
in her plan of her region, the coordinates of all our
lives." She suggests that "not only God ... is dead now
--history, as a common secular resource and the modern
substitute for God, is as well." Discussion centers on
Ballad.

E55   Haines, Helen E. *Living with Books--The Art of Book
      Selection*. 2nd Edition. New York: Columbia University
      Press, 1950. P. 518.

      Brief mention of *Member*.

E56   Hardy, John Edward. *Commentaries on Five Modern American
      Short Stories*. Frankfurt: Diesterweg, 1962. Pp. 11-14.

      Comment on "The Sojourner," with focus on character
      analysis. The story's theme is "love as defense against
      time and man's mortality." Reprinted in Hardy's *The
      Modern Talent: An Anthology of Short Stories*. See E57.

E57   ———, ed. *The Modern Talent: An Anthology of Short
      Stories*. New York: Holt, Rinehart & Winston, 1964.
      Pp. 436-439.

      Reprinted comment on "The Sojourner." See E56.

E58   Harte, Barbara, and Caroline Riley. *200 Contemporary
      Authors*. Detroit: Gale, 1969. Pp. 183-185.

      Discussion of variety of topics relating to McCullers'
      works: her view of love, her blending of realism and
      symbolism, the musical structures of her novels, and her
      critical reception in America and abroad.

E59   Hassan, Ihab. "Carson McCullers: The Aesthetics of Love
      and Pain." In his *Radical Innocence: Studies in the
      Contemporary American Novel*. Princeton, N.J.: Princeton
      University Press, 1961. Pp. 205-229.

      Essay reprinted in revised form from *Modern Fiction
      Studies*, 5 (Winter 1959-1960), 311-326. See F96.

E60   ———. "The Character of Post-War Fiction in America."
      In Richard Kostelanetz, ed. *On Contemporary Literature*.
      New York: Avon Books, 1964. Pp. 36-47 [38, 40, 41, 44].

      Essay reprinted from *English Journal*, 51 (January 1962),
      1-8. See F97. This essay is also reprinted in Joseph J.
      Waldmeir, ed. *Recent American Fiction*. Boston: Houghton
      Mifflin, 1963. Pp. 27-35.

E61   ─────. *Contemporary American Literature--1945-1972: An Introduction.* New York: Frederick Ungar, 1973. Pp. 67-69.

McCullers and Flannery O'Connor seen as stressing "alienation, collapse of values and traditions, the decay of the South."

E62   Herron, Ima Honaker. *The Small Town in American Drama.* Dallas: Southern Methodist University Press, 1969. Pp. 342, 398-400, 444.

Mention of *Member* as a small-town play.

E63   Hewes, Henry. "Introduction." In his ed. *Famous American Plays of the 1940s.* New York: Dell, 1960. Pp. 7-22 [18-19].

Mention of *Member*, which "requires an intimacy most Broadway playhouses lack."

E64   Hoffman, Frederick J. "Eudora Welty and Carson McCullers." In his *The Art of Southern Fiction--A Study of Some Modern Novelists.* Carbondale: Southern Illinois University Press, 1967. Pp. 51-73.

Analyses of *Heart*, *Reflections*, *Ballad*, and *Member*, with emphasis on her "single theme"--"the loss of love and the attempt of the self to identify with other selves."

E65   Howard, Daniel F. "Carson McCullers." In his *Manual to Accompany "The Modern Tradition--Short Stories--Second Edition."* Boston: Little, Brown, 1972. Pp. 40-42.

Commentary on "The Sojourner" and "The Jockey."

E66   Joost, Nicholas. "'Was All For Naught?': Robert Penn Warren and New Directions in the Novel." In Harold C. Gardiner, S.J., ed. *Fifty Years of the American Novel-- A Christian Appraisal.* New York: Charles Scribner's, 1951. Pp. 273-291 [284-286].

Brief discussion of McCullers' heavily symbolic style and of her use of impersonal narrative.

E67   Kazin, Alfred. *Bright Book of Life: American Novelists and Storytellers from Hemingway to Mailer.* Boston: Little, Brown, 1973. Pp. 51-54.

Material reprinted from Kazin's essay in *New York Review of Books*, 16 (February 11, 1971), 28-34 [29-30]. See F113.

E68   ————. "We Who Sit in Darkness--The Broadway Audience
       at the Play." In his *The Inmost Leaf--A Selection of
       Essays*. New York: Harcourt, Brace, 1955. Pp. 127-135
       [131-133].

       Essay reprinted from *Commentary*, 9 (June 1950), 525-529.
       See F114.

E69   Kiernan, Robert F. KATHERINE ANNE PORTER AND CARSON
       McCULLERS: A REFERENCE GUIDE. Boston: G.K. Hall, 1976.

       Pages 95-169 of this book contain an annotated checklist
       of McCullers criticism, arranged in chronological order
       and including books and book sections, periodical arti-
       cles, book reviews, and play reviews. The checklist is
       indexed on pages 185-194.

E70   Knowles, A.S., Jr. "Six Bronze Petals and Two Red:
       Carson McCullers in the Forties." In Warren French, ed.
       The Forties: Fiction, Poetry, Drama. Deland, Fla.:
       Everett/Edwards, 1969. Pp. 87-98. See also p. 85.

       Reassessment of McCullers' work, with emphasis on *Heart*
       and *Member*, seen here as her best novels. She is essen-
       tially "a writer of the Forties" and "essentially a minor
       writer" because "her vision was often limited and special."
       Her art "was a kind of hybrid, mixing the familiar and
       universal with the strange and personal. Within the
       scope of that vision, she handled her themes of love,
       loneliness, alienation, and identity with precision and,
       at her least morbid and most natural, great tenderness."
       Some mention also of *Ballad*, *Reflections*, and *Clock*.

E71   Kronenberger, Louis. "The Season on Broadway." In his
       ed. *The Best Plays of 1957-1958*. New York: Dodd, Mead,
       1958. Pp. 3-38 [12, 14].

       Brief critical mention of *Square Root*.

E72   Kusuhara, Tomoko. "New Indications in Conventionalism in
       Popular Plays." In *American Literature in the 1950's*.
       Annual Report, 1976. Tokyo: Tokyo Chapter, American
       Literature Society of Japan, 1977. Pp. 147-155 [147,
       149, 151, 153-155].

       Mention of *Member* in discussion of trends in American
       drama of the 1950's. It contains elements which link it
       to the conventional drama of the 1950's as well as other
       aspects which indicate "the way to the Theatre of the
       Absurd in the sixties."

E73   Lawson, Lewis A.   "Kierkegaard and the Modern American
      Novel."   In Thomas G. Burton, ed.   *Essays in Memory of*
      Christina Burleson in Language and Literature by Former
      Colleagues and Students.   Johnson City, Tenn.: Research
      Advisory Council, East Tennessee State University, 1969.
      Pp. 113-125 [123].

      Notes that McCullers used Kierkegaard's *The Sickness Unto*
      Death in *Clock*, but that its use is superfluous and
      "weakens an already unsatisfactory novel."

E74   Lesser, M.X., and John N. Morris.   [Comment on "Wunder-
      kind"].   In their ed. *Modern Short Stories--The Fiction*
      of Experience.   New York: McGraw-Hill, 1962.   P. 229.

      Concerns the theme of the conflict between the artist's
      "exacting necessity of his art and the expanding necessity
      of humanness."

E75   Levidova, Inna.   "Carson McCullers and Her Last Book."
      In Carl R. Proffer, ed.   *Soviet Criticism of American*
      Literature in the Sixties.   Ann Arbor, Mich.: Ardis,
      1972.   Pp. 88-95.   See also p. xxix.

      Review of Russian translation of *Clock*, with mention also
      of *Heart* and *Ballad*.   McCullers' novels exist "in two
      organically united planes--psychological and social real-
      ism, and allegory, fable."   Her theme is "the eternal
      and irreplaceable power of goodness--love, self-sacrifice,
      the striving for beauty, the striving to get closer, even
      if only for a single instant, to a comprehension of the
      meaning of human existence."   This review originally
      appeared, in Russian, in *New World*, No. 10 (1966).

E76   MacDonald, Edgar E.   "The Symbolic Unity of *The Heart Is*
      a Lonely Hunter."   In Frieda Elaine Penninger, ed. *A*
      Festschrift for Professor Marguerite Roberts, on the
      Occasion of Her Retirement from Westhampton College,
      University of Richmond, Virginia.   Richmond: University
      of Richmond, 1976.   Pp. 168-187.

      Analyzes the hagiography, structure, symbolic significance
      of numbers, and Biff Brannon's growth into a godhead
      through Gnosis, concluding that McCullers "created a
      Divine Comedy whose symbolic architecture and symmetry
      are everywhere in harmony and which reveals a profound
      sense of form and artistic completion."

B77   Madden, David.   "Introduction."   In his ed. *Proletarian*
      Writers of the Thirties.   Carbondale: Southern Illinois

University Press, 1968. Pp. xv-xlii [xix, xxv].

Brief passing mention of McCullers.

E78 Magny, Claude-Edmonde. *The Age of the American Novel--
     The Film Aesthetic of Fiction Between the Two Wars*. Tr.
     by Eleanor Hochman. New York: Frederick Ungar, 1972.
     Pp. 226, 229.

McCullers writes about the side of America that is a
country "of despair, of groundswells of insecurity and
boredom, of people who have 'everything to make them
happy,' yet who commit suicide ... or who can only find
existence bearable by dint of getting drunk every night;
the America of the novels about the blacks and 'poor
whites.'"

E79 Malin, Irving. "The Gothic Family." In his ed.
     Psychoanalysis and American Fiction. New York: E.P.
     Dutton, 1965. Pp. 255-277 [258-262].

Discussion of the breakdown or lack of family relations
in *Heart*, *Reflections*, and *Member*, and the subsequent
creation of pseudo-family ties.

E80 ————. *New American Gothic*. Carbondale: Southern
     Illinois University Press, 1962. Pp. 14-15, 21-26, 54-
     57, 83-86, 111-117, 133-137, and passim.

Discussions of various aspects of McCullers' writing, including characters' narcissistic love, distorted or absent
family ties, imagery of rooms and houses, voyages and
traveling, and reflections and images which are fragmented
and distorted.

E81 Mann, Klaus. *The Turning Point: Thirty-five Years in
     This Century*. New York: L.B. Fischer, 1942. Pp. 331-
     332.

Brief reference in Mann's diary to *Heart*.

E82 Meeker, Richard K. "The Youngest Generation of Southern
     Writers." In R.C. Simonini, Jr., ed. *Southern Writers--
     Appraisals in Our Time*. Charlottesville: University
     Press of Virginia, 1964. Pp. 162-191 [184-186].

Discussion of the search for love and close family ties
and the "Southern themes" in McCullers' novels and short
stories.

E83   Miles, Rosalind. *The Fiction of Sex--Themes and Functions of Sex Difference in the Modern Novel*. New York:
Barnes & Noble, 1974. Pp. 85, 87, 108-109, 133-134,
140-142.

Passing mention of *Heart* and its linking of "the oppres-
sion of women with racism in the structure of society";
of McCullers' portraits of negroes and children; and of
her primary theme--"the still sad music of humanity in
all its variations, and the loneliness that that entails."

E84   Miller, Jordan Y. "The Member of the Wedding." In his
ed. *American Dramatic Literature--Ten Modern Plays in
Historical Perspective*. New York: McGraw-Hill, 1961.
Pp. 426-428.

Success of *Member* is attributed to a portrayal of loneliness which does not "move too far from reality or toward
undue sentimentality."

E85   Nathan, George Jean. "The Member of the Wedding." In
his ed. *The Theatre Book of the Year 1949-1950--A Record
and an Interpretation*. New York: Alfred A. Knopf, 1950.
Pp. 164-166.

In *Member*, McCullers "spoiled a commendable novel for the
purposes of a possibly potential play." The "primarily
psychological and passively ruminative" materials of the
play, "invested mainly in a single character," present
"serious difficulties to a playwright, or at least to
one not considerably equipped." Discussion also of per-
formances of Harris, Waters, and De Wilde.

E86   ————. *The Theatre in the Fifties*. New York: Alfred A.
Knopf, 1953. P. 10.

Member mentioned, with *Death of a Salesman* and *The Glass
Menagerie*, as proof that the theatre-going public does
not want to laugh but rather to cry.

Nin, Anaïs. See E105.

E87   O'Connor, William Van. *The Grotesque: An American Genre
and Other Essays*. Carbondale: Southern Illinois University Press, 1962. Pp. 6, 13, 21.

Passing mention of McCullers whose characters are "almost
invariably ... abnormal or perverse, but ... [she] seems
to ask that they be taken as 'normal.'"

*E88   Onkoso, Yoshiko. "Solitary Love: Carson McCullers's
       Novels." In *American Literature in the 1940's.* Annual
       Report, 1975. Tokyo: Tokyo Chapter, American Literature
       Society of Japan, 1976 [?]. Pp. 40-57.

 E89   Peden, William. *The American Short Story--Front Line
       in the National Defense of Literature.* Boston: Houghton
       Mifflin, 1964. Pp. 29, 89, 126-127, 170, 190.

       Brief mentions of McCullers' penchant for the Gothic,
       for grotesque characters, and for "distorted" love and
       loneliness. Capote, McCullers, and Singer are compared
       for their "concern with the contrast between the real
       and the illusory."

 E90   Phillips, Louis. "The Novelist as Playwright: Baldwin,
       McCullers, and Bellow." In William E. Taylor, ed. *Modern
       American Drama: Essays in Criticism.* Deland, Fla.:
       Everett/Edwards, 1968. Pp. 145-162 [153-157].

       Discussion of the themes of isolation, loneliness, and
       failure in *Member* and *Square Root.* Lack of success of
       latter is attributed to its affinity to *The Glass
       Menagerie* and to its quick jumps between tragedy and
       comedy.

 E91   Reed, Rex. "'Frankie Addams' at 50." In his *Do You
       Sleep in the Nude?* New York: New American Library, 1968.
       Pp. 38-43.

       Article-interview reprinted from New York *Times,* April 16,
       1967, Sec. 2, p. 15. See F195.

 E92   Rexroth, Kenneth. "The Younger Generation and Its Books."
       In Robert Richman, ed. *The Arts at Mid-Century.* New
       York: Horizon Press, 1954. Pp. 262-268 [266].

       Passing mention of McCullers, along with Styron.

 E93   Rose, Alan Henry. *Demonic Vision--Racial Fantasy and
       Southern Fiction.* Hamden, Conn.: Archon Books, 1976.
       Pp. 121-122.

       Brief mention of Dr. Copeland in *Heart.*

 E94   Rubin, Louis D., Jr. *The Faraway Country--Writers of
       the Modern South.* Seattle: University of Washington
       Press, 1966. Pp. 13, 195, 240.

       McCullers' fiction is too "limited in scope; it stopped
       short of the tragic, contenting itself with a poignant
       exploration of the surfaces."

E95   Rukeyser, Muriel. "The Watchers." In her *Waterlily Fire--Poems 1935-1962*. New York: Macmillan, 1962. Pp. 159-160.

Poem dedicated to McCullers and her husband.

E96   Sanders, Thomas E. [Commentary on "A Tree. A Rock. A Cloud."]. In his ed. *The Discovery of Fiction*. Glenview, Ill.: Scott, Foresman, 1967. Pp. 323-331. See also pp. 293-295, 296, 298, 303, 333, 559.

Detailed explication, with emphasis on style, character depiction, and symbolism.

E97   Schorer, Mark. "Carson McCullers and Truman Capote." In his *The World We Imagine: Selected Essays*. New York: Farrar, Straus & Giroux, 1968. Pp. 274-296.

Essay reprinted from *The Creative Present*. See E98.

E98   ————. "McCullers and Capote: Basic Patterns." In Nona Balakian and Charles Simmons, eds. *The Creative Present --Notes on Contemporary American Fiction*. Garden City, N.Y.: Doubleday, 1963. Pp. 83-107.

McCullers' theme is seen as "spiritual isolation, universal isolation and loneliness." *Heart* is like a parable; *Reflections* like a dream or nightmare; *Member* is more realistic; *Ballad* is truly ballad-like; and *Clock* seems to be an attempted allegory. This essay is reprinted in Schorer's *The World We Imagine*. See E97.

E99   Scott, Nathan A., Jr. *Modern Literature and the Religious Frontier*. New York: Harper, 1958. Pp. 94, 96, 102.

Scattered references to *Member* and its theme of childhood.

E100   Sievers, W. David. *Freud on Broadway--A History of Psychoanalysis and the American Drama*. New York: Hermitage House, 1955. Pp. 431-433.

Praise for *Member*'s psychological portrait "of the lonely sexually eager and verbally eloquent adolescent girl." Play is called "one of the most notable modern American psychological plays."

E101   Smith, Margarita G. "Introduction." In her ed. *The Mortgaged Heart* by Carson McCullers. Boston: Houghton Mifflin, 1971. Pp. xi-xix. See also Smith's "Editor's Note" to each section of the collection: pp. 3-6, 205-

206, 285; and comments on McCullers' early stories by
Sylvia Chatfield Bates, pp. 37-38, 62-63, 87.

Personal reminiscences and background information about
previously uncollected work, unpublished material; and
comments on three early stories by Bates. See F221.

E102   Starke, Catherine Juanita. *Black Portraiture in American
Fiction: Stock Characters, Archetypes, and Individuals.*
New York: Basic Books, 1971. Pp. 132-134.

Brief discussion of Berenice in *Member* in relation to
other black cooks and mammies in literature.

E103   Stegner, Wallace. *The Writer in America.* Tokyo:
Hakuseido, 1951. Pp. 46-47.

Brief praise for McCullers, "a writer of quite extraordinary merit" whose "precocity has shown no sign of
running down."

E104   Straumann, Heinrich. *American Literature in the
Twentieth Century.* 3rd Edition. New York: Harper &
Row, 1965. Pp. 93-96, 97, 137.

McCullers' work deals with characters who have "under-
developed or anomalous minds" but who have an intimation
of a search for "remote values."

E105   Stuhlman, Gunther, ed. *The Diary of Anaïs Nin--1939-
1944.* New York: Harcourt, Brace & World, 1969. Pp.
270-271.

Brief description of Nin's meeting with McCullers.

E106   Sullivan, Walter. *A Requiem for the Renascence--The
State of Fiction in the Modern South.* Athens: University of Georgia Press, 1976. Pp. xxi, 24, 72.

Passing mention of McCullers and *Clock*.

E107   Symons, Julian. "The Lonely Heart." In his *Critical
Occasions.* London: Hamish Hamilton, 1966. Pp. 106-111.

Essay-review reprinted from *Times Literary Supplement*,
July 17, 1953, p. 460. See F227.

E108   Taylor, Horace. "*The Heart Is a Lonely Hunter*: A
Southern Wasteland." In Waldo McNeir and Leo B. Levy,
eds. *Studies in American Literature.* Louisiana State
University Studies, Humanities Series, No. 8. Baton

Rouge: Louisiana State University Press, 1960. Pp.
154-160, 172-173.

View of *Heart* as sharing the same controlling concept
as "The Waste Land." McCullers' theme is "characteris-
tically modern": "the spiritual isolation and loneliness
of man." The society depicted in the novel "is a secular
one ... which has become a loose aggregate of individuals
bearing little or no intrinsic relation to each other.
The psycho-religious bond of community has been lost and
only the empty forms of communal existence remain."

E109 Tischler, Nancy M. *Black Masks--Negro Characters in
      Modern Southern Fiction.* University Park: Pennsylvania
      State University Press, 1969. Pp. 25, 26, 109, 132-133,
      155, 156, 157, 182, 190, 191.

      Passing mention of McCullers' attempt to break the
      stereotype of blacks in *Heart.* Dr. Copeland is not so
      much a black as an isolated man "cut off from the main-
      stream of life."

E110 ————. *Tennessee Williams: Rebellious Puritan.* New
      York: Citadel Press, 1961. Pp. 10, 134-135, 166, 301-
      302.

      Mentions of Williams' first encounter with McCullers,
      of their first summer together, and a brief discussion
      of their relationship.

E111 Vande Kieft, Ruth M. *Eudora Welty.* New York: Twayne,
      1962. Pp. 168, 174-175.

      Brief comparison of Welty's work with McCullers'.

E112 Van Druten, John. *Playwright at Work.* New York:
      Harper, 1953. Pp. 35-36, 103, 122, 174-175, 181-183,
      187, 189-190.

      Passing references to *Member*, several concerning how it
      could be so successful and still be so unorthodox.
      Attributes McCullers' success to her "total absorption
      in her subject, with no regard for the theatrical con-
      ventions beyond a wish to use the stage as best she
      could."

E113 Vidal, Gore. "Ladders to Heaven: Novelists and Critics
      of the 1940's" and "Carson McCullers' *Clock Without
      Hands.*" In his *Rocking the Boat: A Political, Literary
      and Theatrical Commentary.* Boston: Little, Brown, 1962.
      Pp. 125-146 and 178-183.

Essay reprinted from *New World Writing*, 4 (1953), 303–316 (see F237) and review reprinted from *The Reporter*, 25 (September 28, 1961), 50–52 (see G330).

E114   Voss, Arthur. *The American Short Story—A Critical Survey.* Norman: University of Oklahoma Press, 1973. Pp. 350–351.

Stories in *Ballad* feature characters who "suffer the plight of misfits or outcasts in a world full of loneliness and lacking in love." *Ballad* itself is a "powerfully moving, if extreme, example of 'Southern Gothic.'"

E115   Warfel, Harry R. *American Novelists of Today.* New York: American Book Co., 1951. P. 292.

Biographical sketch and plot summaries of *Heart*, *Reflections*, and *Member*.

E116   Wasserstrom, William. *Heiress of All the Ages—Sex and Sentiment in the Genteel Tradition.* Minneapolis: University of Minnesota Press, 1959. P. 103.

Very brief mention of McCullers' "grotesque women."

E117   Waters, Ethel, with Charles Samuels. *His Eye Is On the Sparrow—An Autobiography.* Garden City, N.Y.: Doubleday, 1951. Pp. 263, 272–276.

Reminiscences of original production of *Member*.

E118   Watkins, Floyd C. *The Death of Art: Black and White in the Recent Southern Novel.* Mercer University Lamar Memorial Lectures, No. 13. Athens: University of Georgia Press, 1970. Pp. 14, 21, 25, 29, 35, 44, 50, 52, 55–56, 57, 63.

Examples of racial and geographical stereotyping drawn from *Clock*.

E119   Weales, Gerald. *American Drama Since World War II.* New York: Harcourt, Brace & World, 1962. Pp. 175–179.

Discussion of how McCullers adapted *Member* from her novel, with emphasis on changes and omissions.

E120   Webb, Constance. *Richard Wright—A Biography.* New York: G.P. Putnam's, 1968. Pp. 194–196, 269–273, 413.

Accounts of McCullers' friendship with Wright.

E121   Wikborg, Eleanor. CARSON McCULLERS' "THE MEMBER OF THE
       WEDDING": ASPECTS OF STRUCTURE AND STYLE. Gothenburg
       Studies in English, 31. Göteborg, Sweden: Acta Universi-
       tatus Gothoburgensis, 1975.

       Structural and stylistic study which relates the symbol-
       ism, structure, and certain stylistic features of the
       novel to the themes of "isolation and the desire to be-
       long," "confinement and the desire to escape," and
       "frustration and bewilderment."

E122   Williams, Tennessee. "This Book." In *Reflections in a
       Golden Eye* by Carson McCullers. New Classics Series.
       Norfolk, Conn.: New Directions, 1950. Pp. ix-xxi.

       Defense of McCullers' use of the grotesque as a means
       to convey her "Sense of the Awful which is the desperate
       black root of nearly all significant modern art."

E123   Witham, W. Tasker. *The Adolescent in the American
       Novel--1920-1960.* New York: Frederick Ungar, 1964.
       Pp. 16, 19, 25, 42, 59, 60, 61, 80, 98, 145-146, 169,
       197, 265, 268, 270, 275.

       Passing references to Mick in *Heart* and Frankie in
       Member, with emphasis on their sexuality, loneliness,
       and ambition.

E124   Wykes, Alan. *A Concise Survey of American Literature.*
       New York: Library Publishers, 1955. P. 175.

       McCullers is "a specialist in the study of solitude."

PERIODICAL ARTICLES

This section lists alphabetically magazine and newspaper articles containing mention of McCullers. Pieces which have been
reprinted in books are cross-referenced to Section E of the
bibliography. Items by the same author are listed alphabetically by title. This section includes reviews of books about
McCullers only when such reviews contain significant critical
comment on her works; all other such reviews have been excluded, as have reviews of Edward Albee's adaptation of *The
Ballad of the Sad Café* and reviews of film adaptations of her
fiction. The two latter types of reviews are included, unannotated, in William T. Stanley's 1970 checklist (F225).
For general articles containing brief mention of McCullers,
the page numbers for the full article are listed first, with
the page numbers for references to McCullers listed next,
in brackets.

F1 Albee, Edward. "Carson McCullers--The Case of the Curious Magician." *Harper's Bazaar*, 96 (January 1963), 98.

Brief tribute to McCullers as a person and as a writer.

F2 Allen, Walter. "London Literary Letter." *New York Times Book Review*, October 28, 1962, pp. 56-57 [56].

Mention that McCullers presented three prizes at the Cheltenham Festival of Literature and that she also participated in a "Sex in Literature" symposium. See also F53, F220, F234.

F3 Alsterlund, B[etty]. "Carson McCullers." *Wilson Library Bulletin*, 15 (June 1941), 808.

Biographical sketch which also includes excerpts from reviews of *Heart* and *Reflections*.

F4 Atkinson, Brooks. "Poetry in a Drama--'The Member of the Wedding' Remains Constant and Unimpaired." New York *Times*, September 17, 1950, Sec. 2, p. 1.

Some of play's success attributed to the popular reception of Williams' poetic dramas. *Member* gives a "vivid impression of life being lived with concentrated vitality by people of force and passions."

F5 "Author Carson McCullers Dies in New York at 50." Atlanta *Constitution*, September 30, 1967, pp. 1, 11.

Extended obituary notice, with biographical sketch and critical comment on her work.

F6 Balakian, Nona. "Carson McCullers Completes New Novel Despite Adversity." New York *Times*, September 3, 1961, p. 46.

Interview in which McCullers discusses her writing block and how Mary Mercer helped her overcome it, her feelings for her former music teacher and the teacher's husband, and her reaction to critics.

F7   Baldanza, Frank. "Plato in Dixie." *Georgia Review*, 12
      (Summer 1958), 151-167 [154-162].

      Examination of the existence of Platonic theories of love
      and Platonic forms and techniques in the works of
      McCullers and Capote. Parallels with Plato's *Symposium*
      and *Phaedrus* are found in "A Tree. A Rock. A Cloud.,"
      Heart, *Reflections*, *Member*, and *Ballad*.

F8   Barry, Jackson G. "Jose Quintero: The Director as Image
      Maker." *Educational Theatre Journal*, 14 (March 1962),
      15-22.

      Discussion of Quintero's contribution to production of
      Square Root in 1958 and description of his methods.

F9   Beja, Morris. "It Must Be Important: Negroes in Con-
      temporary American Fiction." *Antioch Review*, 24 (Fall
      1964), 323-336 [327].

      Brief mention of Sherman Pew in *Clock* as the embodiment
      of two black themes--the search for identity and the
      black man as a "Christ martyr."

F10   Bigsby, C.W.E. "Edward Albee's Georgia Ballad."
      Twentieth Century Literature, 13 (January 1968), 229-236.

      Critique of Albee's adaptation of *Ballad* which focuses
      on common themes that McCullers' and Albee's works share.

F11   Bolsterli, Margaret. "'Bound' Characters in Porter,
      Welty, McCullers: The Prerevolutionary Status of Women
      in American Fiction." *Bucknell Review*, 24 (Spring 1978),
      95-105 [95, 103-105].

      Views the plight of Miss Amelia in *Ballad* as essentially
      the same as those of Welty's and Porter's more traditional
      women. Women characters of the first half of the twen-
      tieth century, like women of that time, were imprisoned
      "in a pattern that dictated that women could neither
      take their lives into their own hands nor achieve self-
      realization outside the roles society had chosen for
      them."

F12   "Books and Authors." *New York Times Book Review*, May 5,
      1940, p. 14.

      Heart is listed for June publication among "Forthcoming
      Books."

F13   Bowen, Elizabeth. "A Matter of Inspiration." *Saturday Review*, 24 (October 13, 1951), 27-28, 64-65 [64].

Brief praise for McCullers.

F14   Box, Patricia S. "Androgyny and the Musical Vision: A Study of Two Novels by Carson McCullers." *Southern Quarterly*, 16 (January 1978), 117-123.

The message of *Heart* and *Member* is that "only androgyns are capable of experiencing the sexless love that can ultimately unite all of mankind and change the condition of humanity from isolation to community." This theme is reinforced through the use of music "as a metaphor for this type of love."

F15   Boyle, Kay. "The Aesthetics of the Future." *Syracuse 10*, 2 (December 1959), 15-16, 33-37 [15-16].

Brief mention of *Member* as one of several recent novels which have "cried out man's longing to be identified with other men."

F16   Breit, Harvey. "Behind the Wedding--Carson McCullers Discusses the Novel She Converted into a Stage Play." New York *Times*, January 1, 1950, Sec. 2, p. 3.

Interview in which McCullers discusses the themes of *Member* and why and how she wrote the play.

F17   Bromley, Dorothy Dunbar. "Boy, Star at 7, Doesn't Know He Is Famous--Brandon De Wilde's Parents, Actors Themselves, Don't Want Him a 'Stage Brat.'" New York *Herald Tribune*, February 3, 1950, p. 22.

Account of how De Wilde got role in *Member* and interview with him and his parents.

F18   Broughton, Panthea Reid. "Rejection of the Feminine in Carson McCullers' *The Ballad of the Sad Café*." *Twentieth Century Literature*, 20 (January 1974), 34-43.

Uses theories of de Tocqueville, Karl Stern, and Theodore Roszak in concluding that *Ballad* "may be interpreted as a fable which shows us that rejecting those characteristics labeled as exclusively feminine bounces back on the rejector and renders men and women alike incapable of loving and thereby escaping the prisons of their own spiritual isolation."

F19   Bryan, Don. "Novelist Had Local Relatives." Columbus
       (Ga.) *Enquirer*, September 30, 1967, pp. 1, 2.

       Several of McCullers' hometown relatives and friends
       reminisce about their memories of her, on occasion of
       her death.

F20   Buchen, Irving H. "Carson McCullers: A Case of Conver-
       gence." *Bucknell Review*, 21 (Spring 1973), 15-28.

       McCullers used as example of how psychology can be used
       in literary criticism. Her works are conducive to such
       an approach, especially from a Freudian perspective:
       incest and the guilt for such illicit desire motivates
       much of the action in her fiction.

F21   ————. "Divine Collusion: The Art of Carson McCullers."
       Dalhousie Review, 54 (Autumn 1974), 529-541.

       Discussion of the collusion between McCullers' aesthetics
       and metaphysics which produces her work. Her art provides
       "the flowering dream by which to measure and portray the
       permanent dream of paradisaical exclusion." Art is "the
       square root of heaven on earth."

F22   Byrne, Mary Margaret. "Columbus-Born Writer--McCullers
       Portrait Here." Columbus (Ga.) *Sunday Ledger-Enquirer*,
       July 21, 1968, p. D-8.

       Article advocates that McCullers' hometown purchase
       Emanuel Romano's portrait because she "has long been
       recognized as a major American literary talent."

F23   ————. "For Famous Writer's Cousin--New Show Has a
       Special Meaning." Columbus (Ga.) *Ledger*, November 2,
       1967, p. 25.

       Ginger Storey, cast as Mick in "The Lonely Hunting," a
       dramatization of excerpts from four McCullers works,
       describes a 1965 meeting with McCullers. See F25 and
       F110.

F24   ————. "Lovable Latimer Watson Like Glass of Sparkling
       Champagne." Columbus (Ga.) *Sunday Ledger-Enquirer*,
       July 30, 1961, Sec. 9, pp. 13, 14.

       Brief reminiscence of McCullers when, as Carson Smith,
       she worked as a reporter on her hometown newspaper.

F25   ————. "A Review--McCullers Tribute Done Well."
       Columbus (Ga.) *Ledger*, November 7, 1967, p. 14.

Favorable review of "The Lonely Hunting." See F23 and F110.

F26 ———. "Wednesday in N.Y.--Carson McCullers Play to Premiere." Columbus (Ga.) *Ledger*, October 25, 1963, p. 6.

Announcement of opening of Albee's adaptation of *Ballad*, which notes which of McCullers' family and Columbus friends will be at premiere.

F27 "Call on the Author." *Newsweek*, 58 (September 18, 1961), 106, 108.

Description of McCullers' physical condition, her home, and her black maid.

F28 Calta, Louis. "McCullers' Play to Open Tonight." New York *Times*, January 5, 1950, p. 29.

Plot summary of *Member* and list of cast, director, and producer.

F29 "Canny McCullers Writes About Self--But Not Much." Atlanta *Constitution*, April 28, 1946, Magazine, p. 20.

Facts about McCullers' life and works to date drawn from material she sent to the newspaper at its request. Includes quotations about her work from critics.

F30 Capes, Reggie. "Carson McCullers Was Author--'Heart Is Lonely Hunter' Filming to End at Selma." Columbus (Ga.) *Ledger*, December 4, 1967, p. 15.

General comments on the adaptation and filming of *Heart*.

F31 Carpenter, Frederic I. "The Adolescent in American Fiction." *English Journal*, 46 (September 1957), 313-319 [316-317].

Discussion of "the problems of adolescence and its confrontations of the evils of experience" in *Heart* and *Member*. *Member* is compared to *Catcher in the Rye*.

F32 "Carson McCullers." Atlanta *Journal*, September 30, 1967, p. 12-A.

Obituary editorial. McCullers' work, while set in the South, has "global qualities."

F33 "Carson McCullers." New Orleans *Times-Picayune*, October 3, 1967, p. 8.

Obituary editorial which praises the quality of McCullers'
writing, her grasp of dialogue and of the "reality of
the Southern mind."

F34   "Carson McCullers." *New York Times Book Review*,
       September 17, 1961, p. 5.

       Brief character portrait and references to her poor
       physical condition. She is described as having "an
       impish humor and philosophical calm and ... three pas-
       sions: people, writing and music."

F35   "Carson McCullers." Norfolk *Virginian-Pilot*, September 30,
       1967, p. 14.

       Obituary tribute: "She is one of the handful of contempo-
       rary writers to claim a lasting place on the shelf."
       This article was reprinted in the Richmond (Va.) *Times-
       Dispatch*, October 4, 1967, p. A-10.

F36   "Carson McCullers." Raleigh *News and Observer*,
       September 30, 1967, p. 4.

       Obituary editorial praising McCullers' ability "to re-
       create, with rich complexity, a small world of sense and
       sensory impressions.... Hers was not the literature for
       a season, and as her artistic penetrations grow, her
       fame will become commensurate with her talent."

F37   "Carson McCullers Dies at 50, Wrote of Loneliness and
       Love." New York *Times*, September 30, 1967, pp. 1, 40.

       Almost entirely biographical obituary article.

F38   "Carson McCullers Has Double Dose of Success in Novel and
       Broadway Play." Nyack (N.Y.) *Journal-News*, February 10,
       1950, p. 1.

       Account of the success of *Member*, with particular focus
       on the excellence of Brandon De Wilde's performance and
       the circumstances of the play's composition.

F39   "Carson McCullers in Coma." New York *Times*, September 3,
       1967, p. 40.

       News article that McCullers, "who has been paralyzed for
       some time," is in a coma now.

F40   "Carson McCullers--Novelist of the Deep South." London
       Times, September 30, 1967, p. 12.

Obituary notice, which includes a biographical sketch, brief discussions of the works, and a comment on her theme of unrequited love.

F41   "Carson McCuller's [sic] Play 'Member of the Wedding' Opens on Broadway Jan. 5." Columbus (Ga.) *Sunday Ledger-Enquirer*, December 4, 1949, Sec. C, p. 8.

Announcement of forthcoming opening, description of McCullers' Christmas article in *Mademoiselle*, and brief account of visit to McCullers in New York by childhood friend.

F42   Casey, Phil. "Author Carson McCullers Dead; Dramatized Human Loneliness." Washington (D.C.) *Post*, September 30, 1967, p. B3.

Description of McCullers' career and praise for her work.

F43   Clark, Charlene. "Selfhood and the Southern Past: A Reading of Carson McCullers' *Clock Without Hands*." *Southern Literary Messenger*, 1 (Spring 1975), 16–23.

Clock "has to do with self-definition, more specifically the individual's attempt at self-discovery through knowledge of the past both public and private." As such, it is "by far Mrs. McCullers' most 'Southern' novel, not in the mere parochial sense that it deals with political and social issues that are peculiar to the region, but in its embodiment of that tragic sense of history that is distinctly Southern."

F44   Clurman, Harold. "'Member of a Wedding' [sic] Upsets a Theory: Director Harold Clurman Says Its Success Calls For a New Definition of an Old Question--What Is a Play?" New York *Herald Tribune*, January 29, 1950, Sec. 5, p. 3.

Clurman's account of how he came to direct *Member* and his defense of it against critics who claim it is not a play because it has no action.

F45   "Contributors." *Story*, 9 (December 1936), 113–114.

Contributor's note on Carson Smith which mentions her studying with Sylvia Chatfield Bates and Whit Burnett. This is the earliest mention of McCullers.

F46   Cordell, Actor, Jr. "Carson McCullers' Movie Teen-Ager." Atlanta *Journal and Constitution*, January 14, 1968, Magazine, pp. 10, 28.

Discussion of movie adaptation of *Heart*.

F47   "Creative Artists Win $1,000 Prizes--Ten Awards Made by
       American Academy of Arts and Letters and National Insti-
       tute." New York *Times*, April 14, 1943, p. 46.

       Mentions that McCullers has received one of the $1,000
       grants.

F48   Crist, Judith. "Call It Sad, Call It Funny." New York
       Herald Tribune, October 27, 1957, Sec. 4, pp. 1, 2.

       Brief discussion of background and story line of *Square
       Root*.

F49   ⸻. "'Member of the Wedding'--Ethel Waters Returns
       Thursday in a Part She Finds Very Much Like Herself."
       New York *Herald Tribune*, January 1, 1950, Sec. 5, p. 1.

       Interview in which Ethel Waters discusses the play and
       her role in it.

F50   Cuniff, Robert. "Famous Failures--Carson McCullers:
       Music for Literature." *Show*, 2 (July 1962), 72.

       Discussion of McCullers' abandonment of music in favor of
       writing at age 16. Includes quotations from McCullers.

F51   Danesi, Natalia. "Georgia Writer Here on Fellowship."
       Rome (Italy) *Daily American*, April 20, 1947.

       Article-interview in which McCullers' career is summarized
       and in which she comments briefly on her life in Rome.
       This item was seen only as a clipping in the University
       of Texas collection.

F52   Dedmond, Francis B. "Doing Her Own Thing: Carson
       McCullers' Dramatization of 'The Member of the Wedding.'"
       South Atlantic Bulletin, 40 (May 1975), 47-52.

       Overview which examines play's departures from the novel
       and the structure of the adaptation.

F53   Dennis, Nigel. "Sex Among the Writers." London *Sunday
       Telegraph*, October 7, 1962, p. 5.

       Brief mention of McCullers' participation in "Sex in
       Literature" symposium at Cheltenham Festival. See also
       F2, F220, and F234.

F54   "Died." *Newsweek*, 70 (October 9, 1967), 65.

       Brief obituary notice.

F55 Diehl, Digby. "Edward Albee." *Transatlantic Review*, 13 (Summer 1963), 57-72 [57, 69, 70].

Interview in which Albee discusses why he chose to adapt *Ballad* for the stage and what he is trying to do with his adaptation.

F56 Doar, Harriet. "'Love ... Is at the Heart'--Battling Ill Health, Carson McCullers Writes On." Charlotte *Observer*, May 5, 1963, p. 10-C.

Interview in which McCullers discusses her home in Nyack, N.Y., her clothes, her maid, her early life, and *Heart*, *Clock*, and *Pickle*.

F57 ————. "A Southern Writer Still Young in Heart." Charlotte *Observer*, January 2, 1966, p. 6F.

Mention that McCullers has won the Prize of the Younger Generation awarded by the German newspaper *Die Welt*.

F58 Dodd, Wayne D. "The Development of Theme Through Symbol in the Novels of Carson McCullers." *Georgia Review*, 17 (Summer 1963), 206-213.

McCullers' "suggestive and developmental symbolism" illuminates her theme of "the discreteness of individuals from each other and from God Himself." Includes discussions of *Heart*, *Reflections*, *Member*, and *Ballad*.

F59 Dorin, Rube. "'Square Root' Opens Tonight." New York *Morning Telegraph*, October 30, 1957, pp. 1, 2.

Lists cast and production staff, gives synopsis of plot, quotes McCullers' description of the theme, and excerpts comment from out-of-town review.

F60 Drake, Robert. "The Lonely Heart of Carson McCullers." *Christian Century*, 85 (January 10, 1968), 50-51.

McCullers' writing often suffers from lack of control when she tries to tell too many stories, has too many grotesque characters or too much social consciousness in a single work. Her best works are *Heart* and *Member*.

F61 Durham, Frank. "God and No God in 'The Heart Is a Lonely Hunter.'" *South Atlantic Quarterly*, 56 (Autumn 1957), 494-499.

In *Heart*, McCullers uses "ironic religious allegory ... to reinforce ... [her] concept of the discreteness of

human beings, not just from each other, but from God
Himself." Perhaps McCullers "is saying [that] with the
destruction of the pagan past, the Christian myth derived
from it collapses."

F62   Dwyer, Rebecca. "McCullers in Baltimore." *Drama
      Critique*, 11 (Winter 1968), 47-48.

      Review of Center Stage production of *Member* which faults
      the director for over-stretching the play's "delicate
      structure of mood and meaning."

F63   "The Editor's Guest Book." *Harper's Bazaar*, 74 (October
      1940), 25.

      Contributor's note which calls McCullers a "writer's
      writer" and praises *Heart* and *Reflections*.

F64   Edmonds, Dale. "'Correspondence': A 'Forgotten' Carson
      McCullers Short Story." *Studies in Short Fiction*, 9
      (Winter 1972), 89-92.

      The story is important in showing the bridge between Mick
      and Frankie, as well as for capturing the language of
      adolescents.

F65   Emerson, Donald. "The Ambiguities of *Clock Without
      Hands*." *Wisconsin Studies in Contemporary Literature*,
      3 (Fall 1962), 15-28.

      Exploration of the themes, characters, and structure of
      Clock, with emphasis on the central symbol--the clock
      without hands. This symbol is "richest in the context of
      Mrs. McCullers' other work, it in turn sharpens the con-
      trasts in her picture of man's fate.... she discloses a
      world in which troubles from eternity do not fail and
      the instrument of their chronology marks no certain hour."

F66   "Ethel Waters to Stay in 'Wedding' to June '51." New York
      Sunday Compass, February 12, 1950, Magazine, p. 16.

      News story that Waters and Brandon De Wilde have both
      had their contracts extended due to the "rapid climb of
      the advance sale, from the original $6,000 to $122,000
      in one month."

F67   Evans, Oliver. "The Achievement of Carson McCullers."
      English Journal, 51 (May 1962), 301-308.

      McCullers' work is so controversial and misunderstood
      because she is a realistic allegorical writer. She

writes so realistically that most readers fail to see
that she is an allegorical writer. See E36.

F68 ———. "The Case of Carson McCullers." *Georgia Review*,
18 (Spring 1964), 40-45.

McCullers' mixed critical reception is due to three
problems: her "message" of loneliness which is only
temporarily relieved through unrequited love is an un-
popular one; her characters' deformities, which are
chosen to underscore her theme of spiritual isolation,
are seen as real--not the symbols they are--and are thus
misunderstood; and she writes so realistically that the
allegory and symbolism of her work is lost on some
readers. See E36.

F69 ———. "The Case of the Silent Singer: A Revaluation of
The Heart Is a Lonely Hunter." *Georgia Review*, 19
(Summer 1965), 188-203.

Discussion of the flaws in *Heart*, with emphasis on the
allegorical meaning of the book--man's isolation from man
and his search for meaning in life which can only come
from love. See E36.

F70 ———. "The Pad in Brooklyn Heights." *The Nation*, 199
(July 13, 1964), 15-16.

Biographical account of McCullers' residency in Brooklyn,
where she lived with Richard Wright, Auden, Gypsy Rose
Lee, and others. See E36.

F71 ———. "The Theme of Spiritual Isolation in Carson
McCullers." *New World Writing*, 1 (April 1952), 297-310.

McCullers' writing has theme of "spiritual isolation"
which can only be broken down by love. This essay is
reprinted in Rubin and Jacobs' *South* (E37); see also E36.

F72 Feibleman, Peter S. "A Play Is Born from Novel." Boston
Sunday Globe, July 8, 1962, p. A-3.

McCullers quoted and *Member* mentioned briefly in discussion of plays adapted from novels.

F73 Fletcher, Mary Dell. "Carson McCullers' 'Ancient
Mariner.'" *South Central Bulletin*, 35 (Winter 1975),
123-125.

Comparison and contrast of McCullers' "A Tree. A Rock. A
Cloud." and Coleridge's poem, with emphasis on use of the

archetypal Cain figure in both as well as differences in
the way a similar theme is handled.

F74   Folk, Barbara Nauer. "The Sad Sweet Music of Carson
      McCullers." *Georgia Review*, 16 (Summer 1962), 202-209.

      Discussion of the use of music as an "architectural
      framework," "extended correlative," and "minor symbol"
      in McCullers' work.

F75   Ford, Nick Aaron. "Search for Identity: A Critical Sur-
      vey of Significant Belles-Lettres By and About Negroes
      Published in 1961." *Phylon*, 23 (Second Quarter 1962),
      128-138 [130-133].

      Discussion of use of suspense and irony and the search
      for identity in *Clock*.

F76   "14 Win Admission to Arts Institute--Waldo Frank, Eudora
      Welty, Carson McCullers Among Those Named Members." New
      York *Times*, February 8, 1952, p. 18.

      News story announcing McCullers' election to the National
      Institute of Arts and Letters.

F77   "Frankie! She's Married!" New York *Sunday Compass*,
      February 5, 1950, Magazine, p. 16.

      Interview with actress Julie Harris who talks of her
      experiences with role of Frankie in *Member*.

F78   Fremont-Smith, Eliot. "The Heart Stands Out." New York
      Times, September 30, 1967, p. 40.

      Obituary tribute which praises *Heart* as McCullers' best
      novel and discusses the realism of Dr. Copeland and the
      juxtaposition of love and loneliness.

F79   Friedman, Melvin J. "*The Mortgaged Heart*: The Workshop
      of Carson McCullers." *Revue des Langues Vivantes*, 42
      (U.S. Bicentennial Issue 1976), 143-155.

      Comparison of McCullers' early work with that of
      Flannery O'Connor. Former, as seen in *The Mortgaged
      Heart*, seems unfinished, amateurish, and miscellaneous;
      unlike O'Connor's early work, McCullers' will not ad-
      vance her reputation but merely gives "the world a long
      look at the mediocre side of the author of *The Member
      of the Wedding*."

F80   Funke, Lewis. "News and Gossip Gathered on the Rialto--
      Praise." New York *Times*, February 19, 1950, Sec. 2, p. 1.

Novelist-playwright John Van Druten is quoted in praise of *Member* as "a new kind of playwriting ... [which projects] mood, and ... inner, rather than the outer lives of the characters."

F81 ———. "News of the Rialto: Major Coup." New York *Times*, May 21, 1961, Sec. 2, p. 1.

Brief mention that producer Kermit Bloomgarden has purchased the stage rights to *Clock* and that Albert and Frances Hackett will do the adaptation, with George Roy Hill as director.

F82 ———. "Rialto Gossip--Ironic Notes on the Critics Circle's Best American Play--Other Items." New York *Times*, April 9, 1950, Sec. 2, p. 2.

Discussion of the problems encountered in finding a producer and director for *Member*.

F83 Gaillard, Dawson F. "The Presence of the Narrator in Carson McCullers' *The Ballad of the Sad Café*." *Mississippi Quarterly*, 25 (Fall 1972), 419-428.

The narrator is not only a representative of the community, but his "presence, his telling, lifts the story beyond the commonplace facts, beyond the immediate, and beyond history"; and the café itself, "because of the narrator's response to it, takes on mythic proportions."

F84 Gardner, Paul. "Rialto News." New York *Times*, August 11, 1963, Sec. 2, p. 1.

Brief mention of progress on Albee's adaptation of *Ballad*, including Albee's statement, "'No one should realize where McCullers stops and Albee starts.'"

F85 Gehman, Richard. "Guardian Angel." *Theatre Arts*, 34 (July 1950), 19-23.

Article on theatrical agent Audrey Wood mentions McCullers as one of her clients.

F86 Gelb, Arthur. "Script Revision Held Increasing: Lantz, Producer, Sees Need for Extensive Rewriting." New York *Times*, October 21, 1959, p. L 49.

Lantz quoted as feeling that "'if I had had "The Square Root of Wonderful" to work on from the beginning, which I didn't, it would have been a much better play.'"

F87   ————. "Story of an Actress Who Gained Fame in Flops."
       New York *Times*, May 14, 1950, p. 2x.

       Article on Julie Harris which notes that McCullers chose
       her for the part of Frankie Addams.

F88   Giannetti, Louis D. *"The Member of the Wedding."*
       Literature/Film Quarterly, 4 (Winter 1976), 28-38.

       Comparison and contrast of novel, play, and film with
       respect to theme ("entrapment, loneliness, and frustra-
       tion") and structure.

F89   Ginsberg, Elaine. "The Female Initiation Theme in
       American Fiction." *Studies in American Fiction*, 3
       (Spring 1975), 27-37 [34-35].

       Brief studies of *Member* and *Heart* as two novels which
       present "young girls who begin a journey toward self-
       awareness, maturity, and womanhood."

F90   Gordy, Mary. "Ledger Reporter Finds Former Columbus
       Girl, Now Celebrated Author, Unspoiled by Fame."
       Columbus (Ga.) *Ledger*, December 16, 1940, p. 7.

       Article-interview in which McCullers talks about her new
       novel (*Reflections*) and about life in New York City.

F91   "The Gregarious Reader." Boston *Sunday Globe*,
       September 10, 1961, p. 64.

       Brief announcement of forthcoming September 18th publica-
       tion of *Clock* and the reissuing on that date of all
       McCullers' books in single editions.

F92   Griffith, Albert J. "Carson McCullers' Myth of the Sad
       Café." *Georgia Review*, 21 (Spring 1967), 46-56.

       Exploration of the characters and events in *Ballad*,
       undertaken to prove the thesis that it is a modern myth:
       "Both the characters and events in 'The Ballad of the
       Sad Café' ... have the remoteness, the mystery, the
       numinousness of myth."

F93   Grinnell, James W. "Delving 'A Domestic Dilemma.'"
       Studies in Short Fiction, 9 (Summer 1972), 270-271.

       "The real irony of Martin and Emily's dilemma was that
       his concern for what others thought rendered him unable
       to show his love ... which she needed in order to be
       well."

F94 Hamilton, Alice. "Loneliness and Alienation: The Life
and Work of Carson McCullers." *Dalhousie Review*, 50
(Summer 1970), 215-229.

Discussion of McCullers' characters' need for expression
and "interior freedom," which is seen as the search for
love and for artistic creation. Emphasis on *Heart* and
Reflections.

F95 Hart, Jane. "Carson McCullers, Pilgrim of Loneliness."
Georgia Review, 11 (Spring 1957), 53-58.

McCullers' characters are not chosen for their grotesque-
ness; rather their deformities accentuate the loneliness
that all human beings feel. They overcome their loneliness by making a pilgrimage to a relationship where they
can give love to someone or something.

F96 Hassan, Ihab. "Carson McCullers: The Alchemy of Love and
Aesthetics of Pain." *Modern Fiction Studies*, 5 (Winter
1959-1960), 311-326.

Analysis of the elements of love and pain as they inter-
act with the themes of loneliness and spiritual isolation
in McCullers' novels. This essay, slightly revised, is
reprinted in Hassan's *Radical Innocence*. See E59.

F97 ————. "The Character of Post-War Fiction in America."
English Journal, 51 (January 1962), 1-8.

Scattered references to McCullers and her works, with
comments on *Heart*, *Member*, and *Ballad*. This essay is
reprinted in *On Contemporary Literature*, edited by
Richard Kostelanetz, and in *Recent American Fiction*,
edited by Joseph J. Waldmeir. See E60.

F98 ————. "Laughter in the Dark--The New Voice in American
Fiction." *American Scholar*, 33 (Autumn 1964), 636-640
[638].

Brief mention of McCullers, along with Welty, Flannery
O'Connor, and Purdy, as creators of freaks and monsters
who "are the subjects of veiled mockery; their abnormality
shocks and shames us into ironic laughter."

F99 ————. "The Victim: Images of Evil in Recent American
Fiction." *College English*, 21 (December 1959), 140-146
[144-145].

In McCullers' works, especially *Heart* and *Ballad*, evil is
the denial and rejection of love, but mankind must offer
love anyway without expecting anything in return.

F100   ————. "The Way Down and Out." *Virginia Quarterly
        Review*, 39 (Winter 1963), 81-93 [87, 88, 90].

        Brief scattered comments about McCullers characters,
        including Singer (*Heart*) and Miss Amelia (*Ballad*).

F101   Hawkins, William. "Theater——Ethel Waters Discloses How
        Religion Helps Her." New York *World-Telegram*, January 4,
        1950, p. 33.

        Interview on eve of opening of *Member* in which Ethel
        Waters tells how she came to accept role in the play
        after meeting McCullers.

F102   Hendrick, George. "'Almost Everyone Wants to Be the
        Lover': The Fiction of Carson McCullers." *Books Abroad*,
        42 (Summer 1968), 389-391.

        Brief discussion of the isolation of the characters in
        each of the novels and of their search for love.

F103   Hewes, Henry. "Ethel Waters and a Hymn——An Actress
        Talks About the Song She Sings in Hit Play." New York
        Times, April 30, 1950, Sec. 2, p. 2.

        Interview in which Ethel Waters talks about the role of
        Berenice and how she, director Harold Clurman, and
        McCullers changed it in production.

F104   Hicks, Granville. "Books." *American Way*, 8 (August
        1975), 34-35.

        In the course of a review of Virginia Spencer Carr's
        biography of McCullers (E17), Hicks reminisces about
        his own contacts with McCullers and gives his estimate
        of her work.

F105   Hutchens, John K. "Carson McCullers." *New York Herald
        Tribune Book Review*, June 17, 1951, p. 2.

        Interview, with comments on *Member*, childhood plays
        that she wrote, and an upcoming novel.

F106   "An Interview with Carson McCullers." *Literary
        Cavalcade*, 9 (February 1957), 15.

        McCullers gives a brief summary of her life to date,
        talks about books she liked when she was younger, and
        discusses her style of writing.

F107   "J.R. M'Cullers Jr. Dies--Husband of Novelist, Play-
        wright, Succumbs in Paris at 40." New York *Times*,
        November 27, 1953, p. 27.

        Obituary of McCullers' husband.

F108   Johnson, Carlton. "Editor's Notebook--'A Golden Hand.'"
        Columbus (Ga.) *Ledger*, October 3, 1967, p. 4.

        Obituary tribute which includes reminiscence of meeting
        McCullers on steps of public library in Columbus in the
        early 1940's.

F109   Johnson, Constance. "Columbus People Remember Carson."
        Columbus (Ga.) *Ledger*, September 29, 1967, pp. 1, 2.

        Four people who knew McCullers, including a former high
        school teacher, and one of her mother's friends, recall
        her sensitivity, shyness, sweetness, talent, and in-
        ability to dress fashionably.

F110   ————. "Tribute to Columbus-Born Writer--Theater Hopes
        to Honor McCullers." Columbus (Ga.) *Ledger*, October 13,
        1967, p. 13.

        Article on planned dramatic memorial to McCullers,
        scenes from her novels and plays. See also F23 and F25.

F111   ————. "With McCullers Presentation This Week--
        Springer Theater to Pay Tribute to Memory of Famous
        Local Author." Columbus (Ga.) *Sunday Ledger-Enquirer*,
        November 5, 1967, p. B-1.

        McCullers' cousin, Mrs. Edward Storey, says that the
        author was self-confident and was raised in a "happy"
        and "normal" home. She praises McCullers' fiction but
        notes that the Columbus she wrote about was of her child-
        hood and that her characters "are products of her
        imagination."

F112   Johnson, James William. "The Adolescent Hero: A Trend
        in Modern Fiction." *Twentieth Century Literature*, 5
        (April 1959), 3-11 [6, 7].

        Brief mention of Frankie's sense of loss, sexual confu-
        sion, awareness of body changes, and flight from reality.

F113   Kazin, Alfred. "Heroines." *New York Review of Books*,
        16 (February 11, 1971), 28-34 [29-30].

McCullers' works present the myth of "the utter disloca-
tion of love in our time" and in "our town." Mentions
how style, setting, deviant sexuality, and characterization contribute to this myth. This essay is reprinted
in Kazin's *Bright Book of Life.* See E67.

F114   ————. "We Who Sit in Darkness--The Broadway Audience
at the Play." *Commentary*, 9 (June 1950), 525-529 [527-
528].

Disparages *Member*, along with other modern plays, for
its neglect of the audience which, with no dramatic action and plot to become absorbed in, must fix its attention on the characters, whose dialogue is not written
to be heard by the audience, but as though there were no
chance of its being overheard. This essay is reprinted
in Kazin's *The Inmost Leaf.* See E68.

F115   Kelley, Marion. "Backstage--Julie Harris Plays Child
Role in Play." Philadelphia *Inquirer*, December 18, 1949,
Society Section, pp. 23, 26.

Interview during pre-Broadway tryout of *Member.*

F116   Kelly, Frank K. "'Lonely' Miss McCullers Coming Home
to Write." Atlanta *Journal*, November 16, 1941, p. 13-A.

Interview in which McCullers discusses *Heart* and
Reflections, how difficult it is to write in a distract-
ing place, the critics' responses to her books, her jobs,
and how she writes.

F117   Klein, Marcus. "The Key Is Loneliness." *The Reporter*,
34 (June 30, 1966), 43-44.

McCullers is criticized for her "severely controlled
fiction" in which there is "the constant and virtually
automatic conversion of character into symbol." Comparison with Sherwood Anderson; she is a more "crafty
writer," but his work has more "drama."

F118   Kohler, Dayton. "Carson McCullers: Variations on a
Theme." *College English*, 13 (October 1951), 1-8.

Lengthy analysis of the recurring themes, symbols, and
the objective style in McCullers' works. Emphasis is
on her sensitivity as a writer and on her ability to
portray characters and events realistically. When her
works fail, it is because she has become less objective,
not because she lacks insight or understanding. This

essay also appeared in *English Journal*, 40 (October 1951), 415-422.

F119 Korenman, Joan S. "Carson McCullers' 'Proletarian Novel.'" *Studies in the Humanities* (Indiana University of Pennsylvania), 5 (January 1976), 8-13.

Heart's "major components--setting, characterization, and plot development--are all shaped by McCullers' disapproval of materialistic values and often reflect, too, her objections to capitalism."

F120 Lahr, John. "The Adaptable Mr. Albee." *Evergreen Review*, 12 (May 1968), 37-39, 82-87.

Discussion of Albee's adaptation of *Ballad*.

F121 Lask, Thomas. "Edward Albee at Ease." New York *Times*, October 27, 1963, Sec. 2, pp. 1, 3.

Mention of Albee's interest in *Ballad*, which he sees as having "great visual possibilities."

F122 ———. "Readings from Swift to Faulkner: Records." New York *Times*, May 4, 1958, Sec. 2, p. 16X.

Review of MGM recording of McCullers reading from her works which "stands apart from the others for it is not so much an introduction to her work as it is to the lady herself. Her occasional waywardness with the text, her emotional involvement in what she is reading, the break in her voice in certain passages--all these give this recording its own special quality though it is not always a literary one."

F123 "The Laurels." *Time*, 55 (April 17, 1950), 80.

Announcement that Drama Critics' Circle Award has been voted to *Member*.

F124 Lee, Harry. "Columbus Girl Thinks South Is 'Sick'-- Carson McCullers Wrote 'The Heart Is a Lonely Hunter.'" Atlanta *Constitution*, March 6, 1941, p. 4.

Article based on an interview in which McCullers comments on the South, both as a section of the country and as an environment from which to draw material, and on the "Southern Renaissance" in American writing.

F125 [Lewis, Emory]. "The Season's Best New Play." *Cue*, 19 (January 28, 1950), 14-15.

Brief descriptive praise of *Member* and photographs of
the production.

F126   "A Lonely Hunter." New York *Times*, September 30, 1967,
       p. 32.

       Obituary editorial which praises McCullers' "allegorical"
       stories which "dignified the individual" and "transcended
       their regional frame." She "reflected the lonely heart
       with a golden hand."

F127   Lowndes, Marion. "That's the Spirit." *Mademoiselle*,
       23 (October 1946), 182-183, 290-292 [290].

       Brief mention of ghost in McCullers' Nyack house.

F128   Lowry, Robert. "It's Still the Village." *Mademoiselle*,
       24 (November 1946), 172-173, 303-308 [306].

       Brief mention of McCullers.

F129   Lubbers, Klaus. "The Necessary Order: A Study of Theme
       and Structure in Carson McCullers' Fiction." *Jahrbuch
       für Amerikastudien*, 8 (1963), 187-204.

       Reevaluation of McCullers' achievement by examining in
       chronological order "the interrelation of themes and
       artistic organization" in *Heart*, *Reflections*, *Member*,
       Ballad, and *Clock*. Emphasis is on the evolution of her
       themes from early works to later ones.

F130   McCord, Bert. "News of the Theater." New York *Herald
       Tribune*, October 10, 1947, p. 15.

       Brief announcement that Mary Anderson has been offered
       the lead in *Member*, a play by McCullers and Greer Johnson
       which has been scheduled for production by the Theatre
       Guild.

F131   ————. "News of the Theater." New York *Herald
       Tribune*, January 5, 1950, p. 18.

       Blurb publicizing the opening of *Member*.

F132   "McCullers Honored." Atlanta *Journal and Constitution*,
       April 30, 1967, p. 16-B.

       Announcement that McCullers has won the "1966 Henry
       Bellamann Award of $1,000 in recognition of outstanding
       contribution to literature."

F133   "McCullers Honored." New York *Times*, December 18, 1965, p. 27.

Announcement that McCullers has won the Prize of the Younger Generation awarded by *Die Welt*.

F134   MacDougall, Sally. "Author, 22, Urges Aid to Refugees." New York *World-Telegram*, July 1, 1940, p. 12.

Interview in which McCullers suggests that all refugees who seek admission to the United States should be let in. She adds that she herself would like to adopt a refugee child from France.

F135   McGill, Ralph. "'Ballad of the Sad Café.'" Atlanta *Constitution*, November 13, 1963, p. 1.

Biographical reminiscences of McGill's friendship with McCullers.

F136   ———. "Ballad of C. McCullers." Atlanta *Constitution*, September 30, 1967, pp. 1, 11.

Obituary tribute. McCullers was "widely considered to be the leading woman writer to come out of the South." Includes biographical sketch and quotations from McCullers.

F137   ———. "Carson McCullers: 1917-1967." *Saturday Review*, 50 (October 21, 1967), 31, 88.

Obituary tribute with personal reminiscences. McCullers "was a very great artist and human being."

F138   ———. "Carson McCullers Conquers New York Again." Atlanta *Constitution*, October 31, 1963, p. 31.

Review-article on New York opening of Albee's adaptation of *Ballad*, with emphasis on the play's relationship to the novel.

F139   ———. "Monument to Courage." Boston *Globe*, October 16, 1961, p. 14.

Praise for McCullers' "spirit in which there dwells courage and resolution" and for *Clock*, in which the "characterizations are magnificent." This article also appeared in Atlanta *Constitution*, October 17, 1961, p. 1.

F140   McNally, John. "The Introspective Narrator in 'The
       Ballad of the Sad Café.'" *South Atlantic Bulletin*, 38
       (November 1973), 40-44.

       Detailed examination of the narrator in *Ballad*. It is
       "a beautifully sculptured piece of writing in which we
       overhear the internal monologue of a character whose
       haunting recollections enable him to overcome his own
       ennui and to resist the atrophying pressure of the
       familiar world."

F141   McPherson, Hugo. "Carson McCullers: Lonely Huntress."
       Tamarack Review, 11 (Spring 1959), 28-40.

       Examination of the spiritual isolation in McCullers'
       works, the characters' problems of sexual identity, and
       the disunity of the spiritual and the physical.

F142   Madden, David. "The Paradox of the Need for Privacy and
       the Need for Understanding in Carson McCullers' *The
       Heart Is a Lonely Hunter*." *Literature & Psychology*, 17
       (Nos. 2-3, 1967), 128-140.

       Psychological interpretations of Singer, Biff Brannon,
       Mick Kelly, Dr. Copeland, and Jake Blount. The para-
       doxical conflict with which McCullers is concerned in
       Heart is that "everyone hungers for human understanding
       while simultaneously desiring an inviolable privacy."

F143   Maddocks, Melvin. "Little Precious." *Time*, 106
       (July 21, 1975), 63-64.

       Review of Virginia Spencer Carr's *The Lonely Hunter*
       (E17) which also includes comment on McCullers: "A poet
       of tall tales of damnation she wrote of a time and
       place that seemed peopled by myths and driven by ob-
       sessions; and she lived as she wrote."

F144   "*The Marquis* Interviews Carson McCullers." *The Marquis*
       (Lafayette College), (1964), 5-6, 20-23.

       Interview in which McCullers discusses her work and
       adaptations of it (especially *Ballad*), her early writing
       experiences, and her taste in literature.

F145   Mathis, Ray. "*Reflections in a Golden Eye*: Myth Making
       in American Christianity." *Religion in Life*, 39 (Winter
       1970), 545-558.

       Reflections explores the secularism, myth-making, and
       religiosity of modern man which "have an interesting

relationship, however unorthodox, to classical
Christianity." The novel lampoons "several traditional
Christian forms and paradoxically reveal[s] a touch of
sympathy for an undefined religious need which point[s]
implicitly toward Christianity."

F146   "'Member of the Wedding' Is Praised by New York Critics."
       Columbus (Ga.) *Ledger*, January 30, 1950, p. 6.

       Summaries of New York reviews of *Member*.

F147   "Memo from the Editor." *Mademoiselle*, 24 (January 1947),
       10.

       Brief mention of a bon voyage party for McCullers and
       Kay Boyle, who have sailed for France.

F148   "Mick." *Literary Cavalcade*, 9 (February 1957), 2-T.

       Student-oriented analysis which asserts that Mick has
       "some universal and unchanging truth about adolescence"
       in her to which students react.

F149   "Milestones." *Time*, 90 (October 6, 1967), 112.

       Obituary notice in which McCullers is hailed as "a
       vibrant voice of love and loneliness in the Southern
       novel."

F150   Millichap, Joseph R. "Carson McCullers' Literary
       Ballad." *Georgia Review*, 27 (Fall 1973), 329-339.

       Analysis of *Ballad* which compares it to a folk ballad,
       with respect to folk traditions, images, and super-
       stitions.

F151   ————. "Distorted Matter and Disjunctive Forms: The
       Grotesque As Modernist Genre." *Arizona Quarterly*, 33
       (Winter 1977), 339-347 [345-346].

       Heart, along with *Winesburg, Ohio* and *The Sound and the
       Fury*, used "to demonstrate the convergence of Grotesque
       matter and disjunctive form in the mode of the Modernist
       Grotesque."

F152   ————. "The Realistic Structure of *The Heart Is a
       Lonely Hunter*." *Twentieth Century Literature*, 17
       (January 1971), 11-17.

       Attempt to demonstrate "through structural analysis the
       psychological and social realism" of *Heart*, McCullers'
       "most typical and successful novel."

F153   "Mlle Passports--News of Other Mlle Writers."
        Mademoiselle, 39 (October 1954), 64.

        "Carson McCullers borrowed Tennessee Williams' New York
        apartment while he was in Rome and is now busy writing
        (mostly poetry); this month she will speak on 'Illumina-
        tion and the Writer' in Philadelphia."

F154   "Miss Baxter Next Star at McCarter--'The Square Root'
        Another Premiere, Thursday Oct. 10." Princeton (N.J.)
        Packet, October 3, 1957.

        Brief notice of the pre-Broadway and pre-Philadelphia
        opening of *Square Root.*

F155   Missey, James. "A McCullers Influence on Albee's *The
        Zoo Story.*" *American Notes & Queries,* 13 (April 1975),
        121-123.

        Comparison of "A Tree. A Rock. A Cloud." with Albee's
        play, with respect to "similar language" and "a similar
        idea about learning to love."

F156   Mitchell, Julian. Review of *Carson McCullers--Her Life
        and Work. London Magazine,* 5 (January 1966), 82-85.

        Review of English edition of Evans' critical biography
        (E36) which includes considerable commentary on
        McCullers' work: she is "an allegorist, whose concern
        is to illustrate the human failure which leads to race
        hatred, unemployment, murder and misery; this failure is
        a failure to love properly." She is "among the foremost
        novelists of our time."

F157   Montgomery, Marion. "The Sense of Violation: Notes
        Toward a Definition of 'Southern' Fiction." *Georgia
        Review,* 19 (Fall 1965), 278-287 [278, 285-286].

        Truly Southern writers have a sense of violation in
        their characters. McCullers' characters are solitary
        and lack the recognition that they are violated and
        must pay for that violation; hence she is more a
        Northern writer than a Southern writer.

F158   Moore, Eugene. "Their Private Battles--Illness Plagues
        Four Georgia Writers." Atlanta *Journal and Constitution,*
        August 15, 1965, p. 6.

        Mention that McCullers, "a quiet meditative girl ...
        [who] has created a body of novels and plays that station
        her high among contemporary writers," is confined to a
        hospital.

F159   Moore, Jack B. "Carson McCullers: The Heart Is a Time-less Hunter." *Twentieth Century Literature*, 11 (July 1965), 76-81.

In *Heart*, McCullers employs the initiation myth "to solve a delicate problem of verisimilitude, and ... re-tells the myth in convincingly contemporaneous terms." Explanation and outline of the traditional pattern of this myth and demonstration of how McCullers' retelling conforms to this pattern, despite its use of the real-istic and the erotic. Mick is "a real girl in a real Southern town, a fairytale princess, and a hero. She learns about sex, experiences a transcendant and temporarily beautiful awakening, and faces her difficult entrance into the adult, real world heroically."

F160   Moore, Janice Townley. "McCullers' *The Ballad of the Sad Café*." *The Explicator*, 29 (November 1970), Item 27.

Note on the description of Cousin Lymon in terms of bird imagery, from the "innocence" of sparrow associa-tions at the beginning to the hawk imagery at the end.

F161   Morehouse, Ward. "Broadway After Dark—Carson McCullers Cuts Her Own Hair." New York *World-Telegram and the Sun*, March 31, 1950, p. 36.

Interview in which McCullers discusses writing *Member*, her illnesses, her early writing and money problems, and the actors in *Member* whom she praises. This article also appeared in Atlanta *Journal*, April 30, 1950, Magazine, p. 5.

F162   ————. "Half Season in Review." New York *World-Telegram and the Sun*, January 7, 1950, p. 7.

Very brief praise of *Member*, which "offered some beauti-ful writing and many tender and poignant moments in a shapeless and formless play."

F163   Morgan, Nonie. "Carson McCullers, Distinguished Novel-ist, and Her Mother Visiting Here." Macon (Ga.) *News*, March 18, 1949, p. 11.

Interview in which McCullers tells of amusing incident in Paris where, due to her ignorance of French, she in-advertently accepted an invitation to speak at the Sorbonne.

F164   ————. "Talkin' It Over." Macon (Ga.) *News*, January 16, 1950, p. 6.

Excerpts from New York reviews of premiere of *Member*.

F165 Morris, Wright. "The Lunatic, the Lover, and the Poet."
      Kenyon Review, 27 (Autumn 1965), 727-737 [734].

      Very brief mention of McCullers and *Reflections*.

F166 "Mrs. Lamar Smith." New York *Times*, June 13, 1955,
      p. 23.

      Obituary notice of McCullers' mother.

F167 "Mrs. McCullers Critically Ill." New York *Times*,
      September 2, 1967, p. 13.

      Brief news item reporting that McCullers, who was brought
      to the Nyack Hospital on August 15th, is in critical
      condition.

F168 "Mr. Willkie Buys Copy of Mrs. McCullers' Book."
      Charlotte *Observer*, July 10, 1940, p. 1.

      Brief AP squib reporting that *Heart* was one of five
      books Wendell Willkie purchased to read on his upcoming
      Colorado vacation.

F169 Nance, William L. "Variations on a Dream: Katherine
      Anne Porter and Truman Capote." *Southern Humanities
      Review*, 3 (Fall 1969), 338-345.

      Very brief mention of McCullers.

F170 "Novelist, Short-Story Writer and Playwright." *New York
      Herald Tribune Books*, September 13, 1961, p. 5.

      Very brief biographical note, with mention of McCullers'
      works, her illnesses, and her husband.

F171 "Obituaries--Carson McCullers." *Variety*, October 4,
      1967, p. 63.

      Brief obituary notice, which gives biographical summary
      and stresses film versions of her novels.

F172 "Obituary Notes." *Publishers Weekly*, 192 (October 9,
      1967), 39, 42 [42].

      Brief summary of her life and works.

F173 O'Brien, Edna. "The Strange World of Carson McCullers."
      Books and Bookmen, 7 (October 1961), 9, 24.

      Brief comments on *Heart*, *Reflections*, "A Tree. A Rock.
      A Cloud.," "A Domestic Dilemma," *Member*, and *Ballad*, and
      praise for the recently published *Clock* ("a very worthy

book") and for its author ("the best living woman writer").

F174   Pachmuss, Temira. "Dostoevsky, D.H. Lawrence, and Carson McCullers: Influences and Confluences." *Germano-Slavica*, No. 4 (Fall 1974), 59–68.

Emphasizes similarities between McCullers and Dostoevsky: the tension between the comic and the tragic, moral isolation with the idea of transcendental love (often accompanied by religious symbols) as an escape from isolation, depressing physical settings, use of crime and violence, a dream-like atmosphere, and symbols and leitmotifs which are dropped and then resumed.

F175   P[aterson], I[sabel] M. "Turns with a Bookworm." *New York Herald Tribune Books*, June 23, 1940, p. 11.

McCullers quoted about *Heart* as a parable about fascism.

F176   Perrine, Laurence. "Restoring 'A Domestic Dilemma.'" *Studies in Short Fiction*, 11 (Winter 1974), 101–104.

Explication which blames the problems in the family's relationship on the move from the South to the North. Martin Meadows is viewed as a compassionate but complex man.

F177   Phillips, Robert S. "Carson McCullers: 1956–1964—A Selected Checklist." *Bulletin of Bibliography*, 24 (September–December 1964), 113–116.

Listing of awards received, selected checklist of writings, reviews, and criticism. Updates Stanley Stewart's earlier checklist (F226).

F178   ————. "Dinesen's 'Monkey' and McCullers' 'Ballad': A Study in Literary Affinity." *Studies in Short Fiction*, 1 (Spring 1964), 184–190.

Cites Dinesen's story as a probable source for *Ballad* by noting such similarities as Amazonian women with incestuous feelings for their fathers, a group of gossips, and the similar functions of the hunchback in *Ballad* and the monkey in "The Monkey."

F179   ————. "Freaking Out: The Short Stories of Carson McCullers." *Southwest Review*, 63 (Winter 1978), 65–73.

Exploration of the theme of "personal dissociation" in the nineteen short stories in *Ballad* and *Mortgaged Heart*.

Suggestion is that there is "less physical abnormality
in the stories" than in the novels; rather there are
"people isolated by circumstance rather than physical
appearance or malady. Instead of freaks, ... [there is]
an inner freaking out."

F180   ———. "The Gothic Architecture of *The Member of the
Wedding*." *Renascence*, 16 (Winter 1964), 59-72.

Discussion of the Gothic elements in McCullers' works,
with emphasis on the themes of spiritual isolation and
the failure of love. *Member* contains these elements,
along with an emphasis on death, sexual fear, and violence, and hence is not "a novel of tender adolescence"
but belongs to the Gothic tradition.

F181   ———. "Painful Love--Carson McCullers' Parable."
Southwest Review, 51 (Winter 1966), 80-86.

Rejection of idea that *Ballad* is typically Gothic, because its grotesqueries are ridiculous and "burlesque."
Rather it is a didactic parable and the characters have
symbolic rather than realistic meaning.

F182   "Play Tells How a Lonely Girl Yearns to Belong with
People." *Life*, 28 (January 23, 1950), 64-65.

Picture-story on premiere production of *Member*: "it is
too diffuse to make a continually perfect play, but it
provides the Broadway season with its first dash of
literary distinction and one of its most entertaining
evenings."

F183   Pollock, Arthur. "Theater Time--Carson McCullers Talks
About Self and First Play." New York *Daily Compass*,
October 7, 1949, p. 18.

Topics include résumé of McCullers' life and work to
date and the writing of *Member*.

F184   ———. "Theater Time--Child Actors No Longer Curly
'Awful Little Things.'" New York *Daily Compass*,
February 15, 1950, p. 22.

Brief approving mention of Brandon De Wilde and of
Member, a "splendid achievement."

F185   ———. "Theater Time--A Play Is a Play Is a Play As
Long As It's Interesting." New York *Daily Compass*,
January 11, 1950, p. 18.

Approving mention of *Member*: "It brings a new and very
sensitive talent to the theater, tells a story that is
no story at all if you believe that the thoughts and
feelings of a lonely girl of twelve can never be a story.
It is a beautiful play."

F186   Pollock-Chagas, Jeremy E. "Rosalina and Amelia: A
Structural Approach to Narrative." *Luso-Brazilian
Review*, 12 (Winter 1975), 263-272.

Ballad and Autran Dourado's *Opéra dos Martos* are examined
with reference to their linear structure, secondary
structure ("based on social and/or psychological relations between the protagonists"), progression (juxta-
position of the beginning and end of the narrative "in
order to determine to what extent the original situation
has progressed"), and "the position of the narrator and
the division of the story into 'voices.'"

F187   Pomeranz, Regina. "Self-Betrayal in Modern American
Fiction." *English Record*, 14 (April 1964), 21-28
[26-27].

Mention of *Clock* and of Malone's not questioning the
"sterility" of his existence as analogous to our betrayal of ourselves (cheating ourselves out of the meaning of life). The hope of the future is in Jester, who
searches for meaning.

F188   Post, Constance. "Three Essentials Cited for Aspiring
Novelists by Carson McCullers." Nyack (N.Y.) *Journal-
News*, August 13, 1963, p. 6.

Biographical sketch.

F189   Powers, Clare. "Chicago Footlights." *Chicago Stagebill*,
September 17, 1951, p. 3.

Article on *Member* which appears in playbill for Chicago
production.

F190   Presley, Delma Eugene. "Carson McCullers and the South."
Georgia Review, 28 (Spring 1974), 19-32.

Discusses McCullers' lack of knowledge of the South.
Although she felt stifled by it and felt the need to
criticize it in her works, she did not know it well
enough to give her fiction a real place, with the exception of *Heart* and *Ballad*.

F191   ————.   "Carson McCullers' Descent to the Earth."
Descant (Texas Christian University), 17 (Fall 1972),
54-60.

Examination of *Clock* which claims that "this novel's
ideology indicates nothing less than her discovery of
the fresh abstraction of hope to replace the stale abstraction of nihilism which buttressed her early literary efforts. Her last novel is not successful because
she attempted to write the new abstraction in the style
of the old; she did not discover a new technique by
which to express her new subject matter."

F192   ————.   "The Man Who Married Carson McCullers." *This
Issue* (McKee Publishing Co., Atlanta), 2 (No. 2, 1973),
13-16.

Discussion of importance of Reeves McCullers to his
wife's work; he is "a significant man who has been
strangely ignored by the students of Carson McCullers."

F193   ————.   "The Moral Function of Distortion in Southern
Grotesque." *South Atlantic Bulletin*, 37 (May 1972),
37-46 [40-42, 45].

The grotesqueries of McCullers' characters show their
"need of the salutary quality of a human love which
transcends the limitations of the flesh."

F194   Rechnitz, Robert M. "The Failure of Love: The Grotesque
in Two Novels by Carson McCullers." *Georgia Review*, 22
(Winter 1968), 454-463.

The grotesque world in McCullers' fiction is caused by
moral failures in the characters. In *Heart*, it is the
characters' inabilities to see and know both the physical
and the intellectual sphere; in *Reflections*, it is the
characters' refusals to know themselves.

F195   Reed, Rex. "'Frankie Addams' at 50." New York *Times*,
April 16, 1967, Sec. 2, p. 15.

Article-interview in which McCullers speaks about the
filming of *Reflections*, Albee's stage version of *Ballad*,
the film version of *Member*, her health, and her feelings
about writing. This essay is reprinted in Reed's *Do
You Sleep in the Nude?* See E91.

F196   ————.   "Movies--The Stars Fall on Alabama Again." New
York *Times*, December 10, 1967, Sec. 2, p. 19.

Discussion of the filming of *Heart*.

F197   ————. "Tennessee Williams Turns Sixty." *Esquire*, 76
        (September 1971), 105-108, 216, 218, 220, 222-223 [220,
        222].

        Williams mentions his deep friendship with McCullers,
        recounts anecdotes about her, and calls her "the only
        real writer the South ever turned out."

F198   Rice, Vernon. "Curtain Cues——A Changed and Unchanged
        Waters." New York *Post*, January 4, 1950, p. 56.

        Interview with Ethel Waters on eve of opening of *Member*.
        She tells how and why she came to accept role in the
        play.

F199   ————. "Curtain Cues——Lowe Warming Up on the Side-
        Lines." New York *Post*, January 11, 1950, p. 52.

        Brief praise for *Member* and for McCullers in column of
        miscellaneous theater news.

F200   ————. "A Little Southern Girl Speaks from a Well of
        Despair." New York *Post*, January 29, 1950, p. 8M.

        Interview with McCullers in which she talks about writing
        Member in tandem with Tennessee Williams who was writing
        Summer and Smoke and about the autobiographical aspects
        of her play.

F201   ————. "She Runs a Nursery for Ideas and Talent." New
        York *Post*, February 5, 1950, p. M11.

        Profile of theatrical agent Audrey Wood, with brief men-
        tion of *Member* and McCullers, who is one of her clients.

F202   Rich, Nancy B. "The 'Ironic Parable of Fascism' in
        The Heart Is a Lonely Hunter." *Southern Literary
        Journal*, 9 (Spring 1977), 108-123.

        Using McCullers' own description (F175) of the novel,
        approaches it as a parable with "a conventional pro-
        tagonist [Biff Brannon] pitted against specific forces,
        but [it] develops in thematic patterns rather than in
        traditional plot formation, treating successively the
        ideas of the nature of government, the failure of
        democracy, and the condition of freedom.... The parable's
        theme is an affirmation of the democratic process."

F203   Robinson, W.R. "The Life of Carson McCullers' Imagina-
        tion." *Southern Humanities Review*, 2 (Summer 1968),
        291-302.

Discussion of the dichotomies in McCullers' work--the
instinct toward both life and death, the dream of the
world and love as opposed to reality. Hers is "a moral
art, severe originally, humane finally; it defines the
walls with which man must exist and affirms that he can
live within them."

F204   Robinson, Wayne. "The Living Theater--Anne Baxter Stars
        Tomorrow in Carson McCullers' Play." Philadelphia
        Sunday Bulletin, October 13, 1957, Sec. 5, pp. 9, 10.

        Article on *Square Root* on eve of its pre-Broadway open-
        ing in Philadelphia.

F205   "Role Is Triumph for Ethel Waters." Providence *Sunday
        Journal*, April 20, 1952, Sec. 6, p. 2.

        Note that Waters is to play in touring production of
        Member scheduled to be in Providence for three days.

F206   "Roses Are Red, Violets Are Blue." *Mademoiselle*, 16
        (February 1943), 84-85 [84].

        Brief mention of McCullers in long poem for various
        celebrities on Valentine's Day.

F207   Ross, Dorothy. "About 'The Square Root of Wonderful.'"
        Playbill (National Theatre, New York), 1 (October 28,
        1957), 13.

        Brief article in the program for the New York
        production.

F208   Rubin, Louis D., Jr. "Carson McCullers: The Aesthetic
        of Pain." *Virginia Quarterly Review*, 53 (Spring 1977),
        265-283.

        The aesthetic of McCullers' work is based on the pain
        that "could arise only out of a social situation in
        which the patterns and forms and expectations of con-
        duct and attitude are very firmly and formidably present
        [as in the South], so that the inability or failure to
        function within those patterns seems crucial." Her best
        work, *Heart* through *Member*, transforms the pain of being
        different and the inability to conform into art which
        depicts "maimed, misfitting, wounded people" as
        "exemplars of the wretchedness of the human condition."

F209   Rutherford, Marjory. "New Broadway Hit for Carson
        McCullers?" Atlanta *Journal and Constitution*,
        September 29, 1963, Magazine, pp. 10, 12.

Interview in which McCullers comments on Albee's adaptation of *Ballad*. She says she made few suggestions about adaptation but believes it will be "'interesting and compelling and add a new beauty to an already beautiful work.'" She also mentions a new novel she is writing.

F210   Sachs, Viola. "Contemporary American Fiction and Some Nineteenth Century Patterns." *Kwartalnik Neofilologiczny* (Warsaw), 13 (November 1, 1966), 3-29 [15, 28].

Brief mention of *Heart* which "reveals the terrible hopelessness of man's quest for understanding and love" as an example of a modern novel resembling the nineteenth century's concern with "man's inability to communicate" and his "hopeless and pathetic search for love and understanding."

F211   Schaefer, Ted. "The Man in the Gray Flannery McCuller-Alls." *Saturday Review*, 46 (February 23, 1963), 6.

Parody of McCullers and Flannery O'Connor.

F212   Selby, John. "Mrs. McCullers of Carolina Puzzles Gotham Lit'ry Set." Charlotte *Observer*, July 10, 1940, Sec. 2, p. 1.

Syndicated AP interview with McCullers, who, after success of *Heart*, has recently moved to New York from Fayetteville, North Carolina. She comments on *Heart*, on living in the country and in the city, and on her next novel.

F213   Sellers, Tom. "Valley Echoes--Carson Has New Story in Works." Columbus (Ga.) *Ledger*, December 15, 1964, p. 15.

Review of McCullers' career to date, with emphasis on her childhood in Columbus and on a new story with a Columbus background which she is writing, according to a letter recently received by her first cousin.

F214   Shanley, J.P. "Deaf Mutes' Son, 7, Is a Theatre 'Find'--Boy Discovered While Aiding Mother in Store--Now Gets $75 as an Understudy." New York *Times*, February 16, 1950, p. 50L.

Article on understudy for Brandon De Wilde in *Member*.

F215   ————. "M'Cullers' Drama Wins Critics Prize--'Member of the Wedding' Voted Best American Play of Year by the New York Circle." New York *Times*, April 5, 1950, p. 41.

Article announcing award to *Member* and noting which
critics voted for the play.

F216   "She Belongs with 'Rare Group.'"   Charlotte *Observer*,
        October 1, 1967, Sec. B, p. 2.

Obituary editorial: "The deeply personal world of her
imagination has become universal and symbolical and at
the same time stays touchingly close. She is a permanent part of the American idiom."

F217   Sherrill, Rowland A.   "McCullers' *The Heart Is a Lonely
        Hunter*: The Missing Ego and the Problem of the Norm."
        Kentucky Review, 2 (February 1968), 5-17.

Heart is an "ironic document of an age in which the
death and disappearance of God is dismally conceded, in
which the loneliness of human beings is *a priori*, and
in which the responsibility for man's worth is thrust
rudely into his own hands." The characters are people
without egos, living in a world without norms, and can
discover only their own loneliness, isolation, and the
absurdity of their aspirations in the face of these
realities.

F218   Shorris, Earl. "Books--Literary Life Among the Dinka."
        Harper's, 245 (August 1972), 104-107 [104-105].

Reminiscence of meeting with McCullers towards the end
of her life which emphasizes her frail condition and
her courage in the face of her illness.

F219   Sibley, Celestine. "43 Georgians in 'Who's Who' for
        First Time--18 Atlantans Added to List in New Edition."
        Atlanta *Constitution*, March 17, 1942, p. 5.

McCullers mentioned as one of those newly listed.

F220   Sinclair, Andrew. "A Choice of Festivals." *The
        Listener*, 68 (October 11, 1962), 573.

Report on Cheltenham Festival of Literature and on
McCullers' appearance at a "Sex in Literature" symposium
in which she "deplored the tragedy of exclusive love."
See also F2, F53, and F234.

F221   Smith, Margarita G. "A Girl Named Carson." *Redbook*,
        137 (October 1971), 90, 166.

McCullers' sister's reminiscences. This is basically
similar material to that in the Introduction to *The
Mortgaged Heart* (E101).

F222 "Something to Talk About." *Mademoiselle*, 24 (January 1947), 186-187, 248-249 [249].

Very brief praise for McCullers.

F223 "South Nyack Playwright Acclaimed--Carson McCullers' Work Stars Actress from Summer Plays." *Rockland County Journal-News* (Nyack, N.Y.), January 10, 1950, p. 6.

Summary of Brooks Atkinson's review of *Member*. See H4.

F224 "The Southern Revival--A Land and Its Interpreters." *Times Literary Supplement*, September 17, 1954, p. xvi.

Ballad is briefly cited as an example of the "folk-inspired literature of the modern South." McCullers is one of the Southern writers who "transmute the folk narrative into an examination of a universal moral circumstance."

F225 Stanley, William T. "Carson McCullers: 1965-1969, A Selected Checklist." *Bulletin of Bibliography*, 27 (October-December 1970), 91-93.

Selected checklist of criticism, which includes reviews of the Evans critical biography (E36), as well as of movie versions of *Heart* and *Reflections*. This listing updates Phillips' (F177) and Stewart's (F226) earlier checklists.

F226 Stewart, Stanley. "Carson McCullers, 1940-1956: A Selected Checklist." *Bulletin of Bibliography*, 22 (January-April 1959), 182-185.

Checklist of works by and about McCullers. See also F177 and F225.

F227 [Symons, Julian]. "Human Isolation." *Times Literary Supplement*, July 17, 1953, p. 460.

Discussion of McCullers' vision of mankind's loneliness and of her use of freaks to underscore alienation and the desire to belong. McCullers writes from her personal perspective, rather than trying to set down the perspective of her age. This essay is reprinted, under the title "The Lonely Heart," in Symons' *Critical Occasions* (E107).

F228 Teltscher, Herry O. "Write--As You Are." *Mademoiselle*, 13 (May 1941), 166-167, 270-272 [271-272].

Analysis of McCullers' handwriting shows her to be genuine, realistic, "spontaneously creative, visionary, organized, artistic, critical."

F229   "Ten Artists Win $1000 Grants for 1943 Work." New York *Herald Tribune*, April 14, 1943, p. 23.

News story announcing that McCullers is one of recipients of stipends from the American Academy and the National Institute of Arts and Letters.

F230   Thorp, Willard. "Suggs and Sut in Modern Dress: The Latest Chapter in Southern Humor." *Mississippi Quarterly*, 13 (Fall 1960), 169-175 [174].

Mention of Amelia's relationship with her husband in *Ballad* and how it fits into the pattern of Southern humor.

F231   Tinkham, Charles B. "The Members of the Side Show." *Phylon*, 18 (Fourth Quarter 1958), 383-390 [386-389].

Discussion of Frankie's feeling of exclusion, her desire to belong somewhere, and her rejection of anyone or anything that opposes her belonging.

F232   Torrens, James, S.J. "Whatever Will Be ... Or Will It?" *Today*, 19 (May 1964), 25-28 [26-27].

Clock cited as work which shows clearly "that the effort to cope with meaning and to tell a good story at the same time puts high demands on all the author's powers."

F233   "Tot in Buskin." *New Yorker*, 25 (January 28, 1950), 20-21.

Interview with Brandon De Wilde and his parents; considerable mention of *Member*.

F234   Tuohy, Frank. "Cheltenham Festival--Writers and Patrons." *The Spectator*, No. 7007 (October 12, 1962), 557.

Report on Cheltenham Festival and on McCullers' participation in "Sex in Literature" symposium: her "strange and suffering presence" reminded all "that the creation of art can still be a tragic and desperate endeavour, worthy of the last resources of the human spirit." See F2, F53, and F220.

F235   Vickery, John B. "Carson McCullers: A Map of Love." *Wisconsin Studies in Contemporary Literature*, 1 (Winter 1960), 13-24.

Discussion of the total vision of love conveyed in four
McCullers novels: "she probes beneath the surface of
romantic love parodied" in *Ballad*, of "fraternal love"
in *Heart*, of "convoluted sexual relationships" in
Reflections, and of "familial love" in *Member*. The "sum
of human wisdom momentarily grasped by Amelia Evans, by
Biff Brannon, by Anacleto, and perhaps by little John
Henry is that love is a matter of loving unaltered by
not being loved and that the dream of one's life is a
matter of faith not fact."

F236 Vickery, Olga W. "Jean Stafford and the Ironic Vision."
      South Atlantic Quarterly, 61 (Autumn 1962), 484-491
      [484].

      The work of Stafford, Welty, and McCullers can be com-
      pared in their use of the images of the adolescent, mis-
      fit, and freak to dramatize alienation.

F237 Vidal, Gore. "Ladders to Heaven: Novelists and Critics
      of the 1940's." *New World Writing*, 4 (1953), 303-316.

      Scattered comments on McCullers' writing, mostly praise.
      This essay is reprinted in Vidal's *Rocking the Boat*
      (E113) and in Richard Kostelanetz's *On Contemporary
      Literature*.

F238 Walker, Sue B. "The Link in the Chain Called Love: A
      New Look at Carson McCullers' Novels." *Mark Twain
      Journal*, 18 (Winter 1976), 8-12.

      The "central and controlling metaphor" of McCullers'
      work is "a chain constructed with links of love." The
      chain, "built with links of perverted love, becomes a
      restraining device; it bends and imprisons man within
      himself.... When man masters the 'science of love,'
      when he learns to really 'love his neighbor as himself,'
      the chain paradoxically becomes a ladder ... a means of
      ascent to the highest of perfect forms."

F239 Walter, Eugene. "A Rainy Afternoon with Truman Capote."
      Intro Bulletin, 2 (December 1957), 1-2.

      Interview in which Capote praises McCullers' work.

F240 Watson, Latimer. "Carson McCullers Gets Guggenheim
      Fellowship." Columbus (Ga.) *Enquirer*, April 6, 1942,
      pp. 1, 3.

      Interview in which McCullers speaks of her novel-in-
      progress and her plans.

F241   ————. "How Latimer Sums It Up: 'Wonderful! Every Day
        of It!'" Columbus (Ga.) *Sunday Ledger-Enquirer*, July 30,
        1961, Sec. 10, p. 7.

        Retiring Women's Editor of Columbus newspaper reminisces
        briefly about McCullers' days as a reporter.

F242   ————. "Ovation Greets Opening of Carson's Play in
        N.Y." Columbus (Ga.) *Ledger*, January 6, 1950, pp. 1, 2.

        Account of triumphant opening night of *Member* and
        Watson's own praise for the play: "above all it stands
        as a poignantly beautiful and moving play with a remark-
        able understanding of its subjects."

F243   Watts, Richard, Jr. "Two on the Aisle—Random Notes on
        This and That." New York *Post*, January 10, 1950, p. 34.

        Very brief praise for *Member* at beginning of column de-
        voted to miscellaneous news of the theater.

F244   "We Hitch Our Wagons." *Mademoiselle*, 33 (August 1951),
        248-249 [249].

        McCullers gives advice to young aspiring writers—con-
        tinue writing despite rejection slips, critics are
        always unpredictable, and put aside manuscripts that
        have gone "stale."

F245   Weiler, A.H. "View from a Local Vantage Point." New
        York *Times*, August 6, 1961, Sec. 2, p. 5.

        Notes that both *Ballad* and *Clock* are being adapted for
        the stage and *Member* and *Reflections* being made into
        movies.

F246   Welles, Violet. "About Carson McCullers." *Playbill*
        (National Theatre, New York), 1 (October 28, 1957),
        43-44.

        Biographical sketch included in program for New York
        premiere of *Square Root*.

F247   White, Terence de Vere. "With Carson McCullers:
        Terence de Vere White Interviews the American Novelist
        at the Home of Her Host, John Huston." *Irish Times*
        (Dublin), April 10, 1967, p. 12.

        McCullers talks of Auden, Katherine Mansfield, and her
        own writings. Much of the article is a description of
        McCullers and of her courageous journey to Ireland
        despite her frail health.

F248   Williams, Tennessee. "The Author." *Saturday Review*,
       44 (September 23, 1961), 14-15.

       Williams discusses McCullers' spirit, her courage against
       physical handicaps, her friendship with him, and calls
       her "the greatest living writer of our country, if not
       the world."

F249   Wilson, Barbara L. "Stage Activities--Romantic Play at
       Walnut." Philadelphia *Inquirer*, October 13, 1957,
       Amusements and the Arts Section, pp. 1, 4.

       Article previewing upcoming pre-Broadway run of *Square
       Root*, "a product of one of the finest talents in American
       theatre."

F250   Wilson, Zane. "'The Heart Is a Lonely Hunter' May Be
       Filmed Partly in Columbus." Columbus (Ga.) *Ledger*,
       July 26, 1967, p. 1.

       Speculation that film version of *Heart* may be shot in
       Columbus because script mentions town.

F251   Winer, Elihu. "Broadway's 50-Dollar Angel." New York
       Herald Tribune, February 12, 1950, *This Week Magazine*,
       pp. 7, 32.

       Account of person who invested $50 in *Member*, which,
       after six weeks, will begin to show a profit.

F252   Woodall, W.C. "Author's Girlhood Days Here." Columbus
       (Ga.) *Ledger*, March 30, 1966, p. 19.

       Material, mostly drawn from Evans biography (E36),
       about McCullers' life until she moved to New York after
       high school.

F253   ————. "Our Town--A Broadway Play Hit 16 Years Ago."
       Columbus (Ga.) *Sunday Ledger-Enquirer*, April 18, 1966,
       p. C-1.

       Material on original production of *Member* drawn from
       Evans biography (E36).

F254   ————. "Our Town--Story of 'February House.'" Columbus
       (Ga.) *Ledger*, May 11, 1966, p. 31.

       Material on McCullers' residence in Brooklyn drawn from
       Evans biography (E36).

F255   "Writers Attend M'Cullers Rites." New York *Times*,
       October 4, 1967, p. 51.

Brief account of McCullers' funeral and of mourners who attended.

F256   Zolotow, Sam.   "Guild to Produce M'Cullers Novel--'Member of Wedding,' Made into Play by Author and Greer Johnson, Acquired by Unit."   New York *Times*, May 30, 1947, p. 24.

Announcement that Theatre Guild will produce stage version of McCullers novel as soon as cast is chosen.

SECTION G

REVIEWS OF BOOKS BY CARSON McCULLERS

This section lists reviews of Carson McCullers' books. They
are listed by book reviewed (in chronological order of publication) and alphabetically within the listings for each title.
Because this section is based primarily on clipping files at
the University of Texas and at Houghton Mifflin, it makes no
claim to completeness. Undoubtedly, numerous reviews, especially of English editions, are not included; but what is
here represents the fullest such listing yet published. For
general reviews containing mention of McCullers, the pages of
the full review are listed first, with the pages on McCullers
following, in brackets.

1. THE HEART IS A LONELY HUNTER

G1 Berry, Lee. "This World of Books." Toledo *Blade*, June 15, 1940, p. 5.

"There are flaws in the book, of course, of which a tendency towards over-romanticization of the theme is most apparent, but by and large this is a superlative piece of story-telling, powerful, deeply moving and strikingly original."

G2 Butcher, Fanny. "22 Year Old Girl Writes Strange, Haunting Novel." Chicago *Daily Tribune*, June 5, 1940, p. 20.

"There is not only the delicately sensed need that one might expect youth to know but an even more delicately sensed ironic knowledge."

G3 B[utler], G[eorge] O.] "Fayetteville Woman Produces First Novel About Deep South." Greensboro (N.C.) *Daily News*, June 2, 1940, p. D-3.

McCullers' writing is compared to that of Hemingway, Steinbeck, and Wolfe. *Heart* deserves "to rank among the best [novels] that have been written in America in recent years."

G4 Case, Elizabeth N. "Powerful Novel Probes Strange Group." Hartford *Courant*, June 9, 1940, Magazine, p. 6.

McCullers is called a greater writer than Faulkner or Caldwell, but she is criticized for her "use of certain words and phrases ... which are unessential to her story, and which are questionable in the extreme."

G5 *Catholic World*, 152 (November 1940), 252.

"It is astonishing that a twenty-two year old girl could produce a first novel so fraught with power and understanding, so adroitly selective and so technically

competent." Reviewer disapproves of "the free use of very
coarse language" and "the defeatist philosophy indicated."

G6   Clare, Tullis. "New Novels." *Time and Tide*, 24 (April 10,
        1943), 302.

        The characters in *Heart* "are so sensitively observed, and
        their creator has endowed their doings with such a kind of
        mystical drive, that they more than atone for any jerki-
        ness or minor lapses in construction and give to her novel
        its unusual vitality and subtle flavour."

G7   Cleveland, Elizabeth. "The Bookstall." *Holland's*, 59
        (August 1940), 13.

        Heart is "a queer slice of life" and "a back-breaking load
        of serious concerns for one so young."

G8   Daniel, Frank. "'The Heart Is a Lonely Hunter.'" Atlanta
        Journal, May 26, 1940, Magazine, p. 10.

        It is "a stirring and deeply-felt story of a small Southern
        mill town."

G9   Fadiman, Clifton. "Books--Pretty Good for Twenty-Two."
        New Yorker, 16 (June 8, 1940), 77-78.

        "Though there are plenty of technical faults in this book,
        it seems unimportant to list them. It's more valuable
        just to call attention to the fact that here is a new
        voice speaking about new American spiritual country."

G10   Feld, Rose. "A Remarkable First Novel of Lonely Lives."
        New York Times Book Review, June 16, 1940, p. 6.

        McCullers "writes with a sweep and certainty that are
        overwhelming. From the opening page, brilliant in its
        establishment of mood, character and suspense, the book
        takes hold of the reader."

G11   "First Novel." *Time*, 35 (June 10, 1940), 90.

        "As a candidate for high honors ... Mrs. McCullers flunks
        out flat on a crucial matter. As a writer of words, she
        is never distinguished, never in one glint verbally
        original."

G12   Gannett, Lewis. "Books and Things." Boston *Evening
        Transcript*, June 5, 1940, p. 13.

        Heart is "a strange and uneven book, at times almost
        miraculous in its concise intensity, at times baffling
        in its meandering immaturity." This review also ap-
        peared in New York *Herald Tribune*, June 5, 1940.

G13 Garner, Maxine. "On a Most Appealing Theme." Raleigh *News and Observer*, June 9, 1940, Sec. M, p. 5.

The "appealing" theme of wanting to be understood is undermined by superfluous commentary on social injustices. There is, however, promise for McCullers' future unless she insists on "upsetting our digestion as she grows up."

G14 Gibson, Wilfred. "Books of the Day--New Novels." Manchester *Guardian*, March 26, 1943, p. 3.

"Miss [sic] McCullers's insight into character and the emotional intensity of her writing give her harrowing narrative the significance of an individual reading of life which is even touched with an indefinable sense of beauty."

G15 Goldstein, Albert. "Literature and Less." New Orleans *Times-Picayune and States*, June 9, 1940, Sec. 2, p. 11.

Heart is "sensitively conceived and expertly told." "Its quality as writing and the intensity of its theme combine to make it one of the outstanding novels of recent years."

G16 Hansen, Harry. "The First Reader." New York *World-Telegram*, June 5, 1940, p. 27.

"The author writes with scientific precision, and her ability to keep within the frame of this small community of maladjusted human beings promises well for her future." McCullers writes of "people of a different world--the people we so often pass by as uninteresting."

G17 Hyde, Fred G. "Groping Folk in the South: A First Novel." Philadelphia *Inquirer*, June 5, 1940, p. 13.

"Besides telling a good story, the author has peopled it with a small group of characters so powerfully drawn as to linger long in memory."

G18 "In the Deep South." *Times Literary Supplement*, March 27, 1943, p. 153.

"It is not a novel of any real imaginative power or distinction.... Mrs. McCullers undoubtedly has her moments, but she obscures her picture of the darker side of life in the deep South by the convention compassionate."

G19 Jackson, Katherine Gauss. *Harper's*, 181 (July 1940), unpaged.

"It is a magnificent piece of compassionate satire. Miss [sic] McCullers writes with an extraordinary intensity."

G20 Jones, Dorothy. "Strange Novel Is Soul-Study." Dallas *Morning News*, June 9, 1940, Sec. 4, p. 5.

"It is a strange book, and a rather haunting one. The social implications, though perhaps lacking in subtlety, ... are given forcibly and with some power."

G21 K., E.C. "Young Novelist Writes Unusual Tale of Longing." Milwaukee *Journal*, June 23, 1940, Editorial Section, p. 3.

Mostly descriptive review.

G22 Littell, Robert. "Outstanding Novels." *Yale Review*, 30 (Autumn 1940), vi-xii [viii, x].

"It is a queer, sad book that sticks in one's mind, full of odd but very living people." McCullers should "broaden her scope."

G23 Loewinsohn, Joseph A. "Loneliness of the Human Spirit Is the Theme of Magnificent Story--Young Author's First Novel Is Called Masterpiece." Atlanta *Constitution*, June 2, 1940, Magazine and Feature Section, p. 6.

"Utterly frank in her description of some of the intimate little details of her characters and yet unbelievably tender and touching throughout the length of the book, 'The Heart Is a Lonely Hunter' will cast a spell on you and the magnificent story of the loneliness of the human spirit will hold you enthralled for a long, long time."

G24 McDonald, Edward D. "Mirroring Stream of Fiction." *Virginia Quarterly Review*, 16 (Autumn 1940), 612-614 [612-613].

"To be brief, in *The Heart Is a Lonely Hunter*, form and matter meet and blend, and shape a well-nigh perfect whole."

G25 Merlin, Milton. "Lonely Individuals Almost Make God of Puzzled Mute." Los Angeles *Times*, May 26, 1940, Part 3, p. 7.

McCullers is "an author of exceptional penetration and substance."

G26 Molloy, Robert. "The Book of the Day." New York *Sun*, June 7, 1940, p. 27.

Heart is "strange, serious, occasionally awkward" and
has "some of the insight that characterized Sherwood
Anderson."

G27   Nourse, Joan. "The South of the Mills." San Francisco
      Chronicle, July 14, 1940, *This World* Magazine, p. 20.

      Mostly descriptive review.

G28   O'Brien, Kate. "Fiction." *The Spectator*, No. 5988
      (April 2, 1943), 324.

      Heart is "a curious, uneven book, not for everyone; but
      it has heart and truth in it, and it promises highly for
      the future of its author."

G29   Pruette, Lorine. "She Understands Lonely Hearts." *New
      York Herald Tribune Books*, June 9, 1940, p. 4.

      Mostly descriptive review. This review also appeared in
      Washington (D.C.) *Post*, June 9, 1940, p. B8.

G30   Pryce-Jones, Alan. "New Novels." *The Observer* (London),
      March 28, 1943, p. 3.

      McCullers is "a writer to watch." If "she can discipline
      what is at present a sentimental approach to reality she
      will write a very good novel indeed."

G31   Putzel, Max. *Accent*, 1 (Autumn 1940), 61-62.

      "This novel might be arresting if it didn't conform
      entirely to a tired formula. The people who live here
      inhabit an America clipped of beauty, humor, freedom and
      ethics."

G32   R., B. "Four Discoveries of a Personality." Kansas City
      Star, June 22, 1940, p. 14.

      "Although it exhibits an artificial simplicity of style
      and a blurred intent, it has a queer sort of fascination."

G33   Redman, Ben Ray. "Of Human Loneliness." *Saturday
      Review*, 22 (June 8, 1940), 6.

      "With firm mastery of her medium, the author exposes and
      evaluates an unusual complex of human emotions." She is
      "never commonplace."

G34   Roberts, Mary-Carter. "Young Georgia Woman's First Novel
      Achieves Literary Distinction." Washington (D.C.)
      Sunday Star, June 9, 1940, p. F7.

McCullers is a "genius" and *Heart* is "a virtual volcano
of feeling and, in execution, shows a powerful intellectual grasp on its materials."

G35   Russell, Cara Green. "The Literary Lantern." Norfolk
      Virginian-Pilot, June 2, 1940, Part 1, p. 6.

      "The story is unusual and always fascinating." McCullers
      "can write ... with so much sympathy and such clear see-
      ing, that she comprehends the searing grief that can come
      of a deep friendship and write of it in a way that cannot
      be soon forgotten."

G36   Salomon, Louis B. "Someone to Talk to." *The Nation*, 151
      (July 13, 1940), 36.

      Heart is "a book flavored with compassion and a gentle
      melancholy but never with despair."

G37   Sarton, May. "Pitiful Hunt for Security--Tragedy of
      Unfulfillment Theme of Story That Will Rank High in
      American Letters." Boston *Evening Transcript*, June 8,
      1940, Sec. 4, p. 4.

      After finishing *Heart*, one has a "feeling of having been
      nourished by the truth." Its only flaws are the two
      accidental tragedies--when everything else is inevitable
      --and the neatly worked-out ending.

G38   "Simple Story Has Drama." Pittsburgh *Press*, June 23,
      1940, Fourth Section, p. 8.

      Heart "will probably be recognized as one of the most
      unusual novels of the year." In telling about everyday
      life, McCullers "has spun a yarn far more dramatic than
      polysyllabic adjectives could possibly accomplish."

G39   "Southern Mill Town and Frustrated Group." Springfield
      (Mass.) *Sunday Union and Republican*, June 9, 1940, p. 7E.

      Heart "holds to its excellent limitations, observing,
      discussing, dramatizing."

G40   Spring, Howard. "Dynamite Chambers Lie Ready to Blow Up
      Hitler's Glass Eyrie, 1,800 ft. High." London *Daily
      Mail*, March 27, 1943, p. 2.

      Heart depicts the South of "industrial underpaid workers,
      and slum houses and mean cafés, and a lot of people with
      desperate personal problems that modern life doesn't
      answer."

G41 "Strange Novel Is Effective." Columbus (Ohio) *Sunday Dispatch*, June 9, 1940, First Magazine Section, p. 7.

"It is unfortunate that the theme of her novel is diffuse and scarcely recognizable. She is obviously anxious to arrive at some important conclusion, but what is the conclusion? Perhaps it is sufficient that she has created characters who will not be easily forgotten."

G42 Straus, Ralph. "Novels of the Week." London *Sunday Times*, March 21, 1943, p. 3.

"Faults there may be, exaggerations, unfinished corners and the like, but to my mind it is a remarkable novel, and I warmly recommend it."

G43 Thompson, Ralph. "Books of The Times." New York *Times*, June 4, 1940, p. L 21.

McCullers "has written a book with clever and pleasant characters." As she writes about the effect the five major characters have on each other, "their personal qualities become more and more nearly clear--but they never become wholly clear [because] ... Mrs. McCullers blurs over difficult meanings here."

G44 Tobias, Rowena W. "Lonely Hearts in Georgia." Charleston (S.C.) *News and Courier*, July 7, 1940, Sec. 3. p. 3-iii.

"Miss [sic] McCullers has made a powerful novel out of a very powerful theme, and her entrance into the writing ranks should be heralded with trumpets."

G45 Townend, Marion. "First Novel Is Raw Picture of Southern 'Peasant' Life." Charlotte *Observer*, June 9, 1940, Section Three, p. 5.

"Like an artist who myopically paints a wretched shack ... and forgets to paint in any blue sky," McCullers "may have stayed too close to her subject." But, "despite its shortcomings," *Heart* "shows marked ability in the realistic portrayal of all characters."

G46 Toynbee, Philip. "Novels and Stories." *New Statesman and Nation*, n.s. 25 (May 1, 1943), 292.

McCullers "writes with a bitter compassion which gives deep humanity to her characters."

G47 Wilson, William E. "The Lonely Heart." Providence *Sunday Journal*, June 9, 1940, Sec. 6, p. 6.

"The first half of the book is written with both ...
acute observation, broad knowledge of humankind, and
maturity of style and form." But, toward the end, "the
immaturity of the book becomes apparent."

G48   Wright, Richard. "Inner Landscape." *New Republic*, 103
      (August 5, 1940), 195.

      McCullers' "picture ... is perhaps the most desolate
      that has so far come from the South." Her unique quality
      of despair "seems ... more natural and authentic than
      that of Faulkner"; she can "embrace white and black
      humanity in one sweep of apprehension and tenderness."

G49   "Youthful Writer Displays Amazing Knowledge of Life."
      Boston *Sunday Globe*, June 16, 1940, p. 45.

      "Carson McCullers- is no prude. She writes with a calm
      and factual realism, and with a deep and abiding insight
      into human psychology. She does so without an iota of
      vulgarity and bawdiness, in a manner which many a present
      day novelist would do well to study."

                    2.   REFLECTIONS IN A GOLDEN EYE

G50   Barish, Mildred. "Murder at Army Post Has Weird Backdrop
      of Passion." Los Angeles *Times*, March 2, 1941, Part 3,
      p. 7.

      Reflections "offers to those who relish psychological
      drama a memorable passport to excitement." It is "a
      story that will not easily be forgotten."

G51   Berry, Lee. "This World of Books." Toledo *Blade*,
      February 22, 1941, p. 5.

      "Mrs. McCullers combines a superb narrative technique,
      an exceptional imagination and truly remarkable powers
      of observation." *Reflections* is "a deeply moving emo-
      tional experience."

G52   "Book to Forget with Promptness." Hartford *Courant*,
      February 23, 1941, Magazine, p. 7.

      "This is the sort of book I like to think most persons
      wish to spew out of the mind as rapidly as possible."

G53 B[utcher], F[anny]. "Miss [sic] McCullers Writes Another
     Unusual Novel." Chicago *Daily Tribune*, February 19, 1941,
     p. 15.

     Reflections is a "delicately recorded panorama of strange
     and often torturous twistings of the human mind." It is
     "beautifully and skillfully written and brilliantly de-
     signed to compel the reader's attention."

G54 Butler, George O. "Strange Novel of Army Post by Tar
     Heel." Greensboro (N.C.) *Daily News*, February 16, 1941,
     p. 2-D.

     Reflections is "compelling enough to hold your interest,
     ... uncanny enough to give you the mental creeps, and
     sordid enough to shock your every feeling of decency and
     decorum.... This book ends in a murder and one rather
     regrets that it hadn't been a wholesale massacre in the
     first chapter."

G55 Clare, Tullis. "New Novels." *Time and Tide*, 23 (July 11,
     1942), 560, 562 [560].

     The "mystical awareness and the quality of Mr. [sic]
     McCullers' writing ... give ... a new flavour to this odd
     little book." The "literary style ... wear[s] a decep-
     tive dress of simplicity, ... [the] strategy is unexpec-
     tedly subtle."

G56 Clark, Margaret. "Carson McCullers--Eagerly Awaited
     Second Novel of Author Psychological Study of Crime of
     Passion." Boston *Evening Transcript*, February 15, 1941,
     Sec. 5, p. 1.

     McCullers' style "is well-tempered to an exquisite pre-
     cision and expressed with force," but such gifts "should
     be put to more important use." The plot is "too pre-
     occupied with the morbid and the bizarre."

G57 Creekmore, Hubert. *Accent*, 2 (Autumn 1941), 61.

     Most of the novel is "case histories she has tried to
     bring to life by substituting words for character and
     innuendo for blood. The result is, of course, dreary....
     The characters are ... sealed in the pigeonholes of their
     neuroses. None of them reacts on the others."

G58 Daniel, Frank. Atlanta *Journal*, February 23, 1941,
     Magazine, p. 12.

"Mrs. McCullers has looked deeply into the troubled lives
of those people, and tells their story with sureness, re-
sourcefulness, and a wise cold pity."

G59 Davenport, Basil. "McCullers...." *Saturday Review*, 23
     (February 22, 1941), 12.

     Reflections is "a sad disappointment." It "does not cul-
     minate in tragedy, it trails off into futility." The
     characters' "vagaries seem merely something to be cold-
     bloodedly chosen for their bizarrerie, contemplated and
     set down without pity, or comment or any sort of use."

G60 Fadiman, Clifton. *New Yorker*, 17 (February 15, 1941),
     78, 80.

     "The net effect is completely unconvincing." Although
     McCullers "has undeniable talent," *Reflections* "gives an
     effect of falseness which is further strengthened by her
     too obvious desire to create people and situations that
     are strange and startling."

G61 Feld, Rose. *New York Herald Tribune Books*, February 16,
     1941, p. 8.

     One hopes that McCullers "will use her very real powers
     to write a book that does not depend completely upon the
     grotesque and the abnormal for its effect."

G62 Ferguson, Otis. "Fiction: Odd and Ordinary." *New
     Republic*, 104 (March 3, 1941), 317-318.

     Reflections is a "brilliant piece of execution, hard,
     exact and graceful in likeness, a sort of cameo in
     fiction."

G63 Goldstein, Albert. "Literature and Less." New Orleans
     Times-Picayune and States, February 16, 1941, Sec. 2,
     p. 9.

     "Contrary to ... the ordinary horror piece, her charac-
     ters impress you far more by what they are than by the
     situations they are made to create for themselves."
     There is "a peculiar atmosphere of tragedy from the
     first line of her story and she sustains it with an
     amazing consistency."

G64 H., P. "What Reflections These Are, Beautifully Written."
     Providence *Sunday Journal*, February 16, 1941, Sec. 6,
     p. 6.

McCullers "is not an author who will be grasped fondly
to the heart of the reading public.... She is about as
lovable as a black panther, but is as shining, sleek and
fascinating as a panther."

G65   Hansen, Harry. "The First Reader--Literary Qualities
      Command Respect in Carson McCullers' Second Novel." New
      York *World-Telegram*, February 14, 1941, p. 23.

      Although the characters "are disagreeable people, [this]
      does not invalidate the literary qualities of the story....
      This sort of writing claims respect."

G66   Harbour, Edith. "Books and Book-Makers." Raleigh *News
      and Observer*, February 16, 1941, p. M-5.

      "The story is a disappointment and doesn't live up to the
      promise of the first novel." But "even those who don't
      like the story cannot but admire the writer's technique."

G67   "In Brief." *The Nation*, 152 (March 1, 1941), 247.

      "A remarkable novelette, ... [it has] a haunting origi-
      nality in its probing into the hearts of a half-dozen
      thwarted soul-stunted men and women."

G68   Littell, Robert. "Outstanding Novels." *Yale Review*, 30
      (Spring 1941), viii-xiv [xii-xiv].

      Reflections "is something for her admirers to forget as
      quickly as possible. This isn't easy, for strong traces
      of the talent are still here, and make the novel's in-
      versions and mutilations and nastiness stick in one's
      mind like burrs."

G69   Loewinsohn, Joseph. "Georgia Author Scores Again in
      Novel Probing Human Souls--Tragedy at an Army Post
      Furnishes Theme for Story." Atlanta *Constitution*,
      March 2, 1941, Sunday Magazine and Feature Section, p. 6.

      "Whatever you may think of this weird novel, there is
      no mistake about Miss [sic] McCullers' mastery of the
      difficult art of portraying with compelling force the
      most unexpected twists and mysterious ways of the human
      soul."

G70   Marsh, Fred T. "At an Army Post." *New York Times Book
      Review*, March 2, 1941, p. 6.

      Reflections is "vastly inferior" to *Heart*. "No one
      could say, however, that Miss [sic] McCullers has not

succeeded in making her genuine talent felt, a talent
which is less of subtlety than of infant-terrible insight
expressed with quite grown-up precision, as yet un-
mellowed and unhallowed."

G71 "Masterpiece at 24." *Time*, 37 (February 17, 1941), 96.

"Carson McCullers tells her tale with simplicity, insight
and a rare gift of phrase." *Reflections* is "the
Southern school at its most Gothic, but also at its best."

G72 Molloy, Robert. "The Book of the Day." New York *Sun*,
February 15, 1941, p. 25.

McCullers "has written a story of murder and abnormality
as hard as Hemingway and as morbid as Faulkner." One
"would like to see what the author could accomplish with
more conventional characters."

C73 "No Book for Fingernail Biters Is This Exciting New
Novel." Dallas *Morning News*, February 16, 1941, Sec. 3,
p. 12.

Reflections is "forever straining towards the borders of
madness.... It is exciting and memorable, but hardly
permanent."

G74 "Novels of the Week." *Times Literary Supplement*, May 30,
1942, p. 269.

"You are left at the end with the feeling that everybody
is frustrated in one way or another, but for the rest
there seems insufficient point in this collection of arbi-
trary psychological violences."

G75 "Of Morbid Persons." Springfield (Mass.) *Sunday Union
and Republican*, May 4, 1941, p. 7E.

Mostly descriptive review.

G76 Poore, Charles. "Books of The Times." New York *Times*,
February 15, 1941, p. 13.

If *Reflections* "never comes any too persuasively to life,
it is because it is far too mechanically contrived." It
is too "overloaded" with "clinical data" and "episode is
piled on episode."

G77 Price, H. Bruce. "Brilliant Work--Carson McCullers Writes
Her Second Novel." Louisville *Courier-Journal*, March 9,
1941, Sunday Magazine, p. [7].

"Each story, taken separately, is perfectly constructed
for suspense, surprise, drama and a curious irony. Every
piece of both of them, of the whole book, is exquisite."

G78   R., B. "Novelist Repeats Success." Kansas City *Star*,
      February 15, 1941, p. 14.

      "Her second novel is less than half the length of her
      first. It is approximately twice as good, although it
      may not appear so to those who exhausted themselves with
      praise for 'The Heart.'"

G79   Roberts, Mary-Carter. "Carson McCullers Produces Second
      Fine Story of the Loneliness of Humans." Washington
      (D.C.) *Sunday Star*, February 23, 1941, p. F-7.

      "The reviewer cannot think of anyone since Nathaniel
      Hawthorne who has produced an atmosphere of profound
      psychic trouble as finely as Carson McCullers."

G80   Russell, Cara Green. "The Literary Lantern." Norfolk
      Virginian-Pilot, February 16, 1941, Part 1, p. 6.

      Although *Reflections* is not as good as *Heart*, "judged by
      itself alone it stands among the most vital novels we
      have read in some time. Mrs. McCullers has all the genius
      necessary to become one of America's greatest writers."
      This review also appeared in Charlotte *Observer*,
      February 16, 1941, Section Three, p. 5.

G81   S., F.M. "Into the Murky Depths of Six Human Souls."
      Milwaukee *Journal*, March 9, 1941, Editorial Section,
      p. 3.

      Mostly descriptive review.

G82   Straus, Ralph. "Novels of the Week." London *Sunday
      Times*, May 31, 1942, p. 3.

      Reflections, "while no masterpiece, ... strikes a note at
      once impressive and entirely peculiar to itself." There
      is "something fine and individual here."

G83   Swinnerton, Frank. "New Novels--A Psychological Week."
      The Observer (London), May 24, 1942, p. 3.

      Reflections is "extremely original and interesting."

G84   Toynbee, Philip. "New Novels." *New Statesman and Nation*,
      n.s. 24 (July 11, 1942), 27-28.

Reflections is "a success which is uncomfortably a *tour de force*." By "sheer technical ability Miss [sic] McCullers carries off her *tour de force* and compels her reader to accept it."

G85   W., C. "Only Normal Thing in Carson McCuller [sic] Novel Is a Horse." Columbus (Ohio) *Sunday Dispatch*, February 16, 1941, Third Magazine Section, p. 5.

Reflections is "one of the queerest of the queerest stories ever written." "This reviewer is sitting on a fence admitting that it is well-written and wondering why on earth Miss [sic] McCullers felt compelled to write it.... We would like to see [her] ... write a nice normal story about nice, normal people."

G86   Weeks, Edward. "First Person Singular." *The Atlantic*, 167 (April 1941), unpaged.

Praise for "the vivid economy" of McCullers' "best writing"; criticism for her lack of reality and her tendency "to stick labels on her people and to keep them thereafter in a state of suspended animation."

3.   THE MEMBER OF THE WEDDING (NOVEL)

G87   Alford, Sally. "Frankie Grows Up." *New Masses*, 59 (June 4, 1946), 25.

Member is "thoughtful and deeply felt, with no sign of hurry in it. It was written by a craftsman whose tools are words, and if you have a few hours you can call your own, you could do worse than read it."

G88   Appel, David. "Books and Authors--Carson McCullers Looks at Childhood." Chicago *Daily News*, May 8, 1946, p. 21.

McCullers "proves herself a consistently forceful writer. This probing into a child's deepest thoughts produces a story that is as unforgettable as it is unique."

G89   Boatner, Maxine Tull. "Life in the Heart of a Child." Hartford *Courant*, April 7, 1946, Magazine, p. 12.

"Reading 'The Member of the Wedding' is like living a day in some other person's life. It is honest, true and real, more wonderful than any kind of fiction."

G90 Bond, Alice Dixon. "The Case for Books: Two Widely
     Different New Novels and a Thrilling Book of Adventure."
     Boston *Herald*, April 10, 1946, p. 17.

     "This is a small book, more tightly knit than either of
     the author's two previous ones. It is poignant and
     arresting, amazingly perceptive and exquisitely wrought."

G91 Bower, Helen. "The Book Shelf--The Heart Still Searches."
     Detroit *Free Press*, March 24, 1946, Part Two, p. [6].

     "This is a marvelous study of the agony of adolescence,
     the fierce desire which breeds fierce denial, the inner
     loneliness which expresses itself perversely in violence."

G92 Brady, Charles A. "Bewildered Soul of Youth Is Explored
     Once More." Buffalo *Evening News*, April 13, 1946,
     Magazine, p. 5.

     "Carson McCullers here joins the ranks of that growing
     band of fictioneers who explore, with tenderness and
     understanding, the bewildered psyche of the adolescent."

G93 Brandeis, Adele. "Portrait of a Lonely Adolescent--
     Twelve-Year-Old's Longing to 'Belong' Is Theme of Carson
     McCullers' Unusual Novel." Louisville *Times*, April 5,
     1946, p. 6.

     McCullers "has produced a tour de force in maintaining
     one tone throughout.... The book is quite beautifully
     though often surprisingly written."

G94 "Call of the Highlands." *Times Literary Supplement*,
     March 15, 1947, p. 113.

     "The story has its humorous felicities, even though they
     seem a shade too deliberately contrived, but too seldom
     leaves an impression of considered imagination."

G95 Cheney, Frances. "Of Human Loneliness." Nashville
     Banner, March 27, 1946, p. 16.

     "Mrs. McCullers has skillfully rendered her scenes,
     cleverly heightened her atmosphere of suspense and
     pathos...."

G96 Clare, Tullis. "New Novels." *Time and Tide*, 28 (May 3,
     1947), 458, 460 [460].

     Member, "an unacademic study of American adolescence, is
     as queer and subtle as the other two novels which Miss

[sic] Carson McCullers already has to her credit." Her
"inarticulate people live and she has managed to put into
this child's tragedy ... human warmth."

G97   Cornwell, Dorothea. "Life Says 'Come In' to a Child."
        Louisville *Courier-Journal*, April 14, 1946, Sec. 3, p. 14.

        Mostly descriptive review which calls *Member* McCullers'
        best work to date.

G98   Cournos, John. "A Case History by Carson McCullers."
        New York *Sun*, March 20, 1946, p. 23.

        If McCullers "could only rid herself of her grotesqueries,
        she might be a distinguished writer worthy of the un-
        deserved attention she has now received."

G99   Craig, Helen Pride. "Books in Review." Columbia (S.C.)
        Record, April 4, 1946, p. 8-A.

        Member "will be read ... not for pure enjoyment, but for
        an appreciation of good writing." There is, however, "a
        sordidness about the book ... that cannot be denied."

G100   Dangerfield, George. "An Adolescent's Four Days."
        Saturday Review, 29 (March 30, 1946), 15.

        Member is a "marvelous piece of writing. Not only does
        it sustain the interest all the way through, but it does
        so under circumstances which demand the utmost delicacy
        and balance from the author."

G101   Derleth, August. "Some Outstanding Novels." *Capital
        Times* (Madison, Wis.), April 21, 1946, p. 30.

        Brief mention: "a very fine performance."

G102   Douglas, Marjory Stoneman. "Books--The Member of the
        Wedding." Washington (D.C.) *Times-Herald*, April 21,
        1946, Sec. D, p. D-3.

        McCullers "has never done anything better than this."

G103   Downing, Francis. *Commonweal*, 44 (May 24, 1946), 148.

        "It is difficult to convey the sense of skill with
        which this so-called 'novella' is written.... The tre-
        mendous feeling of the world lost, and meaning lost, of
        life discovered and meaning recovered, the merciful power
        of the young to forget, and thus be healed of fractures,
        is one of the realest things of this fine book."

G104 Dunkel, Wilbur. "Books of the Week--As Adolescent Sees." Rochester (N.Y.) *Democrat and Chronicle*, March 17, 1946, p. 7D.

"This is a book for persons who wish to understand child delinquency as well as for readers who appreciate artistry in fiction."

G105 "The End of F. Jasmine Addams." *Time*, 47 (April 1, 1946), 98-100.

Member is "often touching, always strictly limited by the small scope of its small characters ... full of incident but devoid of a clear plot."

G106 Engle, Paul. "Warm, Poetic, Live Story of a Little Girl." Chicago *Sunday Tribune*, March 31, 1946, Part 4, p. 10.

"There is an almost perfect harmony between the theme of this book and the prose in which it is expressed, for the prose is lyrical and sensitive and always fresh."

G107 F., C. "Childhood in Dixie." *Irish Times* (Dublin), April 19, 1947, p. 6.

McCullers "has handled her study of lonely girlhood with unusual sensitivity and with intense seriousness."

G108 Field, Ben. "Story of the Crisis in the Life of a Lonely Young Girl." *Daily Worker* (New York), April 7, 1946, Magazine, p. 11.

"It seems to me that had the author busied herself more with the forces outside her characters she would have given us a more satisfying novel, one that would have led us to the sources responsible in the main for the growing pains and little tragedies of youth."

G109 "Fine Novella." Brooklyn (N.Y.) *Citizen*, March 29, 1946, p. 4.

"This is a carefully planned book ..., filled with passages both tender and sharp."

G110 Frank, Joseph. "Fiction Chronicle." *Sewanee Review*, 54 (Summer 1946), 534-539 [536-537].

The "really important part of the book is a quality of sensibility which ... the main theme [adolescence] is too weak to support." McCullers "is fascinated by the

revolting and the perverse to an almost morbid extent."
This "quality of sensibility ... in the context of the
present work, adds up to very little because it remains
unfocused and purposeless." If McCullers can continue
to create impressive characterizations like Berenice,
"and place them in a situation where their very gro-
tesqueness takes on symbolic value, American literature
may find itself with a really important writer on its
hands."

G111   G., M.A. "Emotions Take Strange Turn for Youthful
       Girl." Greensboro (N.C.) *Daily News*, March 24, 1946,
       Sec. 2, p. 3.

       "Although employing a flimsy framework for so ambitious
       an attempt, the extent to which [McCullers] develops the
       character [of Frankie] ... provides reading that is
       rarely encountered."

G112   Gannett, Lewis. "Books and Things." New York *Herald
       Tribune*, March 20, 1946, p. 23.

       Member is "a tighter-knit book than 'The Heart Is a
       Lonely Hunter' and far better than the exotic 'Reflec-
       tions in a Golden Eye.'... It is a 'novella,' planned on
       a small scale, but what it essays to do it accomplishes
       with an exquisite nervous tension."

G113   Gould, Ray. "Carson McCuller's [sic] Haunting New Book
       Brilliant Novel of a Girl Growing Up." Montgomery
       (Ala.) *Advertiser*, April 14, 1946, Second Society Sec-
       tion, p. 12.

       "This latest effort of the sensitive young author has
       depth and a unique and subtle style that proves her
       originality. It is a haunting story."

G114   Govan, Christine Noble. "Emotions of Tomboy at Twelve
       Told with Sympathy, Restraint." Chattanooga *Times*,
       April 7, 1946, p. 21.

       Member "is one of those rare small books to which nothing
       can be added, from which nothing can be taken away."

G115   Gray, James. "The Book Shelf." Duluth *News-Tribune*,
       April 7, 1946, Cosmopolitan Section, p. 6.

       "This is a disarming study, much the best that Carson
       McCullers has yet achieved. For though it is still a
       tormented imagination which she explores, it is one in

which a reader recognizes the landmarks of a troubled
journey from childhood into adolescence."

G116   Hamilton, Charles. "Girl Craves to 'Belong.'" Worcester
       (Mass.) *Sunday Telegram*, March 31, 1946, p. 4.

       "Even those who enjoy the book will find it repetitious
       and it seems that Miss [sic] McCullers might have pro-
       duced the same effect more poignantly, if she had writ-
       ten a 40-page short story rather than the present 195-
       page short novel."

G117   Hunter, Anna C. "Books in Review--Lonely Childhood."
       Savannah *Morning News*, April 7, 1946, p. 21.

       McCullers is "an artist of style," has "a tremendous
       sensitivity, especially as regards impressions of the
       world of images, impressions and their relation to
       mood." *Member*, except for its confusing use of two
       themes and "the tendency to exaggerate the case, would
       have been a strong psychological study."

G118   Jackson, Joseph Henry. "Bookman's Notebook--The New
       Aloneness." San Francisco *Chronicle*, March 22, 1946,
       p. 14.

       Mostly descriptive review.

G119   Kapp, Isa. "One Summer, Three Lives." *New York Times
       Book Review*, March 24, 1946, p. 5.

       "The writing is internalized, the characters eccentric,
       and the effect entirely winning.... Rarely has emotional
       turbulence been so delicately conveyed."

G120   King, Robin. "New Novels." *New Statesman and Nation*,
       n.s. 33 (April 5, 1947), 241-242 [241].

       Frankie is "the strangest little monster who ever
       opened her eyes to a bottle of coca-cola.... What Mrs.
       McCullers is driving at is difficult to understand, and
       where she will end up is hard to say."

G121   *Kirkus*, 14 (January 15, 1946), 20.

       "An odd, unhappy little story, with the bizarre,
       neurotic atmosphere Carson McCullers achieves."

G122   Kolenich, Betty. "Girl Wants to 'Belong.'" Columbus
       (Ohio) *Sunday Dispatch*, March 31, 1946, p. E-7.

"Mrs. McCullers' descriptions are vivid and original,
and her narration is startling and straightforward. It
is a 'can't-lay-it-down' book."

G123 "The Literary Guidepost." Trenton (N.J.) *Sunday Times-
Advertiser*, March 31, 1946, Part 2, p. 17.

"Some readers may complain of the ending that, where
there was so much smoke, there ought to have been fire.
But up to the last few paragraphs, this is an inordinately
thrilling picture of a few tremendously hazardous days,
and the most eloquent condemnation imaginable of the
silly notion that ignorance is bliss." This review also
appeared in Council Bluffs (Iowa) *Nonpareil*, March 30,
1946.

G124 "The Literary Lantern." Charlotte *Observer*, March 17,
1946, Sec. B, p. [10].

Member "displays technical brilliance" and "a superb
understanding of the bewilderments of adolescents."
McCullers "knows better than almost any author how to
catch the dream-like quality that is at the root of
most people's private existence."

G125 L[yon], M[aclay]. "Artist's Touch in Fiction." Kansas
City *Star*, March 30, 1946, p. 5.

McCullers' writing "is a special treat to those who
read a good many books because it is something special
of itself, and because it is not ... self-conscious or
striving. It does not depend on tricks for effect."

G126 McGill, Ralph. "Frankie and a Georgia Town." Atlanta
Constitution, March 23, 1946, p. [4].

Member is McCullers' "best." "It is an unusual story
of a very sensitive child, and I think you will find it
holds you by the very brilliance of its writing."

G127 Match, Richard. "No Man's Land of Childhood." *New
York Herald Tribune Weekly Book Review*, March 24, 1946,
p. 5.

While it lacks breadth, *Member* is "a tender subtle
little tragicomedy of the no-man's-land between childhood and adolescence."

G128 Murray, Marian. "Perceptiveness in New Novel of
Adolescent." Hartford *Times*, March 23, 1946, p. 5.

In *Member*, McCullers' "concern is with depth rather
than breadth." She "has a kind of intensity that catches
up the reader, making him take an active part in her
voyage of discovery."

G129   Myrick, Susan. "Books in the News." Macon (Ga.) *News*,
       March 20, 1946, p. 6.

       "This is Carson McCullers at her best; her writing is
       similar in style to such masters of prose as Virginia
       Woolf and D.H. Lawrence...."

G130   N., F.A. "One Summer in the Life of a Little Girl."
       Philadelphia *Inquirer*, April 28, 1946, Society Section,
       p. 19.

       "This novel, her third, is fully as eloquent in its
       treatment of a new dimension of human experience."

G131   North, Sterling. "A Difficult Girl at a Difficult Age."
       Chicago Sun Book Week, March 24, 1946, p. 2.

       Member "is near enough to being completely successful
       (for all its labyrinthine self-assignments) so that it
       will create intelligent controversy." This review also
       appeared in Washington (D.C.) *Post*, March 24, 1946,
       Sec. 4, p. 17S; New York *Post*, March 27, 1946, p. 25;
       Knoxville (Tenn.) *Journal*, March 24, 1946, Sec. D, p. 2;
       Indianapolis *News*, April 2, 1946; Columbus (Ohio)
       Citizen, March 31, 1946; Bridgeport (Conn.) *Herald*,
       March 24, 1946.

G132   "Novels in Variety of Techniques." Providence *Sunday
       Journal*, April 7, 1946, Sec. 6, p. 8.

       "The wonder is poignant, and Miss [sic] McCuller [sic]
       gets a good deal out of it. Her style is still mannered,
       her perception narrow, her expression oversensitized....
       Miss [sic] McCullers' chiefest danger is in overweight of
       manners, compared to her material."

G133   P., W. "New Novel by Carson McCullers." Raleigh *News
       and Observer*, March 31, 1946, Sec. 4, p. 5.

       "The book is entertaining for all its brevity, worth
       reading."

G134   Powell, Dawn. "An Australian Novel and 3 from the
       U.S.A." *PM* (New York), April 14, 1946, p. m13.

"No other contemporary writer since Glenway Wescott has
had the complete artist's equipment.... the extraordinary
gift of seeing, remembering, understanding, assimilating
and conveying in one magic process.... Mrs. McCullers
has achieved a difficult and remarkable effect in giving
us her three principals in three *persons*."

G135   Prescott, Orville. "Books of The Times." New York
        Times, March 19, 1946, p. 25.

        Member "is written so well that it must be classified
        as a success," even though the theme is worn.

G136   Rayburn, Otto Ernest. "Child's Need to 'Belong' Is
        Theme of Story of Adolescent Psychology." Memphis
        Commercial Appeal, April 7, 1946, Sec. 4, p. 12.

        Brief descriptive review.

G137   "The Reading Lamp." South Bend (Ind.) *Tribune*, March 31,
        1946, p. 12.

        Mostly descriptive favorable review.

G138   Roberts, Mary-Carter. "The New Books--Carson McCullers
        Offers a Genuine Work of Art." Washington (D.C.)
        Sunday Star, April 21, 1946, p. C-3.

        "The power of her work is great and in that work she
        reaffirms the already extraordinary evidence of
        artistry."

G139   Rosenfeld, Isaac. "Double Standard." *New Republic*, 114
        (April 29, 1946), 633-634.

        "The interest here is more readily maintained than in
        Eudora Welty's novel [*Delta Wedding*]; the dramatic line
        is stronger and more clearly drawn, the anticipation
        mounts in spite of some padding with which Miss [sic]
        McCullers has filled out her slender story, and there
        is an over-all irony and detachment that reinforces the
        emotional quality of the writing. But in relation to
        the South and the folk material that is so liberally
        used," *Member* is also "oblique and self-centered. It
        presents not so much Southern life, as a parable on the
        life of a writer in the South, the alienation and with-
        drawal the sensitive Southerner must feel."

G140   Savage, D.S. "Fiction." *The Spectator*, No. 6193
        (March 7, 1947), 250.

Member is "remarkably insensitive, written in a clogged
and turgid prose reminiscent of the worst of Faulkner
and Gertrude Stein, with not a single clear visual image
or pure emotional perception."

G141 Scruggs, Philip Lightfoot. "A Southern Miscellany."
Virginia Quarterly Review, 22 (Summer 1946), 448-453
[451, 453].

In *Member*, "there is a quality in handling its very
special theme that is rare.... Miss [sic] McCullers
gives heartening proof that we have some gifted young
writers who accept fully the responsibility of their
exceptional endowment."

G142 Straus, Ralph. "New Novels." London *Sunday Times*,
March 9, 1947, p. 3.

"It is a tender and gracious and oddly impressive little
study."

G143 Sturges-Jones, Marion. "Exploring the Mind of a 12-
Year-Old Girl." Philadelphia *Record*, March 31, 1946,
p. M11.

"F. Jasmine is such a convincing portrait that no one
reading 'The Member of the Wedding' will ever again be
able to think of a junior miss in terms of Sally Benson's
Judy." McCullers "has already reached a point where
she must be regarded as a major American novelist."

G144 Taylor, Glenn. "Books & Authors." Bridgeport (Conn.)
Post, March 31, 1946, Sec. B, p. 2.

Mostly descriptive favorable review.

G145 Trilling, Diana. "Fiction in Review." *The Nation*, 162
(April 6, 1946), 406-407.

McCullers is "too close to the adolescent state of mind"
and she makes Frankie "too specific" for her to be "a
universal child case."

G146 *United States Quarterly Book List*, 2 (September 1946),
180-181.

"Though the book does not have the dimensions of a full
novel, being concentrated in time as well as form, it
is a brilliant and discerning piece of writing."

G147   Weiss, Renée. "Interior Decorating." *Quarterly Review of Literature*, 3 (1946), 195-199 [195, 197-199].

McCullers, "despite her faltering conclusion, within the clear and limited margins of the microscopic [world] she has confined herself to, has created a beautiful and intricate piece of work."

G148   West, Mary Ellen. "A Feeling of Futility Runs Through This." Oklahoma City *Daily Oklahoman*, April 21, 1946, p. D-3.

"This third book, like the other two, gives the reader the feeling that the author has met and carefully observed the characters about whom she writes; in the reviewer's opinion, it is fast-moving, convincing, and of considerable depth."

G149   Wilson, Edmund. "Two Books That Leave You Blank: Carson McCullers, Siegfried Sassoon." *New Yorker*, 22 (March 30, 1946), 87-88 [87].

The kitchen scenes create an "atmosphere and ... the characters are droll and natural.... But they have no internal structure and do not build up to anything. The whole story seems utterly pointless."

G150   Young, Marguerite. "Metaphysical Fiction." *Kenyon Review*, 9 (Winter 1947), 151-155.

Member is not merely "a study of turbulent adolescence," it is symbolic of "the confusions of life." McCullers' writing is controlled, logical, and impressionistic.

4.   THE MEMBER OF THE WEDDING (PLAY)

G151   *Booklist*, 47 (May 15, 1951), 325.

Mostly descriptive review.

G152   Freedley, George. "Off Stage--and On." New York *Morning Telegraph*, May 3, 1951, p. 2.

"Her play is really better than the novel on which it was based, despite the fact that she hurled all the melodrama into the last act after the genuinely enjoyable meandering quality of the first two.... you'll certainly want to read it."

G153   ————. "Off Stage--and On." New York *Morning
         Telegraph*, June 6, 1951, p. 2.

         "It seems to me that she made a finer play than novel."

G154   ————. "The Theatre." *Library Journal*, 76 (May 15,
         1951), 866-868 [867].

         "Excellent adaptation of Mrs. McCullers' novel. Highly
         recommended for theatre and drama collections."

G155   *Kirkus*, 18 (April 1, 1951), 198.

         The play is "of more interest for reading groups than
         production."

                  5. THE BALLAD OF THE SAD CAFÉ

G156   Allison, Elizabeth. "A Mirror at the Carnival."
         Arkansas Gazette (Little Rock), July 8, 1951, p. 2F.

         Reflections is "the finest in the collection"; *Ballad*
         is "also Carson McCullers at her best."

G157   Ashford, Gerald. "Carson McCullers Collection Shows
         Steady Development." San Antonio *Express*, June 3, 1951,
         p. 9B.

         "Through all these works, so far as their chronology
         can be determined, there is a steady trend of develop-
         ment in sureness of touch, and in the human sympathy
         which seemed to be lacking in the second novel,
         'Reflections,' even though its apparent absence was
         probably only the result of insufficient skill in the
         youthful author."

G158   "Attitudes and Emotions." *The Scotsman* (Edinburgh),
         July 31, 1952, p. 9.

         McCullers' characters "fail to convince because they
         become too peculiar.... Her viewpoint is one of hyper-
         sensitive perception, always interesting but producing
         an effect of unreality."

G159   Barkham, John. "Brief Reviews of Leading New Books--
         The Ballad of the Sad Café." Buffalo *Evening News*,
         June 16, 1951, Magazine, p. 7.

"This opportunity for an over-all appraisal of Miss [sic]
McCullers confirms the impression that at her best she
is a sensitive and perceptive artist, with compassion
for, and understanding of, human frailties, and one
possessing a clear and poetic voice."

G160   Beals, Helen. "Book Is Great Literary Triumph." Boston
       Sunday Herald, May 27, 1951, Sec. C, p. 3.

       Ballad (the novel) is "one of Mrs. McCullers' greatest
       literary triumphs."

G161   Betjeman, John. "New Fiction--Drawings Add Distinction
       to Story of Antique Trade." London *Daily Telegraph &
       Morning Post*, August 1, 1952, p. 6.

       "The stories are written in an exciting style." But
       they are "too well written, too sensitive. The pleasure
       of each vivid sentence of description, each tenuous
       thought and feeling captured in black and white, can
       cover obscurity and weak construction."

G162   Bradley, Van Allen. "An Extraordinary Talent--Novels,
       Short Stories of Carson McCullers in a Collected Edi-
       tion." Chicago *Daily News*, June 6, 1951, p. 48.

       The "main body" of McCullers' work, "read together in
       this convincing volume, ... offers very nearly conclu-
       sive evidence that Mrs. McCullers has no peers among
       U.S. women writers today."

G163   C., E. "Carson McCullers at Her Eerie Best." Hartford
       Times, August 4, 1951, p. 14.

       "Mrs. McCullers is one of our best."

G164   C., V. "Carson McCullers' Collected Works." Pasadena
       (Calif.) *Star-News*, July 22, 1951, p. 37.

       McCullers is "one of the greatest portrayers of
       tortured lonely persons, particularly of children, ever
       to have been written in English."

G165   Calder-Marshall, Arthur. "New Novels." *The Listener*,
       48 (August 7, 1952), 235.

       McCullers "matches the freshness of her observation with
       simple language.... She is one of the few writers of
       today whose vision opens up a new world."

G166   Carroll, Mark. "Fiction of the Week." Boston
       Post, July 1, 1951, p. 55.

       "Mrs. McCullers writes with depth and artistry and her
       talent is to be reckoned with in American contemporary
       writing."

G167   "Chambers of Horrors." *Times Literary Supplement*,
       July 25, 1952, p. 481.

       McCullers "is in the front rank of the younger American
       writers." Although she is connected with the Southern
       and Gothic traditions, she is "original and independent";
       and she is "keenly interested in the analysis of love,
       and writes well on this subject, but it is generally
       love of an unusual, outlawed sort."

G168   Chapin, Ruth. "A Writer of Compassion." *Christian
       Science Monitor*, July 5, 1951, p. 7.

       McCullers "has mapped the heights and depths of human
       affections--capricious, absurd, even magnificent. But
       of the values beyond the accidents of being human she
       gives no sign."

G169   Clancy, William P. *Commonweal*, 54 (June 15, 1951), 243.

       McCullers produces "an almost terrifying sense of the
       tragic aloneness of man"; her "fusion of horror and com-
       passion ... [is] equalled by few other contemporary
       writers."

G170   Connolly, Cyril. "Southern Lights." London *Sunday
       Times*, July 20, 1952, p. 5.

       "Those who like a good big chunk of somewhere else and
       are as yet unacquainted with the Southern American
       renaissance should make at once for this book and become
       the guests of an exquisite talent and fascinating mind."

G171   Creekmore, Hubert. "The Lonely Search for Love." *New
       York Times Book Review*, July 8, 1951, p. 5.

       McCullers' works "indicate a specialized talent for a
       sharp, controlled revealing style of fiction which
       since its debut has ... never matched the quality of
       the first novel."

G172   Derleth, August. "Minority Report." *Capital Times*
       (Madison, Wis.), June 28, 1951, p. 26.

McCullers is "one of the top score of American writers
of today." Her work has "an undeniable kinship" with
that of Sherwood Anderson and Thomas Wolfe; and this
collection is "one of the year's outstanding books."

G173   Dowling, H.M.   "Southern Mirror." *Western Mail & South
       Wales News* (Cardiff), August 13, 1952, p. 4.

       McCullers "is undoubtedly a fine and significant writer,
       substituting sensitivity for the blatancy and stridency
       of much modern writing, examining curiously and sym-
       pathetically the odd reflections in her southern mirror."

G174   E., P.   "Carson McCullers Creates Vivid Portrait of
       Oddities."   Washington (D.C.) *Times-Herald*, June 24,
       1951, Metropolitan Section, p. M2.

       "The quality of her art is that out of the grotesque
       and the unreal she creates structures which make the
       most accurate comments on normal existence."

G175   Engle, Paul.   "An Original Gift; Unique and Incredible."
       Chicago Sunday Tribune Magazine of Books, June 10, 1951,
       p. 5.

       McCullers "writes with genuine insights and proved
       emotions."

G176   "For the Southern Bookshelf."   *Holland's*, 71 (January
       1952), 6.

       "While many of Mrs. McCullers' characters are eccentric
       to the point of freakishness and some of her situations
       improbable, her skill is such that she manages to make
       them convincing most of the time, and highly interesting
       all of the time."

G177   Freehafer, John.   *Philadelphia Forum*, 30 (June 1951),
       20-21.

       Mostly descriptive brief review.

G178   G., F.   "McCullers' Works in New Anthology."   Lewiston
       (Me.) *Evening Journal*, July 14, 1951, Magazine, p. 8-A.

       The collection contains "some of the very best fiction
       being produced in this country."   Specific praise for
       "A Domestic Dilemma."

G179   Gannett, Lewis.   "Books and Things."   New York *Herald
       Tribune*, July 9, 1951, p. 13.

"There is a quality and a concern with loneliness in
Carson McCullers' writing which inevitably suggests the
best work of William Saroyan and of Tennessee Williams,
but there is more restraint. She never struts; she
never intrudes herself; she never strains--except in
the 'Golden Eye'--for dramatic effect. She understates;
she refrains from over-writing. If hers is a thin vein,
the ore within that vein assays high."

G180   Govan, Christine Noble. "Lonely Creatures." Chattanooga
Times, July 29, 1951, p. 17.

"This is a fine idea, to bring this writer's work together ... for study and comparison, and above all for
enjoyment and appreciation."

G181   Graham, Joan. Buffalo *Courier-Express*, June 10, 1951,
Sec. D, p. 6.

"Not for a moment does this collection, as do so many,
bog down. It would be difficult for this reviewer to
choose a favorite selection."

G182   H., A.S., Jr. "Omnibus in Big Type." Worcester (Mass.)
Sunday Telegram, June 17, 1951, Sec. C, p. 7.

The novellas "appear as good as ever"; several of the
stories are "mannered, labored, lifeless."

G183   H., J.A. "Thumbnail Reviews--Mrs. Keith's Third Novel
Heads Late Autumn List." *Deseret News* (Salt Lake City,
Utah), October 28, 1951, Society and Family Section,
p. 14s.

"The writing is beautiful with each word precisely chosen
to permit three to do the work of one."

G184   Heth, Edward Harris. "'Ballad of the Sad Café'--Carson
McCullers' Novels and Stories, New and Old, Offered in
One Exciting Volume." Milwaukee *Journal*, June 3, 1951,
Editorial Section, p. 5.

McCullers "deserves" the "honor" of having "her collected
works published."

G185   Hill, Bob. "Looking at Books." Spokane *Chronicle*,
July 5, 1951, p. 38.

Collection "contains some of the best reading of this or
any year," although McCullers "has made the range of
experience touched upon in her books (and touched upon
so authentically) a very narrow one."

G186   Hughes, Riley. *Catholic World*, 173 (August 1951), 391.

       Collection represents "the reworking of a few themes.
       The overriding one is loneliness, specifically that
       separateness brought about by the tensions and violence
       inherent in the South."

G187   "Human Behaviour." London *Times*, July 26, 1952, p. 6.

       McCullers' fiction "is among the most interesting
       phenomena of contemporary American literature.... She
       has a poetic quality all her own and these qualities are
       married to a firm sense of narrative and an eye for ob-
       jective detail."

G188   Hunt, Mary Fassett. "Bit of Life to Hold in the Hand."
       Birmingham (Ala.) *News*, July 15, 1951, p. E6.

       "Carson McCullers' writing achieves a unique atmospheric
       effect. By that she is most closely related to Tennessee
       Williams and Eudora Welty, but she is more deeply search-
       ing than either, and she is more capable of breaking
       your heart."

G189   Hunter, Anna C. "Books in Review." Savannah *Morning
       News*, June 10, 1951, p. 22.

       "This is a significant volume."

G190   Johnson, Pamela Hansford. "Style Is Not Enough." *John
       O'London's Weekly*, 61 (August 1, 1952), [17].

       McCullers "does not observe people--she makes them up;
       and if one bears this in mind and reads the work purely
       for the poetry, it is not unrewarding." But "beautiful
       writing in itself can be sterile, and this kind of
       American art--at its best in Miss [sic] McCullers-- ...
       is a sterile one."

G191   Jones, Carter Brooke. "Carson McCullers' Collected
       Works." Washington (D.C.) *Sunday Star*, May 27, 1951,
       p. C-3.

       The short stories in the collection are, "like all
       first-rate short stories, fragments of life--as it is
       lived, not as people would like it to be--and yet none
       is a mere vignette, a detached mood, as some non-
       formula stories are."

G192   Kee, Robert. "Near-Genius." *The Spectator*, No. 6481
       (September 12, 1952), 340.

The short stories "are of straightforward adult *New Yorker* quality"; *Ballad* and *Reflections* excessively emphasize abnormality; *Member*, whose central character is "not a freak," is a "minor masterpiece."

G193 K[elley], J[ames] E. "McCullers Shines in New Edition." Denver *Post*, May 27, 1951, p. 6E.

The collection reveals McCullers' uncanny insight into the mores of the South and the tremendous vitality of her writing--compassionate and "happily devoid of stylistic excess."

G194 Laws, Frederick. "Brilliant, Sincere, But Not for Me." London *News Chronicle*, August 15, 1952, p. 4.

"I agree with my betters that Carson McCullers is technically brilliant and utterly sincere, but I wish I could like her work a little." The "violence, the sudden turns of emotions, the burst of lyricism, even the sensibility," remind one of Faulkner.

G195 "Lonely and Unusual People Wandering in a Dream World." Miami (Fla.) *Herald*, June 10, 1951, p. 4-F.

Mostly descriptive favorable review.

G196 MacGregor, Martha. "McCullers' Collection." New York *Post*, May 27, 1951, Sec. 2, p. 12M.

"The whole volume shows an unusually high, even level, particularly for the forties, a literary decade of dubious distinction."

G197 M[ahoney], W.J., Jr. "Carson McCullers's Collected Works." Montgomery *Advertiser-Alabama Journal*, May 27, 1951, Sec. D, p. 6.

McCullers' "viewpoint" and "stories" are "novel and interesting." This collection "will be welcomed."

G198 Massingham, Hugh. "The Invisible Worm." *The Observer* (London), July 20, 1952, p. 7.

McCullers is "the true interpreter of the common man.... Her ordinary people are dead right because they are extraordinary." She is "such a mature writer that she makes most of her American contemporaries seem almost crude."

G199 Miller, Nolan. "Mr. Jones and Others...." *Antioch Review*, 11 (June 1951), 237-241 [239].

McCullers has "this rare gift"--"focus, the ability to
direct the attention and to evoke emotions and control
them.... She is at her best with children, adolescents;
her adults are perhaps too odd and hurt, and thus com-
mand false sympathy."

G200 Murphy, Pat. "Such Beauty in the Fisherman's Tale."
London *Daily Mail*, July 26, 1952, p. 2.

This is a "grand collection of tales recounted by a
mistress of her craft. They will endure.... There is a
fluent ease in her writing ... her characters grow out
of the fluid words."

G201 *New Yorker*, 27 (June 9, 1951), 114-115.

"The situations and sentiments are so artistically
evoked that it is no doubt carping to remark that her
innocents often seem a shade too receptive ... and that
the atmosphere of hurt and betrayal often becomes merely
sticky."

G202 O'Connor, Madeleine. "Books on the Table--Collections."
San Francisco *Argonaut*, July 6, 1951, p. 18.

Brief descriptive favorable review.

G203 O'Dell, Scott. "Amelia Ditches Mate on Wedding Night."
Los Angeles *Daily News*, May 26, 1951, p. 8.

Ballad (the novel) is "glowingly impressive, informed
with feeling and humor and poetry, a sure knowledge of
the strange forces that bind together all humanity--
whether for good or for evil."

G204 O[lofson], P[hilip] H. "Discriminating Reader Rewarded
by This Author." Fort Wayne *News-Sentinel*, July 14,
1951, p. 4.

"Her prose is delicate and painstaking and often gives
the impression that each word was hand-picked and reviewed for defects before becoming part of the story in
which it appears. Yet there is a superb fluidity in
reading."

G205 O'Neill, Lois Decker. "Looks at Books." Louisville
Courier-Journal, June 3, 1951, Sec. 3, p. 13.

"It takes a full reading of her work to realize on what
a wide range of perception and sympathy she can play,
how always accurate is her ear, how always clear her
own golden eye."

G206   Poore, Charles. "Books of The Times." New York *Times*,
        May 24, 1951, p. 33.

        Ballad (the novel) is "brilliant"; the collection is "a
        panorama of a remarkable talent that has already gone
        beyond promise to fulfillment."

G207   Pritchett, V.S. "Books in General." *New Statesman and
        Nation*, n.s. 44 (August 2, 1952), 137-38.

        This collection makes "an impact which recalls the im-
        pressions made by such different writers as Maupassant
        and D.H. Lawrence." McCullers has a "courageous imagi-
        nation" and an "original, fearless and compassionate
        mind."

G208   *Punch*, 223 (August 13, 1952), 242.

        "Sensitive, haunting and very efficient studies of dream
        and reality in America.... The delicacy of the prose
        does not soften the firmness of the narrative and
        characterization."

G209   Redman, Ben Ray. "New Editions." *Saturday Review*, 34
        (June 23, 1951), 30.

        Novels and stories "are ever more impressive on second
        reading than they were when first read." McCullers is
        "one of the truly original writers of our time."

G210   "The Revolving Bookstand ... Brief Comments." *American
        Scholar*, 20 (Autumn 1951), 494.

        Collection "demonstrates convincingly Mrs. McCullers'
        claim to a major position in contemporary American
        fiction."

G211   Rosenberger, Coleman. "A Carson McCullers Omnibus."
        New York Herald Tribune Book Review, June 10, 1951,
        pp. 1, 13.

        Each of the works collected "takes its place in an ex-
        panding structure in which each part augments and
        strengthens the rest." *Ballad* (the novel) is McCullers'
        work at its "most intense" level.

G212   Sackett, Russ. "A Bigger Audience." *Oregon Journal*
        (Portland), June 17, 1951, Magazine, p. 8M.

        "This particular collection offers a considerable variety
        of story forms and subject matters. But it's Carson

McCullers from beginning to end--which makes it ... the
finest fiction value on the market today."

G213   Scott, Eleanor. "Carson McCullers and the Theme of
       Loneliness." Providence *Sunday Journal*, June 17, 1951,
       Sec. 6, p. 8.

       McCullers' "externality leads her to an over-emphasis
       upon freaks and perversions; more importantly it results
       in her work lacking the inevitability that would make
       her as great a writer as her materials and fine skill as
       a writer should dictate."

G214   Sherman, John K. "Carson McCullers Achieves Classic
       Status in 15 Years." Minneapolis *Sunday Tribune*,
       June 24, 1951, Feature-News Section, p. 10.

       Ballad (the novel) "illustrates the author's sympathetic
       preoccupation with thwarted and warped people, and in
       this and other stories she explores a subterranean world
       of feelings and inhibitions rarely acknowledged."

G215   Sherman, Thomas B. "Reading and Writing--Carson
       McCullers in One Large Volume." St. Louis *Post-
       Dispatch*, June 17, 1951, Part 2, p. [4].

       McCullers, "one feels, is concerned with the stigmatized
       members of humanity because she knows what concealed
       agonies the outward blemish may signify."

G216   "The Shy & the Lonely." *Time*, 57 (June 4, 1951), 106.

       Taken together, these writings "pretty well establish
       Novelist McCullers as one of the top dozen among con-
       temporary U.S. writers." *Ballad* (the novel) "is told
       with quietness and simplicity ... there streaks through
       it a ribbon of sympathy for the shy and the lonely, the
       eccentrics who wait on the margins of life for a touch
       of love."

G217   Spain, Nancy. "How the Witch Cult is Growing!" London
       Daily Express, August 7, 1952, p. 4.

       McCullers "is certainly the best writer to come out of
       America for years, which makes her subject matter all
       the more deplorable."

G218   Spearman, Walter. "Omnibus Volume Is Issued by Mrs.
       Carson McCullers." Asheville (N.C.) *Citizen-Times*,
       June 3, 1951, Sec. B, p. 5.

McCullers' "sure touch of characterization, her telling
bits of dialogue, her sharp depiction of the Southern-
town background, her brilliant evocation of sentiment
without any lapse into sentimentality attest that Mrs.
McCullers is one of our most gifted Southern writers."

G219 T., C.V. Dayton *News*, July 15, 1951, Sec. 3, p. 15.

Collection is "rewarding to anyone who appreciates rare
artistic talent and insight, operating through an impeccable style."

G220 Taylor, Glenn. "Carson McCullers' Two Worlds--Of the
Mind and the Emotions." Bridgeport (Conn.) *Post*,
June 3, 1951, Sec. B, p. 4.

Mostly descriptive review. This collection "should go a
long way toward stilling the plaint that" the present-
day state of American letters is "an arid one."

G221 Thesmar, Sarah. "McCullers' Pen Gains Power--'Ballad
of Sad Café' and Other Stories Warmly Hailed." Memphis
Commercial Appeal, July 22, 1951, Sec. 5, p. 12.

"A perfect vacation is between the covers of this 791-
not-one-unimportant-page book."

G222 Tunstall, Caroline Heath. "Carson McCullers--'Among
Leading American Writers.'" Norfolk *Virginian-Pilot*,
May 27, 1951, Sec. 4, p. 4.

Novels in the collection are "entertaining, sharply ob-
servant and witty and, thoughtful as they are, they are
written with clarity, rich in concrete images, entirely
free of that muggy impressionism that is so often the
hallmark of studies of the heart."

G223 Urquhart, Fred. *Time and Tide*, 33 (August 16, 1952),
940.

The characterizations in this collection are "what makes
Carson McCullers' work so worth watching for. She
peoples a real world with characters which probably
stepped straight from her imagination, but which are no
stranger than the ones we see continually around us."

G224 Wasson, Ben. "Georgia Author in Collected Work Proves
Tops Among Contemporaries." Greenville (Miss.) *Delta
Democrat-Times*, June 3, 1951, p. 16.

"All true lovers of writing as an art will treasure
this, the collected works of Carson McCullers. Her lack
of the maudlin, her keen perceptivity, her ability to
create vital and thwarted characters, her spartan manner
of speech, her deep and lovely compassion, make her one
of the truly brilliant authors of our time."

G225   Wiener, Max. "Portable McCullers." Newark (N.J.)
       Sunday News, June 17, 1951, Sec. 3, p. 48.

       All the "fragments" of McCullers' work "brought together"
       in this volume "emerge as bits of mosaic which fit into
       a brilliantly integrated design."

G226   *Wisconsin Library Bulletin*, 47 (June 1951), 166.

       "Carson McCullers wrote like a mature person even at the
       age of twenty-three, and subsequent productions, while
       not maintaining the depth and poignancy of *Hunter*, do
       retain her central theme which seems to be the tragedy
       of people's misunderstanding one another."

              6.   THE SQUARE ROOT OF WONDERFUL

G227   Alvarez, A. "Circling the Squares." *The Observer*
       (London), March 15, 1959, p. 23.

       McCullers' characters, "when stripped of their prose
       setting and set down nakedly to talk and act, seem a
       fey, dispiriting lot." She is "an extremely talented
       writer--but only of prose fiction."

G228   *Booklist*, 55 (September 1, 1958), 16.

       "An adroitly written play about modern marriage and
       divorce which under its prevailing tone of Southern
       charm and entertaining banter makes some significant
       points about the realities of love, loyalty, and family
       relationships."

G229   "Coups de Théâtre." *Times Literary Supplement*,
       February 27, 1959, p. 110.

       "As a piece of sentimental theatrecraft *The Square Root
       of Wonderful* may be judged successful; but as an emo-
       tional experience it falls short." McCullers' "hand is
       so evident that the play thereby loses much tension;

her men and women are so clearly a dramatist's puppets
that there is a wistful predictability about their
every speech and action."

G230 Freedley, George. "The Theatre." *Library Journal*, 83
(June 1, 1958), 1800-1801 [1800].

"Although this play was a Broadway failure, Mrs.
McCullers has filled it with lovable and most attrac-
tively written characters which should make it a community theatre favorite."

G231 Gregory, Sister M., O.P. *Best Sellers*, 18 (August 15,
1958), 183.

"The play is implausible, unconvincing and earthbound ...
a case-history in three acts."

G232 *Kirkus*, 26 (May 1, 1958), 348.

"While the Broadway record of this second of Carson
McCullers' plays was not impressive, the quality of
the writing makes the play in book form worth reading."

G233 Maslin, Marsh. "What Makes Authors Turn to Writing?"
San Francisco *Call-Bulletin*, June 21, 1958, p. 10.

It is "a warm and lovely play, well worth reading."

G234 O'Mara, Roger. "Literary Lantern--McCullers Play Probes
Life's Tragedy, Comedy." *Arizona Daily Star* (Tucson),
June 29, 1958, p. 6D.

"After a fumbling start in which the dialogue is strained
as two characters go through silly explanations of
occurrences both are aware of--but which are being put
forth for the reader's or viewer's benefit--she moves
into comic and other scenes with a sure hand."

G235 Watson, Latimer. "'Square Root'--New McCullers Play Is
Out in Book Form." Columbus (Ga.) *Ledger-Enquirer*,
June 29, 1958, Sec. M, p. 7.

"You can't see a play in 'The Square Root of Wonderful.'
We rather agree with the critic who said the only good
thing about it, or possibly he said the best thing
about it, was the name."

7. CLOCK WITHOUT HANDS

G236 Allen, Morse. "Time Does Not Register." Hartford
      Courant, September 24, 1961, Magazine, p. 14.

      While *Clock* is entertaining, "it will not greatly add
      to its author's high reputation."

G237 B., A.M. "Book Reviews--Death's Light Is Clear." St.
      Louis *Advocate*, September 21, 1961, p. 10.

      "There remains in Mrs. McCullers' book, when all is con-
      sidered, a certain sterility. Death might have been
      more acceptable as a hero, if there had been some place
      in the plot for God."

G238 B., O.T. *Wisconsin Library Bulletin*, 57 (September-
      October 1961), 306-307.

      "Segregation in the South with its strife between the
      generation that resists and the generation that is
      gradually learning is well-portrayed in character and
      situation. Certain to be one of the year's outstanding
      novels."

G239 Balliet, Whitney. *New Yorker*, 37 (September 23, 1961),
      179.

      Mostly descriptive review.

G240 Barkham, John. "Novel of Change in the Old South."
      New York *World-Telegram and Sun*, September 19, 1961,
      p. 25.

      "This new novel of Carson McCullers, though not the
      best of her books, still makes most current fiction
      seem trifling."

G241 Beau-Seigneur, Jay. "Books: From Milan, Georgia...."
      Burlingame (Calif.) *Advance Star*, September 24, 1961,
      Peninsula Living, p. 24.

      "This brilliant, haunting novel undoubtedly will be
      marked hereafter as one of the very best works of fic-
      tion ever written by an American."

G242 Boger, Mary Snead. "Ill Author's 'Livingness' Enters
      Book." Charlotte *Observer*, October 1, 1961, p. 6-F.

Clock is a "masterpiece" because the people "are simple, sometimes pathetic, but always believable people." McCullers' "'livingness' flows into her book and illumines with a strange hollow light on every page."

G243 *Booklist*, 58 (September 1, 1961), 23.

"With her customary perception, the novelist gives focus and meaning to personal lives and relationships and in them sees reflected the love, loneliness, and tragedy of man's existence. Not quite so compelling as some of McCullers' earlier works but a strong novel that deals with important themes."

G244 *Bookmark*, 20 (July 1961), 233.

"This powerful and original novel with striking portrayal of Southern characters deals with the voice of conscience and the need for reaffirmation of faith in the dignity of man."

G245 Bowen, Robert O. *Catholic World*, 194 (December 1961), 186-188.

"The shallowness of the narrative is obscured by direct action and occasional stylistic play-pretties and the narrative nowhere penetrates to the depth of the soul."

G246 Bradbury, Malcolm. "New Fiction." *Punch*, 241 (November 8, 1961), 696.

Although McCullers is criticizable for "the sickly, sentimental generosity with which she can sometimes treat children, and a desire ... to treat all people and all opinions as if they too were overgrown children," nevertheless, "in spite of its flaws, the book is of undoubted substance."

G247 Buckmaster, Henrietta. "The Break-Through and the Pattern." *Christian Science Monitor*, September 21, 1961, p. 7.

Clock is a novel "which comes, with a startling vividness, to a dead end." The writing is "artful" but "it skims over honest confrontations."

G248 Butcher, Fanny. "Georgia Ways, Caricatured from Life." *Chicago Sunday Tribune Magazine of Books*, September 17, 1961, p. 3.

McCullers "writes with an intense feeling for words and the patterns of thought they can make and record and she does it without making the reader overly conscious of the beauty of her prose."

G249   Cheney, Frances Neel. "Loneliness Continues to Intrigue Southern Writer." Nashville *Banner*, September 15, 1961, p. 23.

"One misses a certain maturity which would allow this woman ... to turn her talents to some song other than 'None But the Lonely Heart.'"

G250   Culligan, Glendy. "McCullers Mixture as Before." Washington (D.C.) *Post*, September 17, 1961, Sec. E, p. 6.

Clock is "outrageously direct, insinuatingly oblique, sad, funny, tender. In short, it is as hard to resist as the confidences of a child."

G251   Dawkins, Cecil. "Carson McCullers Recasts a Golden Eye on the South." Milwaukee *Journal*, September 17, 1961, Part 5, p. 4.

Without comparing *Clock* to McCullers' earlier fiction, "on its own it is a better than average novel with rewarding moments."

G252   De Mott, Benjamin. "Fiction Chronicle." *Hudson Review*, 14 (Winter 1961-1962), 622-629 [625-626].

Clock is "depressingly underdone" and without details. It "tells two stories but both have little substance."

G253   Didion, J[oan]. *National Review*, 12 (January 30, 1962), 69.

McCullers' early fiction showed "the chasm between some people and the circumstances of their lives ... the condition in which some social cog is missing." In *Clock*, however, "she has tried to make believe that those Gothic characters of hers make up society itself, rather than exist outside of it."

G254   Emerson, Donald. "Disjointed Novel." *The Progressive*, 25 (November 1961), 42-43.

"It is uncertainty about her objective that weakens *Clock Without Hands*.... The understanding, the tenderness, the humor and pathos are evident ... but the plot is loose.... Although the total effect is below her own standard, Mrs. McCullers writes separate scenes which compare well with her best."

G255 Fancher, Betsy. "Dilemma of Man Unfolds in 20th Century Masterpiece." Atlanta *Journal and Constitution*, September 17, 1961, p. 13-D.

"Great themes and unforgettable characters are masterfully compressed and interwoven in this slender volume."

G256 "Free from the Fetters of Dogma." *Times Weekly Review* (London), October 26, 1961, p. 10.

"A vital and tireless imagination distinguishes Miss [sic] Carson McCullers's fiction; it is also marvellously free from the fetters of dogma and of literary fashion." Her portrayal of the judge "is surely among the best studies to have been made of aggressive and tragic old age."

G257 "From Life into Death." *Times Literary Supplement*, October 20, 1961, p. 749.

"She has been able by dint of honesty as much as by technical skill to write a good and moving book which comes up to all the demands raised by her reputation."

G258 Fuller, John. "New Novels." *The Listener*, 66 (November 9, 1961), 783.

"In this very good novel by Miss [sic] McCullers there is a bad novel ... struggling to get out, a kind of melodrama that tends to rise darkly to the surface where the author is being least vigilant in avoiding the Colour Problem...."

G259 Galloway, David D. "Dying Man--Novel's Hero--Ponders Life Responsibility." Buffalo *Courier-Express*, September 17, 1961, p. 13.

"As usual, Carson McCullers has written with the intensity and the whimsical tenderness which make her one of the most successful writers living today."

G260 Godden, Rumer. "Death and Life in a Small Southern Town." *New York Herald Tribune Books*, September 17, 1961, p. 5.

"Not a word could be added or taken away from this marvel of a novel by Carson McCullers." She is

"transcendental," a "master of peculiar penetration,"
and "an incomparable storyteller."

G261   Govan, Christine Noble. "Study in a Southern Town
Lacking in Creative Spark." Chattanooga *Times*,
September 24, 1961, p. 18.

The novel has its good parts, but on the whole it
leaves the reader "unconvinced or frankly bored."

G262   Green, Peter. "Recent Fiction--Growing Up in Two
Jungles." London *Daily Telegraph and Morning Post*,
October 20, 1961, p. 21.

"It is a remarkable, if muted, achievement."

G263   Greenwood, Walter B. "Carson McCullers Writes of a
South in Midst of Change." Buffalo *Evening News*,
September 16, 1961, p. B-8.

Clock is "more than well told.... Carson McCullers
writes with an effortless grace and precision ... she
sees deeply with a poet's vision of the human condition."

G264   Griffin, Lloyd W. *Library Journal*, 86 (August 1961),
2682.

"A perceptive and colorful study of the change in
Southern mores. A thoughtful, intermittently brilliant
book for a fiction collection."

G265   Gross, John. "Past Masters." *New Statesman*, n.s. 62
(October 27, 1961), 614-615 [614].

"This is the author's weakest book to date: the writing
is surprisingly slack, the symbolism creaks, the
climax ... doesn't come off. But Mrs. McCullers ...
still has a wonderful eye, and an unsurpassed feeling
for the unfledged, the broken down, the estranged."

G266   Grumbach, Doris. *America*, 105 (September 23, 1961), 809.

"A novel lacking any distinction except the name of its
author, it tells a story studded with the clichés of
current events and is written in a style ... forced and
flat."

G267   Haddican, James. "In Another Small Town in the South."
New Orleans *Times-Picayune*, September 24, 1961, Sec. 2,
p. 2.

"Although it has its moments, the novel doesn't have enough of them to sustain interest from one situation to the next.... Her style alone doesn't establish the essential rapport between the writer and the reader...."

G268 Hall, Ted. "Timepiece Beyond Repair." Newark (N.J.) *Sunday News*, September 17, 1961, p. 48.

"In the climate of the times, 'Clock Without Hands' will probably hit the best-seller lists. But if it does, it will [be] because of its political correctness, not because it is a great--or even good--literary work."

G269 Hartt, J.N. "The Return of Moral Passion." *Yale Review*, 51 (December 1961), 300-308 [300-301].

"This account ... of the flesh-trammeled spirit is as confused philosophically as the movement of the novel is mechanical."

G270 Hicks, Granville. "The Subtler Corruptions." *Saturday Review*, 44 (September 23, 1961), 14-15, 49.

Clock is a "fine novel." Although it does not equal *Heart*, the characterizations and the insights are very good.

G271 Hobby, Diana Poteat. "Unsweetened South." Houston *Post*, September 17, 1961, *Houston Now*, p. 20.

Mostly descriptive review.

G272 Hogan, William. "A Bookman's Notebook--The Georgia Scene by Carson McCullers." San Francisco *Chronicle*, September 18, 1961, p. 39.

"An even novel of power, subtlety and confusion.... the beautiful individual scenes here add up to something less than a whole."

G273 Howe, Irving. "In the Shadow of Death." *New York Times Book Review*, September 17, 1961, p. 5.

Although *Clock* is "more robust, realistic, and conventional" than McCullers' earlier works, it is "also less successful." It is poorly constructed with an "absence of inner conviction and imaginative energy."

G274 Hughes, Catharine. "A World of Outcasts." *Commonweal*, 75 (October 13, 1961), 73-75.

Clock is criticized for its lack of character development and for McCullers' "inability to focus ... attention where she seemingly wishes it to be, on J.T. Malone."

G275 Hunter, Anna C. "Tragedy of the Unregenerated." Savannah *Morning News*, September 17, 1961, Magazine, p. 12.

"There is little new to enlighten those concerned with the Southern dilemma, but the powerful voice of a master raised on the issue, is of paramount importance to her people.... Each scene is etched; each denunciation is acidly bitten in the fabric of her medium."

G276 Hutchens, John K. "Daily Book Review--'Clock Without Hands.'" New York *Herald Tribune*, September 18, 1961, p. 21.

The effect of the book is of "dazzling unrelated patches in a contrived narrative that wanders between realism and fantasy.... [It] occasionally shines but more often is wayward."

G277 Idema, Jim. "Heresy! C. McCullers Lays Egg." Denver *Post*, September 17, 1961, *Roundup*, p. 10.

"The plot is a confusion of undeveloped extensions, blind alleys, unsatisfied questions.... When people talk to each other and act out their lives against each other they are just not very interesting."

G278 Jackson, Katherine Gauss. "Books in Brief." *Harper's*, 223 (October 1961), 111-112.

Mostly descriptive review.

G279 Jennings, Elizabeth. "Human Loneliness." London *Sunday Times*, October 15, 1961, Magazine, p. 31.

Clock is "a very fine novel."

G280 Kennedy, John S. "Time Runs Out." *Our Sunday Visitor* (Huntington, Ind.), September 3, 1961, p. 7.

Clock is "hardly" McCullers' "best": Malone "is all but eclipsed because of the author's preoccupation with the Judge, who, although a character rich in comedy and pathos alike, is scarcely deserving of the attention paid him."

G281 Kilts, Donald L. Saginaw (Mich.) *News*, September 19, 1961, Sec. B, p. 6.

"Mrs. McCullers' people in *Clock Without Hands* sometimes slide beyond believability, at times seem stereotypes. But they are there as they are for a purpose. They tell their story. They make their point."

G282 *Kirkus*, 29 (July 15, 1961), 627.

Clock "embellishes an already fine literary reputation though it lacks the sting of her previous work." It is written "with great narrative skill and precise characterization."

G283 Kirvan, John J. *The Sign*, 41 (January 1962), 61.

Clock is "placid, subdued, controlled, ordinary and even bland.... This is a novel with its moments but conspicuously lacking in the force, tautness, and emotional impact that we have come to expect of Miss [sic] McCullers."

G284 K[lein], [Francis A.] "McCullers New Novel Memorable." St. Louis *Globe-Democrat*, September 17, 1961, p. 4F.

Clock is "by far the best thing ... [McCullers] has done so far, and that is very good indeed.... You can't get her characters out of your mind.... There is humor here, and compassion, irony and power--in short, Carson McCullers at the top of her form."

G285 L[aycock], E[dward] A. "McCullers Sadness." Boston *Sunday Globe*, September 24, 1961, p. B-7.

Clock is "not the best McCullers, but its McCullers touches raise it far above most recent fiction."

G286 *Life*, 51 (September 22, 1961), 21.

"Carson McCullers has come back with an absolute gem of a novel.... Miss [sic] McCullers uses her poet's instinct and storyteller's skill to reaffirm her place at the very top of modern American writing."

G287 "Lonely Hunter Hearts." *Newsweek*, 58 (September 18, 1961), 106.

"The separate quests of these lonely hunter hearts do not blend very satisfactorily as a story, but the characters themselves are often piercingly real."

G288   M., T. "Modern Novel at Its Nadir." Houston *Chronicle*,
       September 3, 1961, TV Pullout Section, p. 2.

       "It is one of the most inane, improbable, poorly con-
       ceived pieces of dirty writing to come from a 'name
       novelist' in a good many years."

G289   McConkey, James. *Epoch*, 11 (Fall 1961), 197-198.

       "The novel is uneven; the McCullers aware of separation
       and isolation is more universal than the McCullers who
       hints at an achieved, and mature, sense of responsi-
       bility."

G290   Martin, Jean. "Ways of Telling It." *The Nation*, 193
       (November 18, 1961), 411-412.

       "Warm, funny and readable; its point may not quite
       click, but the writing is quietly superb." It is a
       "step forward" for McCullers "for it eschews the pointed
       and labored allegory of her earlier works."

G291   Maslin, Marsh. "Southerners Are Sure to Curse This
       Novel." San Francisco *News Call-Bulletin*, September 16,
       1961, p. 6.

       "Millions of white Southerners--who do not read her
       novels and think of Carson McCullers as a 'nigger-lover'
       --would curse this novel without reading it and deny
       anything in it could happen. But a few hundred thousand
       Southerners will recognize this picture of dreadful
       adolescence as true."

G292   "The Member of the Funeral." *Time*, 78 (September 22,
       1961), 118-120.

       "Novelist McCullers drops the story thread and comes
       close to losing the entire narrative spool.... Motiva-
       tions are inept and mystifying." *Clock* "shows nothing
       but the absence of life."

G293   Mitchell, Julian. *London Magazine*, n.s. 2 (April 1962),
       91, 93, 95.

       "There has been a paring to essentials ... so that
       nothing seems unnecessary.... *Clock Without Hands* is as
       fine as anything she has written, a meditation on life
       and death, and a long look into the eyes of the South."

G294   Moore, Harry T. "Well-Told Story of Two Men." Boston
       Herald, September 17, 1961, Sec. 3, p. 9.

"Sometimes Mrs. McCullers tells the reader too much instead of dramatizing the material, but for the most part this is a story of assured power." It is "beyond the general run of novels."

G295 Mortimer, Penelope. "Southern Justice." *Time & Tide*, 42 (October 19, 1961), 1757.

Clock "is not a masterpiece.... But it is a very good novel ... it excites emotions of pity and joy which normally are too spent to stir. Miss [sic] McCullers' talent for comedy is unrivaled and I can think of no one whose writing gives more pleasure or whose powers of stimulation are so strong."

G296 "New Fiction." London *Times*, October 19, 1961, p. 15.

"A vital and tireless imagination distinguishes Miss [sic] Carson McCullers's fiction; it is also marvelously free from the fetters of dogma and of literary fashion." *Clock* is "surely among the best studies to have been made of aggressive and tragic old age."

G297 Norris, Hoke. "New Carson McCullers: Life in Midst of Death." Chicago *Sun-Times*, September 24, 1961, Sec. 3, p. 4.

Praise for the realism of the book; but McCullers "is too good a writer to fall into the traps of [sentimentalizing] this theme."

G298 "Novel's Look at South Finds It Dismal Still." Washington (D.C.) *Sunday Star*, September 24, 1961, Sec. C, p. 5.

Clock "lacks cohesion, direction and point. It is little more than an attempt to exploit meretriciously sensational aspects of miscegenation, perversion and race-hatred."

G299 Parker, Dorothy. "*Clock Without Hands* Belongs in Yesterday's Tower of Ivory." *Esquire*, 56 (December 1961), 72-73.

Criticism of the stock characters and situations in the book and of the implausible actions and characters. "It is sharply difficult for me to attempt to explain that Carson McCullers has not, to my mind, again written a perfect book."

G300   Phillippi, Wendell C.   "'Clock Without Hands' Strikes
       Morbid Note."   Indianapolis *News*, October 28, 1961,
       p. 2.

       Mostly descriptive review.

G301   *Playboy*, 8 (October 1961), 52-53.

       "J.T. Malone remains veiled, while the world of mindless
       racism around him comes through vividly in this admir-
       able and ambitious novel."

G302   Powers, Dennis.   "McCullers Novel Ranks Among the
       Year's Finest."   Oakland (Calif.) *Tribune*, September 24,
       1961, p. 2-EL.

       Clock is "unquestionably one of the finest novels of
       the year, and in spite of its imperfections, a resound-
       ing success."

G303   Prescott, Orville.   "Books of The Times."   New York
       Times, September 18, 1961, p. 27.

       It "is not a successful novel."   It is "full of im-
       probable dialogue and improbable situations.... Even
       the prose style, for the most part, is fast and
       pedestrian."

G304   Priestley, Lee.   "Universal Motivation Probed."   Okla-
       homa City *Daily Oklahoman*, September 24, 1961, p. 5D.

       Despite the violence, *Clock* is not grim because McCullers
       "blends much humor with the irony and compassion that
       reveal her characters so powerfully."

G305   Quigly, Isabel.   "In the Mind."   Manchester *Guardian*,
       October 20, 1961, p. 7.

       "Tensions, atmospheres, glories all mount and multiply,
       the atmosphere of the small town in Georgia is so strong
       you can smell the fear and enmity, and see the startling
       physical beauty.... If Miss [sic] McCullers is not the
       major American novelist of the moment, ... she is cer-
       tainly the most attractive...."

G306   Quinn, John J., S.J.   *Best Sellers*, 21 (October 1, 1961),
       253-254.

       "It is easy to predict how the novel will score with
       prize-awarding judges and especially with the dis-
       criminating reader; it is a winner."

G307 Rackemann, Adelaide C. "Deft, Sure and Entertaining."
Baltimore *Sun*, September 17, 1961, p. A-5.

"While the reader may ponder the meaning of it all--and
there is much to ponder--this is a tremendously entertaining story."

G308 Ragan, Sam. "From the Minutes of Our Time." Raleigh
News and Observer, September 17, 1961, Sec. 3, p. 5.

Although McCullers is one of the greatest living novelists, *Clock* fails "to measure up to her work of the
past." However, it "should not be rejected without
reading. There is excitement in it."

G309 Raven, Simon. "Two Kinds of Jungle." *The Spectator*,
No. 6956 (October 20, 1961), 551-552 [551].

"It is never easy to see just how seriously she wishes
to be taken, so blithely does she sprinkle the sugar-
icing of comedy over the grimmest possible events....
you may construe this book with profit, on any level
from the anecdotal to the tragic. I use the latter word
advisedly."

G310 Richter, Harvena. "Carson McCullers' Novel Skirts the
Outrageous." Providence *Sunday Journal*, September 17,
1961, p. N54.

"A sometimes beautiful, often puzzling and perverse com-
bination of classic ideas, Southern violence, and comedy
bordering on the burlesque." There is "brilliance ...
in her combining of the cynical and poetic eye.... But
much is pure celluloid."

G311 "Riddles of Salinger and McCullers." Miami (Fla.)
Herald, September 17, 1961, Sec. F, p. 7.

Nobody in *Clock* "quite lives and the point she strives
to make is obscure."

G312 Rolo, Charles. "A Southern Drama." *The Atlantic*, 208
(October 1961), 126-127.

"Readers who have wished in the past that Miss [sic]
McCullers were a bit less fascinated by abnormality and
grotesquerie may find this the most impressive of her
novels.... The craftsmanship is impeccable.... *Clock
Without Hands* is a strong contender for the 1961 National
Book Award for fiction."

G313   Rubin, Louis D., Jr.   "Six Novels and S. Levin."
       Sewanee Review, 70 (Summer 1962), 504-514 [509-511].

       "The old artistry at creating a pervasive mood and tone
       is missing completely. It is as if Miss [sic] McCullers
       determined to write a novel 'about' the segregation
       issue and fashioned her people entirely with this issue
       in mind. The net result is not a novel but a tract."

G314   Sandrof, Nancy. "Artist at Perfection." Worcester
       (Mass.) *Sunday Telegram*, September 17, 1961, Sec. D,
       p. 11.

       In *Clock*, McCullers "continues to probe and delve deep
       into the secret selves of her characters. What she finds
       and reports is always a rich mine of revelation to the
       reader."

G315   Schott, Webster. "Situations Unrelated to the Spirit."
       Kansas City *Star*, September 23, 1961, p. 7.

       "A poor, unconvincing and wholly regrettable novel.
       Mrs. McCullers repeatedly loses control of her material.
       ... *Clock Without Hands* reads like a plan for a novel or
       a fattened first draft."

G316   Schroetter, Hilda N.   Richmond (Va.) *Times-Dispatch*,
       September 24, 1961, p. 4-F.

       Clock is a "genuine tradegy," inciting "most profoundly
       the emotions of pity and terror." McCullers is "cer-
       tainly one of the outstanding stylists of the day, and
       this seems to me to be her finest work to date."

G317   Scott, Eleanor. "Books in Review--Sunday Books--Quiet
       Desperation." *The New Mexican* (Santa Fe), September
       17, 1961, *Pasatiempo*, pp. 4, 8.

       "In many ways this is Miss [sic] McCullers' finest
       novel. The Gothic quality of her earlier works, peopled
       as they were by deaf mutes, hunchbacks, giantesses, and
       perverts, is subdued. The grotesqueness of the normal
       suffices, and so her symbols slide into the texture of
       her novel more smoothly than heretofore."

G318   Sherman, John K.   "Carson McCullers Tells Parable of
       Loneliness." Minneapolis *Sunday Tribune*, October 8,
       1961, Sec. E, p. 6.

       McCullers "jabs gently but surely at the truth,
       produces a purer and unflourished prose that becomes

a kind of sad compassionate poetry of unfulfilled
lives."

G319 Stilwell, Robert L. "New McCullers Novel." Louisville
Courier-Journal, September 17, 1961, Sec. 4, p. 7.

Criticism of McCullers for stereotyping characters and
situations.

G320 Strasfogel, Ian. "Some of the Recent Fiction."
Cincinnati *Enquirer*, October 1, 1961, p. 4-F.

Although most of *Clock* is "over-explicit," "overlong
and stilted," with "dull boring writing most of the
time," it is recommended because of its "overwhelming
final pages" with their "tragedy-triumph, including one
of the most superb death scenes since Shakespeare."

G321 Sullivan, Margie [Margaret]. "'Clock Without Hands'--
Carson McCullers Pens Major Work of Fiction." Columbus
(Ga.) *Sunday Ledger-Enquirer*, September 17, 1961, Sec. B,
p. 5.

"A remarkable work, 'Clock Without Hands' is Carson
McCullers's most affirmative and most profound novel."

G322 Sullivan, Oona. *Jubilee*, 9 (November 1961), 55-56.

"Her style seems tired here and her characters are
flatter than they should be to convey her deeper intui-
tions about men, society, and change.... there's too
much information, argument and social comment that is
very close to propaganda--which truth doesn't need and
neither does art."

G323 Sullivan, Walter. *Georgia Review*, 15 (Winter 1961),
467-469.

"The trouble with this book is that it is totally contrived. Now and then the characters come to life ...
but Mrs. McCullers is always quick to push them back
into her iron scheme."

G324 Swift, Ruth. "Book About South Leaves One Smiling
Through Tears." Birmingham (Ala.) *News*, September 17,
1961, p. E-6.

McCullers "makes us live with and within her characters....
At the same time it is a book about universal man who is
born with a 'clock without hands,' measuring out the time
of his livingness."

G325 "They Face Death and Decision—Two Old Men of the
      South." Detroit *News*, September 17, 1961, p. 21-E.

      "The story is superb"; McCullers "writes brilliantly
      and tenderly."

G326 Toynbee, Philip. "Mellowing in the South." *The
      Observer* (London), October 15, 1961, p. 29.

      "This is a good novel, funny, sad and beautiful.... the
      writing is sound and serious. Perhaps Miss [sic]
      McCullers's next novel will recover the lost zest and
      freshness of 'Reflections in a Golden Eye' without sur-
      rendering this new-found balance and concern."

G327 Tracy, Honor. "A Voice Crying in the South." *New
      Republic*, 145 (November 13, 1961), 16-17.

      Clock "abounds in detail of brilliance or beauty ...
      but ... there are weaknesses of structure and concep-
      tion" and "just a touch of the commonplace now and
      again."

G328 Turner, Jim. "Good and Evil Tussle in Novel of
      Southern Town's Prejudices." Cleveland *Press*,
      September 19, 1961, p. A7.

      "This fictional bit about a Southern town steeped in
      tradition and prejudice is not a slick, cleverly plotted
      work. It is, in fact, episodic and confusing. It
      seems at times almost a grotesque burlesque, but such
      uncomfortable spots are of short duration."

G329 Tyler, Betty. "The Dying in Search of Eternity."
      Bridgeport (Conn.) *Post*, September 17, 1961, Sec. C,
      p. 4.

      McCullers "still handles man's aloneness but this time
      it is more sardonic, less satisfying, even though, in
      the end, each man has found his own self in life. The
      book closes with a gentle sigh but there is nothing
      gentle in its telling."

G330 Vidal, Gore. "The World Outside." *The Reporter*, 25
      (September 28, 1961), 50-52.

      Clock is "uneven and uncertain," but "even this near
      failure of McCullers is marvelous to read, and her
      genius for prose remains one of the few satisfying
      achievements of our second-rate culture." This review
      is reprinted in Vidal's *Rocking the Boat* (E113).

G331   *Virginia Quarterly Review*, 38 (Winter 1962), viii.

"Readers of Carson McCullers' previous works of fiction will find that her novel maintains the high level of quality they have come to expect."

G332   Walker, Gerald. "Books--Carson McCullers: Still the Lonely Hunter." *Cosmopolitan*, 151 (November 1961), 26-27.

Clock is a "departure from these private melancholy studies in the futility of interpersonal relationships. ... it displays an awareness of a larger social drama."

G333   Wilson, W. Emerson. "McCullers' Latest." Wilmington (Del.) *Morning News*, September 18, 1961, p. 15.

"Carson McCullers is a master of descriptive writing and her strong sense of humor provides many delightful passages in this novel. But by making the judge instead of J.T. Malone the dominating character, she, I feel, greatly weakens the effectiveness of her story.... he remains a caricature rather than a believable human being."

G334   Wolfe, Ann F. "Human Compassion Is Theme of Terse Novel." Columbus (Ohio) *Sunday Dispatch*, September 24, 1961, TAB Section, p. 19.

"Carson McCullers cuts life to the quick.... In the process she clearly exposes the truth.... And that is the achievement of a truly great artist."

G335   Zyskind, Irvin. "Columbus Native's Latest Novel Describes Crucial 15-Month Period in Lives of Four." Columbus (Ga.) *Enquirer*, September 25, 1961, p. 7.

Clock is "a strong, fast-moving novel." J.T. Malone is "perhaps [the] most truly portrayed" character; but the judge "begins and remains a stereotyped southern politician."

8.   SWEET AS A PICKLE AND CLEAN AS A PIG

G336   Blount, Charlotte. "Children's Bookshelf--Not Every Writer Can Do It." Winston-Salem (N.C.) *Journal and Sentinel*, December 27, 1964, p. D3.

"These poems are either ludicrously poor or embarrassing, depending on your mood. The forced rhymes, unpredictable meter, tawdry subjects, stilted ideas—it all adds up to zero.... This may very well be the worst children's book of the season."

G337   Gibson, Walker.   "'We Come to Know a Poem by Some Act of the Heart and Mind.'"   *New York Times Book Review*, November 1, 1964, Part 2, p. 57.

"This book may seem slight and disappointing, from so distinguished a pen, but spaceships and slumber parties will at least remind the children that poetry can speak for any world at all."

G338   Jacobson, Ethel.   "Treasure Chests of New and Classic Poetry."   *Chicago Tribune Books Today*, November 1, 1964, p. 5A.

The poems are "the sort of fun children understand." Very brief review.

G339   *Library Journal*, 89 (December 15, 1964), 59.

"This contrived and unappealing poetry is illustrated with rather crude, cartoon-like drawings. Not recommended."

G340   Waingrow, Hope.   "Notes on Volumes in the Juvenile Sections."   Claremont (Calif.) *Courier*, December 5, 1964, p. 7.

"Being a McCullers fan of long standing, I would have wished her children's verse might have more of the haunting heartbreak the reader is afflicted with through her other works."

G341   "Words to Play With."   *Times Literary Supplement*, December 9, 1965, p. 1141.

The "main interest" of this book is "that it is by Miss [sic] Carson McCullers; but let not devotees think to find more than a grain or two of the novelist's dazzling idiosyncrasy in these musing, amusing, throwaway verses."

9.   THE MORTGAGED HEART

G342   Adams, Phoebe. *Atlantic Monthly*, 228 (November 1971), 153.

"The early stories are notable for their precocious handling of standard adolescent themes."

G343   Alexander, Aimee. "Collection of Unpublished Writings of the Late Carson McCullers." Lexington (Ky.) *Sunday Herald-Ledger*, December 26, 1971, p. 36.

Detailed favorable descriptive review.

G344   Atchitz, Kenneth John. *Mediterranean Review*, 2 (Spring 1972), 63-64.

The early stories reveal McCullers' "struggles with her preferred medium"; the outline of "The Mute" is "a fascinating and sobering documentary of the complex planning necessary to the undertaking." The essays are "overly sentimental and dated. Nor are her poems momentous.... But the articles on writing are valuable contributions to American criticism."

G345   Avant, John Alfred. *Library Journal*, 97 (January 1, 1972), 73.

"The stories are clearly apprentice works ... too slight in these early exercises to hold one's interest.... Readers who aren't especially studying her work should ... not risk losing their affection for her by reading *The Mortgaged Heart*."

G346   Ayres, Jackie. "Carson McCullers' Stories Live Again." Indianapolis *News*, November 6, 1971, p. 34.

The interest of the collection lies in the remarks made by McCullers' teacher, Sylvia Chatfield Bates, and noting "how they influenced the later writings of the author."

G347   Balakian, Nona. "Books of The Times--Love--Perverse and Perfect." New York *Times*, January 3, 1972, p. 25.

"The volume's most obvious usefulness will be to students of literature who will be able to scan her early work for essential patterns and learn the extent to which personal experiences shaped her art."

G348 Bauerle, Ruth. "Carson McCullers." Cleveland *Plain Dealer*, November 7, 1971, p. 8-H.

"*The Mortgaged Heart* is a good book to dip into to catch the savor of an American writer who kept her youthful sensitivity."

G349 Bischoff, Barbara. "Bookmarks." *Oregon Journal* (Portland), January 15, 1972, p. 8J.

"Her loss was a great one to American letters but what she did leave us have become classics and she was a writer who, as a New York Times editorial stated, 're-flected the lonely heart with a golden hand.'"

G350 Charles, Timothy. "Deprived Spirits." *The Scotsman* (Edinburgh), June 3, 1972, *Week-end Scotsman*, p. 3.

This volume is "both a necessity and an enrichment" for those seeking "further information about" McCullers. Her work "results from an unlooked for synthesis of sensitivity and toughness." She "represents the high point of feminine sensibility in American shorter fiction since the war."

G351 Cheney, Charlotte. "Miss [sic] McCullers Works Released." Pittsburgh *Press*, January 2, 1972, p. G-5.

Mostly descriptive review.

G352 *Choice*, 9 (March 1972), 61.

The collection "reveals the early emergence of McCullers' talent and growth as an artist and is an attractive and touching volume that spans 30 years of writing." McCullers is "one of the most gifted but underrated authors of the 20th century."

G353 Chubb, Dell. "The Heart of a Lonely Writer." St. Louis *Sunday Post-Dispatch*, November 14, 1971, p. 4D.

Mostly descriptive review.

G354 Clark, George E. "Volume Features Selected Works of Carson McCullers." Jackson (Tenn.) *Sun*, January 23, 1972, p. 12-C.

This volume "should be a welcome addition to a short but excellent list of modern American classics by this Southern writer."

G355　Clemons, Walter. "A Memento for Collectors." *New York Times Book Review*, November 7, 1971, pp. 7, 12.

　　　　"It's sad to find that none of these [the pieces in the volume] shows Carson McCullers at anything like her best. The book is a memento for collectors."

G356　Dorheim, Jean. "Out in McCullers Country, an Enigma Lies Buried." Milwaukee *Journal*, October 31, 1971, Part 5, p. 4.

　　　　The collection should be "fascinating to the general reader."

G357　Drinnon, Elizabeth. "Carson McCullers--Writer's Development Reflected in Stories." Macon (Ga.) *Telegraph & News*, January 23, 1972, Sec. A, p. 8.

　　　　Mostly descriptive favorable review.

G358　Dunn, Douglas. "Down South." *New Statesman and Nation*, n.s. 83 (June 2, 1972), 756.

　　　　This collection is "more interesting for previously un-published or uncollected stories than for the miscel-laneous journalism written for such papers as *Vogue* and *Mademoiselle* which would have been better forgotten."

G359　Friend, James. "The Enduring Art of Carson McCullers." Chicago *Daily News*, April 8-9, 1972, *Panorama*, p. 6.

　　　　"Not all the work in this volume is vintage McCullers. But that doesn't matter at all. What does matter is that it's Carson McCullers in the first place. Select-ing her sorrows, editing her ironies, she endures."

G360　Fuller, Richard. "McCullers Finding Her Way: A Look at the First Efforts." Philadelphia *Inquirer*, November 28, 1971, p. 6-H.

　　　　Volume is "like seeing a flower bloom into beauty through the technical magic of time-lapse photography."

G361　Gordimer, Nadine. "A Private Apprenticeship." *London Magazine*, 12 (October-November 1972), 134-137.

　　　　In-depth review of this collection as well as of McCullers' full career: "in her work as in Faulkner's the brutality of White Southerners towards black, and the degradation of black and white through this has ...

been brought to life more devastatingly than by any
black writer so far."

G362   Gullason, Thomas A. *Saturday Review*, 54 (November 13,
       1971), 64.

       "While there are no significant successes among the
       stories, essays, and poems in *The Mortgaged Heart*, they
       help to round off Carson McCullers' literary career."

G363   H[all], B[arbara] H[odge]. "New Views of McCullers--
       Collection Reflects Personality, Talent." Anniston
       (Ala.) *Star*, October 31, 1971, Sec. D, p. 2.

       This is "an interestingly mixed collection."

G364   Hardwick, Elizabeth. "Romance vs. Cruelty: The South,
       Seen by Two Famous Women." *Vogue*, 158 (November 1,
       1971), 62.

       "It is naturally not her best, but it completes the
       shelf."

G365   Harrell, Don. "O'Connor and McCullers." Houston
       Chronicle, November 7, 1971, Magazine, p. 15.

       The early stories "are useful primarily to someone
       professionally interested in her development"; and,
       otherwise, "some of the best fiction of the last twenty
       years" is present in the volume.

G366   Hartley, Lodwick. "McCullers and O'Connor Seen Afresh
       in Posthumous Volumes." Raleigh *News and Observer*,
       February 13, 1972, Sec. 4, p. 6.

       The collection is valuable for watching McCullers'
       "upward climb."

G367   Hogan, William. "World of Books--A 'New Book' by
       Carson McCullers." San Francisco *Chronicle*, October 26,
       1971, p. 37.

       Volume "should be essential reading for any serious
       beginning writer.... it could be an illuminating text-
       book in creative writing programs." The outline of "The
       Mute" and the essays are more interesting than the
       stories.

G368   Howes, Victor. "Score for a Typewriter--Alone in a
       Crowd." *Christian Science Monitor*, November 11, 1971,
       p. B7.

Volume "preserves glimpses of her genius for characterization, her ability to shadow forth a vague sense of
disaster, her power to fuse the poles of anguish and
farce."

G369 Huelsbeck, Charles. *The Sign*, 51 (April 1972), 48-49.

"This collection ... illustrates the evolution and
creative process of her sensitive, fertile imagination."
The poems are "rich in evocative metaphors" and the
essays are "the best section of this book."

G370 Kinney, Jeanne. *Best Sellers*, 33 (November 15, 1971),
371.

Volume's main value is "to round out the picture of the
author as a creative person." The essays are "remarkably lucid prose"; but "it would have honored the
author's memory to have left" the poems "buried in a
drawer somewhere."

G371 *Kirkus*, 39 (August 15, 1971), 925.

"The most arresting pieces are the stories, and those
chiefly for their intimation of things to come.... Both
poems and essays might have been more selectively edited
and the interest overall will depend on a special
affection."

G372 Lafferty, Alice P. "Always There's the Heart."
Philadelphia *Sunday Bulletin*, October 31, 1971, Sec. 2,
p. 3.

Mostly descriptive review.

G373 Lloyd, Pat. "For the Avid Fans of Carson McCullers."
Pensacola (Fla.) *News*, April 10, 1972, p. 9A.

"Students of literature will appreciate the essays,
poems, short stories, which show the author's development."

G374 McKenzie, Alice. "Bookshelf." Clearwater (Fla.) *Sun*,
November 21, 1971, Sec. F, p. 9.

Descriptive favorable review.

G375 Madden, David. "Transfixed Among the Self-Inflicted
Ruins: Carson McCullers's *The Mortgaged Heart*."
Southern Literary Journal, 5 (Fall 1972), 137-162.

Extended review-essay which deals with all of McCullers'
major works. Of *Mortgaged Heart*: "The main justifica-
tion for this collection is that it enables us to see
the writer's virtues ineffectively employed in her
early work and her early faults put to good use in her
later work.... As a means of studying her themes, techniques, and style, the book is invaluable."

G376 Mann, Elizabeth L. "McCullers: 'The Marvelous Solitary
      Region.'" Greensboro (N.C.) *Daily News*, January 23,
      1972, p. B3.

      "Altogether there is so much variety and genius in this
      collection of Carson McCullers' 'least-known' works,
      and ... many interesting comments by her sister."

G377 Moody, Minnie Hite. "Two Georgia Writers Who Raced the
      Clock." Columbus (Ohio) *Sunday Dispatch*, December 19,
      1971, TAB Section, pp. 16, 17.

      Choice of the material in the collection is "wise" in
      that it allows the reader to see McCullers' development
      as a writer.

G378 Morton, Tim. "A Ballad Sad and Golden." Norfolk
      Virginian-Pilot, January 16, 1972, p. C6.

      While this is not the best of McCullers, "there is
      nothing that isn't emotionally right on dead center,
      that hasn't been known and lived."

G379 Murray, Michele. "From the Heart, Polished Stories by
      a Craftsman." *National Observer*, November 20, 1971,
      p. 25.

      "The non-fiction collected in *The Mortgaged Heart* is
      trivial and time bound.... But the 14 stories, while
      unequal in quality and achievement, will give lovers of
      good writing the rare pleasure of reading a complete
      well-wrought story."

G380 *Publishers Weekly*, 200 (September 6, 1971), 41.

      "A lovely book containing material that is essential
      reading for any serious student of Carson McCullers'
      writing.... Many of the themes she dealt with at greater
      length in her later work are touched upon in this col-
      lection with gravity and grace."

G381 Rogers, W.G. "Genius of Carson McCullers." Dallas
      Morning News, October 24, 1971, p. 10E.

"The secret of the extraordinary emotional force that boils up in McCullers' pages is largely her unique control of detail." Her "genius ... has never yet been accorded, I think, its full due."

G382   Rowe, William. "Unpublished Works of Carson McCullers Compiled in Volume by Margarita Smith." Columbus (Ga.) *Enquirer*, December 27, 1971, p. 8.

Descriptive favorable review.

G383   Ryan, Michael. "Books & People: The Mind of the South." *The Phoenix* (Boston), December 8, 1971, pp. 26, 28.

Comparison of McCullers and Flannery O'Connor which finds latter stylistically "infinitely superior" but lacking former's depth "of insight into character." *Mortgaged Heart* is "a representative survey of McCullers' work."

G384   S., D. "McCullers Tales Recall Growth." Murfreesboro (Tenn.) *Daily News Journal*, November 21, 1971.

"Here is a book every Carson McCullers fan will want."

G385   Schlueter, Paul. "Struggling in Isolation." Chicago *Sun-Times*, November 7, 1971, *Showcase*, p. 20.

This book will not do very much "to increase McCullers' stature."

G386   Theroux, Paul. "Early Sparks of a Unique Sensibility." London *Times*, June 8, 1972, p. 10.

The collection "has value. The pieces it contains amount to a kind of literary biography, and read straight through one sees the style and perception developing and expressing a unique sensibility."

G387   Thomas, W.H.J. "Current Reading." Charleston (S.C.) *News and Courier*, November 14, 1971, p. 4-D.

It is "a weakened Mrs. McCullers" that is revealed in this collection "but a very true and revealing picture of the artist as well."

G388   Toynbee, Philip. "Full of the Deep South." *The Observer* (London), June 4, 1972, p. 33.

"Nearly all the pieces included in this volume have been published before; but it is useful to have them assembled in a single volume. Or perhaps, it would be

better to say that it is useful to have the two-thirds
of the book which is devoted to short stories; the few
essays of criticism are mildly interesting, but scarcely
worth perpetuating; the occasional essays are often
awful beyond belief...."

G389   Wasson, Ben.   "McCullers Legacy Published." Greenville
       (Miss.) *Delta Democrat-Times*, November 7, 1971, Sec. 1,
       p. 25.

       Mostly descriptive favorable review.

G390   Welch, Susan.   "Carson McCullers--and the Evolution of
       a Writer." Minneapolis *Tribune*, November 28, 1971,
       pp. 10D, 11D.

       This collection "serves to underline a core of sameness
       that runs through all her work." It is possible to see
       McCullers' "thrust ... slant ... predisposition that
       most certainly was the genesis of her creativity."

G391   West, Rebecca.   "When Silent Was the South." London
       Sunday Telegraph, June 18, 1972, p. 12.

       The volume "is to be respected as a matter of familial
       piety." Most of this review is devoted to a discussion
       of *Ballad* and *Member*.

G392   Whaley, Russell G.   "Lonely Heart, Golden Hand." Tampa
       Tribune-Times, January 23, 1972, p. 5-C.

       In this volume, "readers discover Mrs. McCullers' pre-
       cocious talent and observe its rapid development and
       refinement."

G393   Willis, Alan.   "McCullers Collection Revealing."
       Winston-Salem (N.C.) *Journal and Sentinel*, February 6,
       1972, p. D4.

       "Anyone seeking new flesh to fill out what is so often
       for so many a skeletal understanding of this complex
       and difficult author, will find it in the essays and
       poems."

G394   "The Writer's Library." *The Writer*, 85 (May 1972), 46.

       "This volume of the previously uncollected writings of
       Carson McCullers brings together a wide selection of
       short stories, essays, and poetry, including eight
       stories never before published."

G395 Zulch, Betty. "Stories by Carson McCullers." Mt. Pleasant (Texas) *Daily Tribune*, January 23, 1972, Sec. 1, p. 7.

Mostly descriptive favorable review.

SECTION H

REVIEWS OF
CARSON McCULLERS' PLAYS IN PERFORMANCE

Listed in this section are reviews of Carson McCullers' plays
as they were first produced in the United States and Great
Britain. No attempt has been made to list any but reviews of
these original productions; similarly, we have not listed reviews of the touring company of the original production of
The Member of the Wedding. For each play, only its Philadelphia out-of-town tryout, its Broadway premiere, and its first
London production have been included. Reviews by the same
author are listed chronologically.

1. *THE MEMBER OF THE WEDDING*

December 22, 1949, Walnut Theater, Philadelphia

H1   Martin, Linton. "The Call Boy's Chat--Able Acting Aids
     Illusion; Theater Half Century Ago." Philadelphia
     Inquirer, January 1, 1950, Society Section, p. 13.

     "Curiously contradicting in its qualities of keen con-
     vincing and unconvincing character drawing, and often ex-
     citing in its utterly unhackneyed dialogue and details....
     The vitality and veracity of her principal character
     creations triumph over technical deficiencies."

H2   Murdock, Henry T. "McCullers' 'Member of the Wedding'
     Bows at Walnut." Philadelphia *Inquirer*, December 23,
     1949, p. 20.

     "It is long and its physical maneuvering is clumsy," but
     it shows "rich characterization."

H3   Sensenderfer, R.E.P. "'The Member of the Wedding' Opens
     at the Walnut." Philadelphia *Evening Bulletin*,
     December 23, 1949, p. 14.

     McCullers "has been more successful in characterization
     and striking incidents than in constructing a unified
     drama. However, she shows herself a mistress of true
     talk and literate writing as well as having a flair for
     moving climaxes...."

January 5, 1950, Empire Theater, New York

H4   Atkinson, Brooks. "At the Theatre." New York *Times*,
     January 6, 1950, p. 26.

     The play has no "dramatic momentum" but while "it may not
     be a play, ... it is art." The characterizations are
     "superb pieces of work."

247

H5   ——————.   "Three People--'The Member of the Wedding'
        Superbly Acted by an Excellent Company." New York *Times*,
        January 15, 1950, Sec. 2, p. 1.

        The play is "static; it lacks the inner motion of a fully
        resolved piece of theatre work" but McCullers "has a
        genius for the principal characters ... and for the myriad
        nuances and subtleties of their family life together."

H6   Barnes, Howard. "The Theaters." New York *Herald Tribune*,
        January 6, 1950, p. 12.

        "The acting is the chief virtue of the production." The
        play "moves at a snail's pace through two acts in which
        the literary origin is all too apparent to a final burst
        of hysterics and melodrama."

H7   ——————.   "Fine Acting in 'Member of the Wedding.'" New
        York *Herald Tribune*, January 15, 1950, Sec. 5, pp. 1, 2.

        McCullers "has failed to transmute a piece of literature
        into stage terms.... The work scarcely moves from start
        to finish and winds up as contrived a melodramatic ending
        as has been conceived for a long time."

H8   Beaufort, John. "'The Member of the Wedding' on Broadway
        Stage--Simplicity and Composure Fused to Gain Rare Effect."
        Christian Science Monitor, January 14, 1950, p. 4.

        Praise for the play's "searching quality of emotion, the
        depth of inner conflict." McCullers has made an "admir-
        able adaptation of her novel."

H9   Beyer, William. "The State of the Theatre: Actors Take
        Honors." *School and Society*, 66 (April 8, 1950), 213-214.

        "An ingratiating theatrical tidbit, touching and warm,
        with affection and humor, both robust and tender, ... [it]
        succeeds best dramatically when it concerns itself with
        the three main characters."

H10   Bolton, Whitney. "Stage--'Member of the Wedding' Just
        What Theater Needs." New York *Morning Telegraph*,
        January 7, 1950, pp. 2, 3.

        "A play like 'The Member of the Wedding' is just what the
        theater needs and the theater, by the same token, is an
        inexpressibly wonderful medium for 'The Member of the
        Wedding.'"

H11 Brown, John Mason. "Plot Me No Plots." *Saturday Review*, 33 (January 28, 1950), 27-29.

Despite the characters' lack of growth, *Member* is "no ordinary play. It is felt, observed, and phrased with exceptional sensitivity." Although "character and mood" are McCullers' "substitutes for plot," the play is not harmed by that fact.

H12 Callaway, Joe A. "New York Plays ... Deplorable Dependence on Broadway." *Player's Magazine*, 26 (March 1950), 126.

"Perhaps Carson McCullers' 'The Member of the Wedding' comes closest [of the season's new plays] to achieving the aims of the art theatre. Yet it would be a difficult production to attempt except with experienced actors and the most delicately handled direction. It is a rambling play which depends upon characterization rather than plot development."

H13 Chapman, John. "'Member of the Wedding' and Its Cast Earn Cheers at the Empire." New York *Daily News*, January 6, 1950, p. 55.

"As a piece of playmaking it is not ideal, for it reiterates one theme for two acts with scarcely any story or character development." But, "ideal or not, ... [it] is an absorbing study of an adolescent girl."

H14 ————. "An Interesting Member of the Race—In 'The Member of the Wedding' a Girl Faces the Job of Growing Up." New York *Sunday News*, January 15, 1950, Sec. 2, p. 3.

Mostly descriptive favorable review, with praise for the director and the three lead actors.

H15 Clurman, Harold. "Theatre: From a Member." *New Republic*, 122 (January 30, 1950), 28-29.

The director of the New York production of *Member* defends its right to be called a play. It does have action—that action is the characters' "struggle for connection" with a larger world. "The proof is in the doing of it." This review is reprinted in Clurman's *Lies Like Truth* (E20).

H16 Colby, Ethel. "Entertainment: Julie Harris Makes Touching Ingenue." *Journal of Commerce* (New York), January 6, 1950, p. 9.

"Mrs. McCullers was able to intensify the poignancy of
plot and retain the dominance of her major characters,
while highlighting her flair for revelatory dialogue.
The resultant drama is an important 'first play' for the
author and a memorable experience for theatregoers."

H17   Coleman, Robert. "The Theatre--'Member of the Wedding'
      Is a Stirring Hit." New York *Daily Mirror*, January 6,
      1950, p. 34.

      Although *Member* is more a mood than a play, it is success-
      ful and sure to be a hit.

H18   Cooke, Richard P. "Adolescent Problem." *Wall Street
      Journal*, January 9, 1950, p. 12.

      "'The Member of the Wedding' is at once delicate and
      amusing, beautifully written and acted."

H19   Dash, Thomas R. "'The Member of the Wedding.'" *Women's
      Wear Daily*, January 6, 1950, p. 57.

      The "thread of the story ... is thin, and there is little
      action," but *Member* is "a poignant study" of adolescence.

H20   Eaton, Hal. "First Night--'Member of Wedding' Is 1st
      Hit of 1950." *Long Island Daily Press* (Jamaica, N.Y.),
      January 6, 1950, Sec. 5*C, p. 8.

      "Written with heart and depth, Miss [sic] McCullers'
      comedy-drama emerges as a tender and touching tale, its
      characters human and warm. The author doesn't coddle,
      pamper or patronize her people. Nor are they subtle or
      evasive." This review also appeared in Newark (N.J.)
      Star-Ledger, January 6, 1950.

H21   Field, Rowland. "'Member of the Wedding.'" Newark
      (N.J.) *Evening News*, January 6, 1950, p. 20.

      Member is "a most rewarding event to which the season
      can point with justifiable pride." It "matches fine
      writing with superlative acting and directing."

H22   Gabriel, Gilbert W. "New Plays on Broadway--Wend Your
      Way Westward to the Empire." *Cue*, 19 (January 14, 1950),
      20.

      "It is a play written pretty much against the rules, and
      therefore all the rarer. It seldom amounts to more than
      half a play, but this half has a sympathy in it.... It
      is infinitely lovely."

H23 Garland, Robert. "'The Member of the Wedding'--Something
     Special But Not Quite a Play." New York *Journal-
     American*, January 6, 1950, p. 18.

     "As a playwright, she remains a novelist ... so what
     should be the climax of the play ... is no more than off-
     stage action talked about unseen." Even so, the play is
     "something rare and special."

H24 Gibbs, Wolcott. "The Theatre: Brook and River." *New
     Yorker*, 25 (January 14, 1950), 44-49 [44-46].

     McCullers has tried "to transfer her book too literally
     to the stage.... The result is a curiously uneven work--
     sometimes funny, sometimes moving, but also unfortunately
     sometimes just a trifle incoherent and shapeless."

H25 Hassan, Rita. "Reviews--'Member of the Wedding.'" *Show
     Business* (New York), January 10, 1950, p. 6.

     "There is magic on the stage of the Empire Theatre these
     nights and once again the theatre emerges as a form of
     art."

H26 Hawkins, William. "Theater--Waters, Harris Roles Spark
     'Wedding.'" New York *World-Telegram and the Sun*,
     January 6, 1950, p. 32.

     Mostly descriptive review. The script is "richly
     actable."

H27 ————. "Novice Calmly Steals the Show." New York
     World-Telegram and the Sun, January 14, 1950, p. 9.

     Praise for three lead actors, with very little mention
     of McCullers.

H28 Hipp, Edward Sothern. "A Most Precocious Little Girl--
     Frankie Addams of 'Member of Wedding' Is a Fantastic
     Heroine." Newark (N.J.) *Sunday News*, January 15, 1950,
     Sec. 2, p. 38.

     The play's characters are "fantastic," its plot "murky,"
     and much of the dialogue "like a Freudian version of
     'Alice in Wonderland.'"

H29 Mace, Louise. "Here and There in the Theater--'The
     Member of the Wedding.'" Springfield (Mass.) *Sunday
     Republican*, February 5, 1950, p. 16A.

     "If it does not have story it has something far more
     stimulating--a deep-plyed continuity of character

development in which the two poles of mortal striving,
aloneness and oneness, are the beginning and the ending,
and the rounded whole, of her thesis."

H30   Marshall, Margaret. "Drama." *The Nation*, 170 (January 14,
       1950), 44.

       "It is not so much a play as it is whatever in the theatre
       corresponds to the tone poem in music.... an authentic
       experience, deeply felt, has been articulated in authen-
       tic character and speech."

H31   [Morrison], Hobe. *Variety*, January 11, 1950, p. 58.

       Criticism for the "slight and slow-moving plot, the in-
       clusion of non-essential elements ... the faulty dramatic
       structure"; but it is a "perceptive, tender and touching
       drama" which is "undeniably poignant."

H32   "New Play in Manhattan." *Time*, 55 (January 16, 1950), 45.

       "Its virtues are refreshing and uncommon ... [but] Carson
       McCullers' novel suffers from having been made into a
       play--or, rather from not having been."

H33   "New Plays." *Newsweek*, 35 (January 16, 1950), 74.

       "Despite the sketchy story and its hasty resolution, 'The
       Member of the Wedding' is written in wisdom and deep
       feeling." It is "a play of unusual distinction and un-
       expected delight."

H34   Phelan, Kappo. "The Stage--'A [sic] Member of the Wed-
       ding.'" *Commonweal*, 51 (January 27, 1950), 437-438.

       Because of "uncanny theatrical luck," McCullers' play is
       "irresistible" and "a complete delight." She provided
       the "framework that a director can build into a fine
       play; and that actors can play ... to the hilt."

H35   Pollock, Arthur. "Theater Time--'Member of the Wedding'
       Poignant and Sensitive." New York *Daily Compass*,
       January 6, 1950, p. 18.

       It is "a play as simple as a play can be; sensitive,
       poignant and beautiful. And at the same time comic....
       It is a play to remember."

H36   Sheaffer, Louis. "Curtain Time--'Member of Wedding'
       Sensitively Reports on a Girl's Adolescence." Brooklyn
       (N.Y.) *Eagle*, January 6, 1950, p. 10.

"The tragi-comedy of early adolescence ... is brilliantly,
compassionately explored in 'The Member of the Wedding.'"
McCullers is "far more concerned with examining people
than packing in story."

H37 ————. "Curtain Time——About 'Member of the Wedding' and
Whether It Really Is a Play." Brooklyn (N.Y.) *Eagle*,
January 15, 1950, p. 25.

McCullers has substituted an "internal drama ... [for]
the flashier results of a neatly turned plot, the sure
fireworks of actions."

H38 *Theatre Arts*, 34 (March 1950), 13.

"Mr. Clurman's perceptive staging hides the play's technical defects.... The play is a rain from heaven to a
dry theatre season."

H39 Watts, Richard, Jr. "Two on the Aisle——A Striking New
American Play." New York *Post*, January 6, 1950, pp.
45, 46.

It is a "sensitive unusual play of genuine individuality"
whose "weaknesses as a well-rounded theatrical conception
are more than atoned for by its sensitivity of feeling,
its delicacy of treatment, and its understanding warmth
of human sympathy."

H40 ————. "Two on the Aisle——The Stage Has a New Playwright." New York *Post*, January 15, 1950, p. M4.

"There is very little suspense or conflict.... Its concern is basically with good suggestion and implication,
with the capturing of intangible qualities of character
and emotion." Although McCullers is somewhat clumsy in
presenting "conventional theatrical activity," her weaknesses "are more than made up for by the freshness and
loveliness of the mood ... and the richness and humor
and tenderness of the characterization."

H41 Wyatt, Euphemia Van Rensselaer. "Theatre." *Catholic
World*, 170 (March 1950), 467-468.

"A play which lays bare the struggles of the human soul
is the purest drama."

February 5, 1957, Royal Court Theatre, London

H42   Gibbs, Patrick. "First Night--Sensibility and Style--
       Tragi-Comedy with Southern Setting." London *Daily
       Telegraph and Morning Post*, February 6, 1957, p. 8.

       "The author displays rare sensibility and style." The
       play is a "tragi-comedy of mood and atmosphere."

H43   "Plays." *English*, 11 (Summer 1957), 185-186.

       Member is "a prolonged rumination on the nature of exis-
       tence written chiefly for three voices." That it is
       neither mawkish nor boring is a "tribute to the skill of
       Miss [sic] McCullers and of her three main players, who
       succeeded in communicating ... a poignant and haunting
       nostalgia, an underlying awareness of the mystery and
       wonder and sadness of living."

H44   "Royal Court Theatre." London *Times*, February 6, 1957,
       p. 3.

       McCullers achieves balance in her play through the char-
       acter of Berenice and greater emotional depth with the
       part of the "unspectacular father."

H45   Shulman, Milton. "Salute for a Valiant Failure." London
       Evening Standard, February 6, 1957, p. 10.

       "It is charged with ... brooding frustration, and futil-
       ity. Its language ... has the fragile grace of swaying
       cobwebs." *Member* is "a very tender bloom that has failed
       to stand up to the rigours of transplanting."

H46   Trewin, J.C. "One of the Party." *Illustrated London
       News*, 230 (February 16, 1957), 276.

       "This is, essentially, a work for the printed page, or
       for sound-radio--where ... [the] Narrator can be en-
       listed." It "can only be an impression of the book."

H47   Tynan, Kenneth. "At the Theatre--Mood Indigo." *The
       Observer* (London), February 10, 1957, p. 11.

       It is "not so much a play as a tone poem for three voices
       in two colours, black and white.... But Miss [sic]
       McCullers bears a charmed style, and wields it like a
       wand." She "triumphs, partly because her innate tract
       rejects the phoney-primitive and partly because she is
       writing about the South."

H48   Worsley, T.C.   "Growing Up." *New Statesman and Nation*,
      n.s. 53 (February 16, 1957), 201-202.

      "Two acts of stagnation and then a flurry of foreshortened
      activity is nothing more than a mess." *Member* would
      "surely be used as a prime example of How Not to Write
      a Play."

                   2.   *THE SQUARE ROOT OF WONDERFUL*

           October 14, 1957, Walnut Theater, Philadelphia

H49   de Schauensee, Max.   "The Living Theater--Carson McCullers
      Play Opens on Walnut Stage." Philadelphia *Evening
      Bulletin*, October 15, 1957, p. 63.

      While "there is much that remains unsatisfactory and un-
      convincing, the general atmosphere has an amount of
      fascination that only an original artist like Mrs.
      McCullers can generate."

H50   Gaghan, Jerry.   "Anne Baxter Stars at Walnut." Philadel-
      phia *Daily News*, October 15, 1957, p. 43.

      "What we heard last evening seemed too consciously liter-
      ary and almost was devoid of humor."

H51   Murdock, Henry T.   "'Square Root of Wonderful' at Walnut
      --Miss [sic] McCullers' Love Mathematics Doesn't Quite
      Add Up." Philadelphia *Inquirer*, October 15, 1957, p. 17.

      What the characters do and "what happens to them fails to
      grip the emotions or challenge the imagination enough."

H52   ————.   "2d Time Around--Tryout Tremors Observed."
      Philadelphia *Inquirer*, October 20, 1957, Amusements and
      the Arts Section, pp. 1, 4.

      Square Root does not make its points, "vagueness hovered
      over the acting," "sympathy could be distributed only
      meagerly among the characters and then perhaps, in the
      wrong places."

           October 30, 1957, National Theater, New York

H53   Aston, Frank.   "Theatre: A Story of Love--'Square Root'
      Is Like Magic." New York *World-Telegram and Sun*,

October 31, 1957, p. 32.

"Mrs. McCullers has written a sturdy entertainment."

H54   Atkinson, Brooks. "Theatre: 'Square Root.'" New York
      Times, October 31, 1957, p. 40.

      "The basic flaw is probably the lifelessness of the
      characters and the flatness of most of the writing.
      Mrs. McCullers has not been able to impart to this love
      story the other-worldliness of her best writing."

H55   Bolton, Whitney. "Stage Review--'Square Root' Odd,
      Rambling, Verbose." New York *Morning Telegraph*,
      November 2, 1957, p. 2.

      "Carson McCullers can write like a streak. She can, as
      demonstrated here, also write like a smudge."

H56   Chapman, John. "'The Square Root of' Scatters Neuroses
      Along the Psychopath." New York *Daily News*, October 31,
      1957, p. 65.

      Square Root "mostly scatters its neuroses and thereby
      lessens its emotional impact."

H57   ————. "Great Met Performance--Theatre Lagging." New
      York *Sunday News*, November 10, 1957, Sec. 2, p. 3.

      Although *Square Root* does "contain some charmingly
      written scenes, it is generally about as murky as its
      title."

H58   Clurman, Harold. "Theatre." *The Nation*, 185
      (November 23, 1957), 394.

      The failure of the play is due to its stage direction.
      "As a result, lyric writing, beautifully awry, and wonder-
      fully intuitive character sense have been flattened into
      semi-caricature."

H59   Colby, Ethel. "Entertainment--On Broadway." *Journal of
      Commerce* (New York), October 31, 1957, p. 8.

      "Carson McCullers' new play ... is only medium fare."

H60   Coleman, Robert. "'Square Root of Wonderful' Ain't."
      New York *Mirror*, November 1, 1957, pp. 32, 33.

      Square Root "boasts flashes of beauty, embedded in a
      basis of the fumbling and sordid. It starts to soar
      like a bird ... but too seldom gets off the ground."

H61   Cooke, Richard P. "The Theatre--McCullers' Second Best."
      Wall Street Journal, November 1, 1957, p. 8.

      "The occasional flashes of Miss [sic] McCullers' witty
      and penetrating prose are not enough to make up for
      'Square Root's' shortcomings." The play lacks a sense
      of the tragic.

H62   Dash, Thomas R. "'The Square Root of Wonderful.'"
      Women's Wear Daily, October 31, 1957, p. 43.

      The play "adds up to little either as a dramatic stage
      narrative or as an emotional experience." There is "too
      much reminiscence and too little dynamic development."

H63   Driver, Tom F. "Mixed Grill." *Christian Century*, 74
      (November 27, 1957), 1424-1425 [1425].

      "Where Miss [sic] McCullers is content to write comedy,
      the current entry is better than all right. But where
      she turns the script into problem drama, it becomes
      embarrassing."

H64   Field, Rowland. "Broadway: Twisted Tale--'Square Root
      of Wonderful' Tedious Social Exercise." Newark (N.J.)
      Evening News, October 31, 1957, p. 53.

      The play's message "is encased in disappointing second-
      best wordage and appeal." Criticism for its characters'
      lack of motivation and their inability to evoke sympathy.

H65   Gibbs, Wolcott. "The Theatre: Music and Words." *New
      Yorker*, 33 (November 9, 1957), 103-105.

      "Mrs. McCullers' play presents us with a heroine who is
      ... a pinhead, and with a hero and villain who are a
      rather stifling moralist and a boozily grandiloquent
      psychopath, respectively."

H66   Hayes, Richard. "Private Worlds." *Commonweal*, 67
      (December 13, 1957), 288-289.

      "It issues from a sensibility which is genuine, however
      diffuse; it is full, too, of some wreckage of feeling.
      And it excels in a kind of mad compulsive logic of wit....
      It is a play not readily exhausted; always it holds some-
      thing in reserve."

H67   Hipp, Edward Sothern. "Words and Music--Lena Horne, Anne
      Baxter in New Entertainments." Newark (N.J.) *Sunday
      News*, November 10, 1957, Sec. 3, p. E4.

"There are occasional snatches of crisp dialogue ...
[but] most of the new play ... is uninspired treatment
of a routine plot." It is not "much of a play. Just a
catchy title and a germ of an idea."

H68   Kerr, Walter. "First Night Report--'The Square Root of
       Wonderful.'" New York *Herald Tribune*, October 31, 1957,
       p. 22.

       McCullers' tendency to interrupt the "tragic or pathetic
       thread" with "jovial eruption snaps whatever thread we
       may have begun to cling to."

H69   Lewis, Emory. "The Theatre--Elementary Math." *Cue*, 26
       (November 9, 1957), 9.

       "It's all a bit pat and ... dull, save for Mrs. McCullers'
       own special humor and Southern way with language."

H70   Lewis, Theophilus. "Theatre." *America*, 98 (November 30,
       1957), 299-300 [299].

       "In Carson McCullers' script, secondary characters are
       more amusing than the principals."

H71   McClain, John. "'The Square Root of Wonderful'--Diffuse
       Doubletalk Adds Up to Big 0." New York *Journal-American*,
       October 31, 1957, p. 22.

       "The plot is implausible, the people are grotesque....
       It is difficult to understand how the lady who wrote
       'Member of the Wedding' could have drifted into such
       diffuse doubletalk."

H72   [Morrison], Hobe. *Variety*, November 6, 1957, p. 72.

       Square Root is "a curious comedy-drama of cryptic ele-
       ments, uninteresting characters and surprisingly flat
       writing."

H73   "New Plays in Manhattan." *Time*, 70 (November 11, 1957),
       93-94.

       Square Root has "a variety of themes, in a variety of
       tones, at a variety of tempos. Possessing sufficient
       materials for several plays, *Square Root*, for lack of
       integration, largely comes off no play at all."

H74   *Theatre Arts*, 42 (January 1958), 24.

       "The general effect of flatness can be written off as an
       occupational hazard of any author. What is more difficult

to account for in this case is the coarseness of her
style, which was matched by the production's heavy-
handed direction. The only thing that can be safely re-
peated about the cast ... is that it failed to disguise
the play's defects."

H75 Watts, Richard, Jr. "Two on the Aisle--The New Carson
McCullers Play." New York *Post*, October 31, 1957, p. 30.

The play lacks "dramatic effectiveness," but "the gift
for fresh and sympathetic observation of character is
still there."

H76 Wyatt, Euphemia Van Rensselaer. "Theatre." *Catholic
World*, 185 (January 1958), 304-308 [306].

The play "pursues a persistent indelicacy in its factual
details of life with an uxurious husband. The title is
the best part of this seemingly illegitimate theater
child of the very gifted McCullers."

March 9, 1970, Hampstead Theatre Club, London

H77 Barber, John. "Lost Chances of Play by Delicate Writer."
London *Daily Telegraph*, March 10, 1970, p. 14.

"By not taking her gifts quietly enough, by forcing them
to big effects instead of small, Miss [sic] McCullers
has over-reached herself and produced a bad play."

H78 Bryden, Ronald. "A Criminal Talent." *The Observer*
(London), March 15, 1970, p. 35.

The play's characters are "amusing creations, but obviously derived from a different imagination and play.
The uncertain production does nothing to integrate them."

H79 Shulman, Milton. "Darn Agonizing 'Way Down South.'"
London *Evening Standard*, March 10, 1970, p. 17.

"Because Miss [sic] McCullers could write with sensitivity
and concern, these melodramatic posturings [of her characters in this play] have not dated nearly as much as one
might have expected. There is a kind of primness about
the dialogue which is rather unnerving...."

H80 Wardle, Irving. "Drama in Dixie." London *Times*,
March 10, 1970, p. 16.

"The most painful thing about the 'Square Root of Wonderful' ... is to see her fumbling; to see one of America's

finest artists stammering through her A.B.C. in the hope
of turning out something acceptable to Broadway."

H81   ————. "McCullers Drama Has Unhappy Bow on London
Stage." New York *Times*, March 12, 1970, p. 47.

"As a novelist Miss [sic] McCullers was in complete control of her talent, and it hurts to see so fine an artist
stammering imitatively through the ABC's of stage
craftsmanship."

H82   Young, B.A. *"The Square Root of Wonderful."* *Financial
Times* (London), March 11, 1970, p. 3.

"This story is drenched in sentimentality; it is tidied
up at the end like a magazine serial.... I found it warm
and touching.... The faults of the play are faults of
generosity, and I find them easy to forgive."

SECTION I

DISSERTATIONS

This section lists all dissertations entirely about McCullers
or containing significant mention of her work. Only those
dissertations abstracted in *Dissertation Abstracts* and
Dissertation Abstracts International are included. Annotations
are provided only when the title does not make clear which of
McCullers' works is studied.

I1 Agee, William Hugh. "The Initiation Theme in Selected
    Modern American Novels of Adolescence." Ph.D., Florida
    State University, 1966 [Abstract in *Dissertation Abstracts*,
    27 (February 1967), 2521A].

    Deals with *Heart* and *Member*.

I2 Armes, Nancy Ruth. "The Feeder: A Study of the Fiction of
    Eudora Welty and Carson McCullers." Ph.D., University of
    Illinois at Urbana-Champaign, 1975 [Abstract in *Disserta-
    tion Abstracts International*, 36 (November 1975), 2817A].

I3 Bauerly, Donna M. "Patterns of Imagery in Carson McCullers'
    Major Fiction." Ph.D., Marquette University, 1973
    [Abstract in *Dissertation Abstracts International*, 34
    (November 1973), 2606A].

I4 Bluefarb, Samuel. "The Escape Motif in the Modern American
    Novel: Mark Twain to Carson McCullers." Ph.D., University
    of New Mexico, 1967 [Abstract in *Dissertation Abstracts*,
    27 (May 1967), 3863A].

    Deals with *Heart*. See E7.

I5 Carlson, Judith Garrett. "The Dual Vision: Paradoxes,
    Opposites, and Doubles in the Novels of Carson McCullers."
    Ph.D., Case Western Reserve University, 1976 [Abstract in
    Dissertation Abstracts International, 37 (June 1977),
    7749A].

I6 Carlton, Ann Ruth. "Patterns in Carson McCullers' Por-
    trayal of Adolescence." Ph.D., Ball State University, 1972
    [Abstract in *Dissertation Abstracts International*, 33
    (July 1972), 302A].

I7 Carney, Christina F. "A Study of Themes and Techniques in
    Carson McCullers' Prose Fiction." Ph.D., Columbia Univer-
    sity, 1970 [Abstract in *Dissertation Abstracts Inter-
    national*, 34 (July 1973), 307A-308A].

I8   Carr, Virginia Spencer. "Carson McCullers and the Search
      for Meaning." Ph.D., Florida State University, 1969
      [Abstract in *Dissertation Abstracts International*, 33
      (December 1972), 2924A-2925A].

I9   Coale, Samuel Chase, V. "The Role of the South in the
      Fiction of William Faulkner, Carson McCullers, Flannery
      O'Connor, and William Styron." Ph.D., Brown University,
      1970 [Abstract in *Dissertation Abstracts International*,
      31 (June 1971), 6596A-6597A].

I10   Eckard, Ronald David. "The Sense of Place in the Fiction
      of Carson McCullers." Ph.D., Ball State University, 1975
      [Abstract in *Dissertation Abstracts International*, 36
      (February 1976), 5295A].

I11   Edelstein, Arthur. "Realism and Beyond: Essays on
      Twentieth-Century Fiction." Ph.D., Stanford University,
      1977 [Abstract in *Dissertation Abstracts International*,
      38 (September 1977), 1377A-1378A].

I12   Everett, Howard Dean. "Love and Alienation: The Sad,
      Dark Vision of Carson McCullers." Ph.D., University of
      New Mexico, 1975 [Abstract in *Dissertation Abstracts
      International*, 36 (December 1975), 3711A-3712A].

I13   Finger, Larry Livingston. "Elements of the Grotesque in
      Selected Works of Welty, Capote, McCullers, and O'Connor."
      Ph.D., George Peabody College for Teachers, 1972 [Abstract
      in *Dissertation Abstracts International*, 33 (October
      1972), 1721A-1722A].

I14   Gillespie, Sheena. "Dialectical Elements in the Fiction
      of Carson McCullers: A Comparative Critical Study."
      Ph.D., New York University, 1976 [Abstract in *Dissertation
      Abstracts International*, 37 (March 1977), 5804A-5805A].

I15   Gossett, Louise Young. "Violence in Recent Southern
      Fiction." Ph.D., Duke University, 1961 [Abstract in
      Dissertation Abstracts, 23 (July 1962), 233-234].

      See E50.

I16   Hunt, Tann H. "Humor in the Novels of Carson McCullers."
      Ph.D., Florida State University, 1972 [Abstract in
      Dissertation Abstracts International, 34 (August 1973),
      775A].

I17   Johnson, Thomas Slayton. "The Horror in the Mansion:
      Gothic Fiction in the Works of Truman Capote and Carson
      McCullers." Ph.D., University of Texas, Austin, 1973
      [Abstract in *Dissertation Abstracts International*, 34
      (November 1973), 2630A].

I18   Joyce, Edward Thomas. "Race and Sex: Opposition and
      Identity in the Fiction of Carson McCullers." Ph.D.,
      State University of New York at Stony Brook, 1973
      [Abstract in *Dissertation Abstracts International*, 34
      (December 1973), 3403A-3404A].

I19   Millichap, Joseph Robert. "A Critical Reevaluation of
      Carson McCullers' Fiction." Ph.D., University of Notre
      Dame, 1970 [Abstract in *Dissertation Abstracts International*, 31 (March 1971), 4783A].

I20   Radway, Janice Anne. "A Phenomenological Theory of
      Popular and Elite Literature." Ph.D., Michigan State
      University, 1977 [Abstract in *Dissertation Abstracts International*, 39 (July 1978), 288A-289A].

I21   Rechnitz, Robert Max. "Perception, Identity, and the
      Grotesque: A Study of Three Southern Writers." Ph.D.,
      University of Colorado, 1967 [Abstract in *Dissertation Abstracts*, 28 (December 1967), 2261A].

      Deals with McCullers, Welty, and O'Connor.

I22   Rogers, Ann Tucker. "The Search for Relationships in
      Carson McCullers." Ph.D., St. Louis University, 1971
      [Abstract in *Dissertation Abstracts International*, 32
      (February 1972), 4632A].

I23   Shapiro, Adrian Michael. "Carson McCullers: A Descriptive
      Bibliography." Ph.D., Indiana University, 1977 [Abstract
      in *Dissertation Abstracts International*, 38 (November
      1977), 2795A-2796A].

I24   Shaw, Joy Farmer. "The South in Motley: A Study of the
      Fool Tradition in Selected Works by Faulkner, McCullers,
      and O'Connor." Ph.D., University of Virginia, 1977
      [Abstract in *Dissertation Abstracts International*, 38
      (January 1978), 4162A].

I25   Smith, Christopher Michael. "Self and Society: The
      Dialectic of Themes and Forms in the Novels of Carson

McCullers." Ph.D., University of North Carolina at
Greensboro, 1976 [Abstract in *Dissertation Abstracts
International*, 37 (November 1976), 2880A].

I26   Smith, Simeon Mozart, Jr. "Carson McCullers: A Critical
      Introduction." Ph.D., University of Pennsylvania, 1964
      [Abstract in *Dissertation Abstracts*, 25 (December 1964),
      3583-3584].

I27   Sullivan, Margaret Sue. "Carson McCullers, 1917-1947:
      The Conversion of Experience." Ph.D., Duke University,
      1966 [Abstract in *Dissertation Abstracts*, 28 (May 1968),
      4648A-4649A].

I28   Thomas, Leroy. "An Analysis of the Theme of Alienation
      in the Fictional Works of Five Contemporary Southern
      Writers." Ph.D., Oklahoma State University, 1971
      [Abstract in *Dissertation Abstracts International*, 33
      (August 1972), 768A].

      Deals with McCullers, Wolfe, Warren, Welty, and O'Connor.

I29   Wallace, Harry Joseph. "'Lifelessness Is the Only Abnor-
      mality': A Study of Love, Sex, Marriage, and Family in
      the Novels of Carson McCullers." Ph.D., University of
      Maryland, 1976 [Abstract in *Dissertation Abstracts
      International*, 37 (December 1976), 3630A-3631A].

I30   White, Barbara Anne. "Growing Up Female: Adolescent
      Girlhood in American Literature." Ph.D., University of
      Wisconsin-Madison, 1974 [Abstract in *Dissertation
      Abstracts International*, 35 (March 1975), 6167A].

      Deals with McCullers, Stafford, and Suckow. Focus on
      Member.

I31   Wikborg, E.S.M. "Carson McCullers' *The Member of the
      Wedding*: Aspects of Structure and Style." Ph.D.,
      Göteborgs Universitet, 1975 [Abstract in *Dissertation
      Abstracts International*, 37 (August 1976), Vol. C, pp.
      15-16].

      See E121.

SECTION J

FOREIGN-LANGUAGE MATERIAL

This section presents an incomplete and preliminary selection of the commentary on McCullers' works in foreign lan-
guages. Items marked with an asterisk have not been verified
and are listed here as incomplete citations. This section
should be regarded only as a token listing of what surely is
the considerable amount of attention McCullers' work has
received throughout the non-English-speaking world.

BOOKS

J1 Arnavon, Cyrille. "Les Dix Dernières Années (1940-1950)."
    In his *Histoire littéraire des États-Unis*. Paris:
    Hachette, 1953. Pp. 429-438 [436].

J2 Blanzat, Jean. "Préface." In *Reflets dans un oeil*
    d'or by Carson McCullers, tr. by Charles Cestre. Paris:
    Editions Stock, 1946. Pp. 7-14.

J3 Brodin, Pierre. "Carson McCullers." In his *Présences*
    contemporaires--Écrivains américains d'aujourd'hui. Paris:
    Debresse, 1964. Pp. 98-106.

J4 Brown, John. *Panorama de la littérature contemporaine aux*
    États-Unis. Paris: Gallimard, 1954. Pp. 225-227.

J5 Cabau, Jacques. "L'Esthétisme et le 'nouveau roman.'"
    In his *Le Prairie perdue--Histoire du roman américain*.
    Paris: Editions du Seuil, 1966. Pp. 60-73 [73].

J6 Cardwell, Guy. *Der amerikanische Roman, 1850-1951*.
    Vienna: U.S. Information Service, 1953. P. 54.

J7 Dommergues, Pierre. "L'Implacable Géométrie du coeur:
    Carson McCullers." In his *Les Ecrivains américains d'*
    aujourd'hui. Paris: Presses Universitaires de France,
    1965. Pp. 56-59.

*J8 Dorfel, Hanspeter. "Carson McCullers: *The Member of the*
    Wedding (1946)." In Peter Freese and Liesel Hermes, eds.
    Der Roman im Englischunterricht der Sekundarstufe, II:
    Theorie und Praxis. Paderborn: Shoningh, 1977. Pp. 185-
    206.

J9 Erlebach, Peter. "Carson McCullers: Clock Without Hands."
    In Frieder Busch and Renate Schmidt-von Bardeleben, eds.
    Amerikanische Erzählliteratur 1950-1970. Munich: Fink,
    1975. Pp. 102-112.

*J10   Inazawa, Hideo. *America Joryu Sakka Ron: Cather, Buck,
       McCullers no Sekai.* Tokyo: Shimbisha, 1978.

J11   Izzo, Carlo. "Il novecento--La narrativa." In his
       Storia della litteratura Nord Americana. Milan: Nuova
       Accademia Editrice, 1957. Pp. 605-646 [617].

*J12   Katsurada, Shigetoshi. "Carson McCullers, *The Member of
       the Wedding* no Bunsho: Sono Sutairo no Ongakusei." In
       Chiaki Higashida, ed. *Gengo to Buntai: Higashida Chiaki
       Kyoju Kanreki Kinen Ronbunshu.* Osaka: Osaka Kyoiku
       Toshu, 1975. Pp. 275-291.

J13   Lalou, René. "Préface." In *Frankie Addams* by Carson
       McCullers, tr. by Marie-Madeleine Fayet. Paris: Stock,
       1949. Pp. 7-14.

J14   Lenz, Siegfried. "Die Chancen der Frist über Carson
       McCullers: 'Uhr ohne Zeiger' (1963)." In his *Beziehungen
       --Ansichten und Bekenntnisse zur Literatur.* Hamburg:
       Hoffman und Campe, 1970. Pp. 205-208.

J15   Lennertz, Franz. *Auslandische Dichter und Schriftsteller
       unserer Zeit.* Stuttgart: Alfred Kroner, 1955. Pp. 453-
       454.

*J16   Lombardo, Agostino. *Realismo e simbolismo.* Rome: Ed.
       di Storia e Letteratura, 1957.

J17   Magny, Claude-Edmonde. *L'Âge du roman américain.* Paris:
       Editions du Seuil, 1948. P. 245.

J18   Mohrt, Michel. "Les États-Unis." In Jean-Claude Ibert,
       ed. *Les Littéraires contemporaines à travers le monde.*
       Paris: Librairie Hachette, 1961. Pp. 295-314 [306-307].

J19   ————. *Le Nouveau Roman américain.* Paris: Gallimard,
       1955. Pp. 205, 224-231.

J20   Popp, Klaus-Jürgen. "Carson McCullers." In Martin
       Christadler, ed. *Amerikanische Literatur der Gegenwart
       in Einzeldarstellungen.* Stuttgart: Alfred Kroner, 1973.
       Pp. 1-21.

J21   ————. "Carson McCullers, 'A Tree, a Rock, a Cloud'
       (1942)." In Peter Freese, ed. *Die amerikanische Short
       Story der Gegenwart: Interpretationen.* Berlin: Schmidt,
       1976. Pp. 48-53.

J22   Rosati, Salvatore. "La prosa narrativa: 2) Da Farrell ai contemporanei." In his *Storia della letteratura americana.* Tomni: Edizioni Radio Italiana, 1956. Pp. 241-254 [247]. See also p. 290.

J23   Saporta, Marc. "Les Innocents aux mains vides: Carson McCullers (1917-1967), William Goyen (né en 1915)." In his *Histoire du roman américain.* Paris: Gallimard, 1976. Pp. 276-279 [276-278]. See also p. 491.

J24   Simon, Jean. "Conclusion--Aujourd'hui." In his *Le Roman américain au XXe siècle.* Paris: Boivin, 1950. Pp. 181-184 [183].

*J25   Tournier, Jacques. "Préface." In *La Ballade du café triste* by Carson McCullers. Paris: Editions Stock, 1974.

Periodical Articles

J26   Amette, J.-P. "Le Petit Arpent de Miss Carson." *Spécial,* No. 475 (May 8, 1974), no pagination.

J27   Antonini, Giacomo. "Ossessione nella McCullers." *La Fiera Letteraria,* 17 (April 22, 1962), 5.

J28   Bellour, Raymond. "Le Génie inimitable de Carson McCullers." *La Magazine Littéraire,* No. 89 (June 1974), 30-33.

J29   Bianciotti, Hector. "Les Privilèges de la solitude." *Le Nouvel Observateur,* No. 491 (April 8-14, 1974), 56.

       Review of French translations of *Ballad* and *Oeuvres.*

*J30   Blanzat, Jean. "Frankie Addams de Carson McCullers." *Figaro Littéraire,* No. 190 (December 10, 1949), 229-236.

       Review of French translation of *Member.*

J31   ————. "Lignes d'ombre." *Les Nouvelles Littéraires,* No. 2432 (May 6-12, 1974), 9.

       Excerpt from the preface of the French translation of *Reflections.*

J32   Bokanowski, Hélène. "Carson McCullers et le roman métaphysique." *L'Arche,* 7 (May 1947), 155-158.

J33 Bondy, Barbara. "Eine dichterin Amerikas: zu den deutschsprachigen Ausgaben der Werke von Carson McCullers." *Deutsche Rundschau*, 89 (July 1963), 76-79.

J34 Braem, Helmut M. "Das dunkle gelassen Anerkannt--'Preis der Jungen Generation' für Carson McCullers und Peter Hunhel." *Die Welt* (Hamburg), October 9, 1965, p. 51.

J35 ————. "Jetzt Liegen die gesammelten Werke von Carson McCullers." *Die Zeit*, June 21, 1966, p. 27.

J36 *Bulletin Critique du Livre Français*, V (April 1950), 221.

Review of French translation of *Member*.

J37 Cabau, Jacques. "Les Enfantines de Carson McCullers." *Express*, No. 1190 (April 29-May 5, 1974), 74.

Review of French translation of *Ballad*.

J38 "Carson McCullers." *Das Tintenfass*, No. 2 (October 1965).

*J39 "Carson McCullers: Oeuvres romanesques." *Minute*, May 9, 1974.

J40 "Carson McCullers: Le Sud au ras de choses." *Bulletin du Livre*, No. 241 (May 10, 1974), 48-49.

Review of *Oeuvres*.

*J41 "Cette Grande Carson McCullers." *Le Journal du Dimanche* (June 1974).

J42 Christie, Erling. "Carson McCullers og Hjertenes Fangen-skap." *Vinduet* (Oslo), 9 (No. 2, 1955), 55-62.

J43 Dommergues, Pierre. "L'Ambiguité de l'innocence." *Les Langues Modernes*, 59 (January-February 1965), 54-59.

J44 ————. "La Fin d'un age--Les Tristes Ballades de Carson McCullers." *Le Monde*, October 11, 1967, p. 3.

Obituary tribute.

J45 Equchi, Yuko. "Carson McCullers: Human Isolation in America." *Essays and Studies in British and American Literature* (Tokyo Women's Christian College), 7 (Summer 1959), 129-146.

J46 Gozzi, Francesco. "La narrativa di Carson McCullers." *Studi Americani*, 14 (1968), 339-376.

J47 Gresset, Michel. "Carson McCullers." *Nouvelle Revue Française*, 17 (July 1969), 1-2.

*J48 Guigonnat, Henri. "Toute la violence tragique de la vie." *Le Quotidien de Paris*, May 13, 1974, p. 12.

J49 Jaworski, Philippe. "La Double Quête de l'identité et de la réalité chez Carson McCullers." *Nouvelle Revue Française*, 17 (July 1969), 93-101.

J50 Kemp, Robert. "La Vie des livres--Dames hallucinées." *Les Nouvelles Littéraires*, No. 1163 (December 15, 1949), 2.

Review of French translation of *Member*.

J51 Margerie, Diane de. "Carson McCullers ou la separation." *La Quinzaine Littéraire*, 186 (May 15, 1974), 12-13.

Review of French translation of *Ballad* and *Oeuvres*.

*J52 Mertens, Pierre. "Les Milles et une solitude des coeurs transis." *Le Soir de Bruxelles*, April 10, 1974.

J53 Micha, René. "Carson McCullers ou la cabane de l'enfance." *Critique*, 18 (August-September 1962), 696-707.

J54 [Miller, Robert Ellys]. "Chasseurs solitaires." *Les Nouvelles Littéraires*, No. 2432 (May 6-12, 1974), 8.

Review of *Oeuvres*.

J55 Mizuta, J. "Carson McCullers' *The Heart Is a Lonely Hunter*." *Rikkyo Review*, 22 (1961), 79-95.

*J56 Mohrt, Michel. "Le Coeur blessé de Carson McCullers." *Le Figaro Littéraire*, April 20, 1974, p. 8.

J57 P.-L., M. "Revue des livres nouveaux." *Bulletin des Lettres*, No. 241 (October 15, 1962), 353-354.

Review of French translation of *Clock*.

*J58 Parias, Louis-Henri. "Le Besoin d'aimer et d'être aimé." *France Catholique*, April 12, 1974.

*J59 Radu, Aurelia. "Implicatiile initierii sau metafozele singuratatii in universul eroilor lui Carson McCullers." *Analele Universitatu Bucuresti Literatura Universala Comparata*, 19 (No. ii, 1970), 141-148.

J60   Rantavaara, Irma. "Yksinainen Sydan." *Parnasso*, No. 8 (December 1957), 341-345.

*J61   Remacle, André. "Carson McCullers: Oeuvres." *La Marseillaise*, April 14, 1974, p. 10.

J62   Richard, Jean-Pierre. "Reflets dans un oeil d'or." *Fontaine*, 53 (June 1946), 135-136.

      Review of French translation of *Reflections*.

J63   Ríos Ruiz, Manuel. "Carson McCullers, la novelista del fatalismo." *Cuadernos Hispanoamericanos*, No. 228 (December 1968), 763-771.

J64   Rivière, Yvette. "L'Alienation dans les romans de Carson McCullers." *Recherches Anglaises et Américaines*, 4 (1971), 79-86.

J65   Rolin, Gabrielle. "La Ballade de Carson McCullers-- 'Cette chose que je veux, je ne sais pas quoi.'" *Le Monde*, No. 9095 (April 12, 1974), 17.

J66   Rougemont, Denis de. "Une Recherche sensible." *Les Nouvelles Littéraires*, No. 2432 (May 6-12, 1974), 9.

      Excerpt from the preface to the French translation of *Heart*.

J67   Schäffer, Kristiane. "Jeder Starb, keiner Starb--Über 'Uhr ohne Zeiger' von Carson McCullers." *Monat*, 15 (February 1963), 65-66, 68-69.

J68   Schnack, Elisabeth. "Abschied von Carson McCullers." *Neue Zürcher Zeitung* (Zurich), "Feuilleton," October 5, 1967, p. 1.

J69   Skotnicki, Irene. "Die Darstellung der Entfremdung in den Romanen von Carson McCullers." *Zeitschrift für Anglistik und Amerikanistik*, 20 (January 1972), 24-25.

J70   Spens, Willy De. *La Nouvelle Revue Française*, 11 (August 1, 1963), 342.

      Review of French translation of *Clock*.

J71   Toebasch, Wim. "Regionalistiche Literatuur." *De Vlaamse Gids*, 50 (December 1966), 676-677.

J72   Vaal, Hans de.   "Een Middag met Carson McCullers."
      Litterair Paspoort, 8 (April 1953), 80-84.

      Interview.

J73   Valensise, Rachele.   "Tre scrittrici de Sul: Flannery
      O'Connor, Caroline Gordon, Carson McCullers."   *Studi
      Americani*, 17 (1971), 251-289 [263-272, 281-282].

INDEX

This Index is keyed to all sections of this bibliography and
lists: (1) the names of all authors, editors, or translators
of all books and articles by and about McCullers; (2) the
titles of all books and periodicals containing material by
and about McCullers; (3) all appearances, either as primary
or as secondary sources, of all material by McCullers (works
by McCullers are listed in capital letters in the index; item
numbers for essays or sections of books entirely about that
title are italicized in the entries); (4) all subjects mentioned in the annotations of Part II of this bibliography
(the index is keyed to the annotations; thus, only those persons or works mentioned in the annotations are included as
subjects in the index). With respect to category 4, titles
which are subjects are listed with the author's name in paren-
theses following--e.g., "*The Glass Menagerie* (Williams)"--in
order to differentiate them from primary titles. Also, because
most of the entries in Section I of the bibliography are unannotated, this index does not include subject listings for
these entries; the only exceptions to this are for those
dissertations which do have brief annotations.

Abell, Elizabeth, BB8
Abels, Cyrilly, B9, E1
Abrahams, William, BB3, BB52
Accent, G31, G57
Adams, Phoebe, G342
The Adolescent in the American Novel--1920-1960, E123
L'Âge du roman américain, J17
The Age of Anxiety: Modern American Stories, BB60
*The Age of the American Novel--The Film Aesthetic of Fiction
    Between the Two Wars*, E78
Agee, William Hugh, I1
Albee, Edward, D7, F1
Albee, Edward (subject), C48, E13, F10, F26, F55, F84, F120-
    F121, F138, F144, F155, F195, F209
Aldridge, John W., E2
Alexander, Aimee, G343
Alford, Sally, G87
Alice in Wonderland (Carroll), H28
"THE ALIENS," A9.1-A9.2, F179
Allen, Morse, G236
Allen, Walter, E3, F2
Allison, Elizabeth, G156
Alsterlund, Betty, F3
Alvarez, A., G227
America, G266, H70
America Joryu Sakka Ron: Cather, Buck, McCullers no Sekai, J10
American Accent, BB8
American Drama Since World War II, E119
*American Dramatic Literature: Ten Modern Plays in Historical
    Perspective*, BB21, E84
The American Heritage History of the Writer's America, E31
American Literature in the 1950's, E72
American Literature in the 1940's, E88
American Literature in the Twentieth Century, E104
American Models--A Collection of Modern Stories, BB63
American Notes & Queries, F155
American Novelists of Today, E115
American Scholar, F98, G210
The American Short Story--A Critical Survey, E114

The American Short Story--Front Line in the National Defense
    of Literature, E89
American Way, F104
American Writers--A Collection of Literary Biographies, E52
American Writers Today, E27
American Writing Today--Its Independence and Vigor, E4
Amerikanische Erzählliteratur 1950-1970, J9
Amerikanische Literatur der Gegenwart in Einzeldarstellungen,
    J20
Der amerikanische Roman, 1850-1951, J6
Die amerikanische Short Story der Gegenwart: Interpretationen,
    J21
Amette, J.-P., J26
Analele Universitatu Bucuresti Literatura Universala Comparata,
    J59
Anderson, Mary (subject), F130
Anderson, Sherwood (subject), F117, F151, G26, G172
Angoff, Allan, E4
Angus, Sylvia, BB68
Anhalt, Edna, D1
Anhalt, Edward, D1
Anniston (Ala.) Star, G363
Antioch Review, F9, G199
Antonini, Giacomo, J27
Appel, David, G88
L'Arche, J32
Archer, William, E45
Arizona Daily Star (Tucson), G234
Arizona Quarterly, F151
Arkansas Gazette (Little Rock), G156
Armes, Nancy Ruth, I2
Arnavon, Cyrille, J1
"ART AND MR. MAHONEY," A9.1-A9.2, C28, F179
The Art of Fiction, BB38
The Art of Southern Fiction--A Study of Some Modern Novelists,
    E64
The Arts at Mid-Century, E28, E92
Asheville (N.C.) Citizen-Times, G218
Ashford, Gerald, G157
Aston, Frank, H53
"ASTRONAUT," A8.1-A8.2
Atchitz, Kenneth John, G344
Atkinson, Brooks, F4, H4-H5, H54
Atlanta Constitution, F5, F29, F124, F135-F136, F138-F139,
    F219, G23, G69, G126
Atlanta Journal, F32, F116, F161, G8, G58
Atlanta Journal and Constitution, F46, F132, F158, F209, G255
The Atlantic, G86, G312

Atlantic Monthly, G342
Auchincloss, Louis, E5
Auden, W.H. (subject), F70, F247
Auslandische Dichter und Schriftsteller unserer Zeit, J15
Austin, Alex, BB11
"AUTHOR'S NOTE," C45
"AUTHOR'S OUTLINE OF 'THE MUTE,'" A9.1-A9.2, B12, G344, G367
Autumn Light: Illuminations of Age, BB81
Avant, John Alfred, G345
Ayres, Jackie, G346

B., A.M., G237
B., O.T., G238
"THE BABY-KILLER" (see also THE HEART IS A LONELY HUNTER), B4
Balakian, Nona, E98, F6, G347
Baldanza, Frank, F7
Baldwin, James (subject), E90
The Ballad of Carson McCullers, B12, E36
THE BALLAD OF THE SAD CAFÉ (novella), A5.1a-g, A5.2.a-b,
    A5.3-A5.7, B3, BB2, BB40, BB50, BB69, BB75, BB78, C19,
    D11, D15, E3-E5, E9-E10, E17, E25, E34-E36, E50-E52, E54,
    E64, E70, E75, E88, E97-E98, E114, F11, *F18*, *F83*, *F92*,
    F97, F99-F100, F129, *F140*, F144, *F150*, *F160*, F173, *F178*,
    F181, *F186*, F190, F224, F230, F235, F245, G156, G160,
    G192, G203, G206, G211, G214, G216, G391, J25, J29, J37,
    J51
The Ballad of the Sad Café (Albee), D7, E13, F10, F26, F55,
    F84, F120-F121, F138, F144, F209
THE BALLAD OF THE SAD CAFÉ AND OTHER STORIES, A5.4
THE BALLAD OF THE SAD CAFÉ--THE NOVELS AND STORIES OF CARSON
    McCULLERS, A5.1.a-g, A5.3; Reviews: G156-G157, G159-G160,
    G162-164, G166, G168-169, G171-G172, G174-G186, G188-
    G189, G191, G193, G195-G197, G199, G201-G206, G209-G216,
    G218-G222, G224-G226
THE BALLAD OF THE SAD CAFÉ--THE SHORTER NOVELS AND STORIES OF
    CARSON McCULLERS, A5.2.a-b, A5.5; Reviews: G158, G161,
    G165, G167, G170, G173, G187, G190, G192, G194, G198,
    G200, G207-G208, G217, G223
Balliet, Whitney, G239
Baltimore Sun, G307
Barber, John, H77
Barish, Mildred, G50
Barkham, John, G159, G240
Barnes, Clive, BB49
Barnes, Howard, H6-H7
Barry, Jackson G., F8
Bates, Sylvia Chatfield, E101
Bates, Sylvia Chatfield (subject), F45, G346

Bauerle, Ruth, G348
Bauerly, Donna M., I3
Baxter, Anne (subject), F154, F204
Beals, Helen, G147
Beatty, Richmond Croom, BB6, BB46
Beaufort, John, H8
Beau-Seigneur, Jay, G241
Beauvoir, Simone de, E32
Beja, Morris, F9
Bellour, Raymond, J28
Bellow, Saul (subject), E90
Benson, Sally (subject), G130
Berkley, James, BB42
Berkley, Saundra Gould, BB67
Berry, Lee, G1, G51
Best American Plays--Third Series--1945-1951, B7, BB12, E42
The Best American Short Stories--1944, B3
*The Best American Short Stories 1964 and the Yearbook of the
    American Short Story*, B11
*Best Modern Short Stories Selected from "Saturday Evening
    Post,"* BB28
The Best Plays of 1957-1958, E71
Best Sellers, G231, G306, G370
Betjeman, John, G161
Beyer, William, H9
Beziehungen--Ansichten und Bekenntnisse zur Literatur, J14
Bianciotti, Hector, J29
Bigsby, C.W.E., F10
Birmingham (Ala.) *News*, G188, G324
Bischoff, Barbara, G349
Black Masks--Negro Characters in Modern Southern Fiction, E109
*Black Portraiture in American Fiction: Stock Characters,
    Archetypes, and Individuals*, E102
Blanzat, Jean, J2, J30-J31
Block, Maxine, E6
Bloomgarden, Kermit (subject), F81
Blount, Charlotte, G336
Bluefarb, Sam, E7, I4
Boatner, Maxine Tull, G89
Boger, Mary Snead, G242
Bokanowski, Hélène, J32
Bolsterli, Margaret, F11
Bolton, Whitney, H10, H55
Bonazza, Blaze O., BB34
Bond, Alice Dixon, G90
Bondy, Barbara, J33
Bonin, Jane F., E8
Booklist, G151, G228, G243

Bookmark, G244
Books Abroad, F102
Books and Bookmen, F173
"BOOKS I REMEMBER," C9
Boston *Evening Transcript*, G12, G37, G56
Boston *Herald*, G90, G294
Boston *Post*, G166
Boston *Sunday Globe*, F72, F91, G49, G285
Boston *Sunday Herald*, G160
Botteghe Oscure, C32, C35, C39
Bowen, Elizabeth, F13
Bowen, Robert O., G245
Bower, Helen, G91
Boyle, Kay, E9, F15
Boyle, Kay (subject), F147
Box, Patricia S., F14
Bradbury, John M., E10
Bradbury, Malcolm, G246
Bradley, Van Allen, G162
Brady, Charles A., G92
Braem, Helmut M., J34-J35
Brandeis, Adele, G93
"BREATH FROM THE SKY," A9.1-A9.2, C55, F179
Breit, Harvey, F16
Brickell, Herschel, B1-B2, B6, E11
Bridgeport (Conn.) *Herald*, G131
Bridgeport (Conn.) *Post*, G144, G220, G329
Bright Book of Life: American Novelists and Storytellers from Hemingway to Mailer, E67
Brodin, Pierre, J3
Broer, Karl, BB71
Bromley, Dorothy Dunbar, F17
Brooklyn (N.Y.) *Citizen*, G109
Brooklyn (N.Y.) *Eagle*, H36-H37
"BROOKLYN IS MY NEIGHBORHOOD," A9.1-A9.2, BB1, BB4, BB10, C8
Brooks, Cleanth, B8, BB18, E12
Broughton, Panthea Reid, F18
Brown, John, J4
Brown, John Mason, H11
Brustein, Robert, E13
Bryan, Don, F19
Bryant, Jerry H., E14
Bryden, Ronald, H78
Buchen, Irving H., F20-F21
Buckmaster, Henrietta, G247
Bucknell Review, F11, F20
Buffalo *Courier-Express*, G181, G259
Buffalo *Evening News*, G92, G159, G263

Bulletin Critique du Livre Français, J36
Bulletin des Lettres, J57
Bulletin du Livre, J40
Bulletin of Bibliography, F177, F225–F226
Burlingame (Calif.) *Advance-Star*, G241
Burnett, David, B11
Burnett, Hallie, BB30, BB33
Burnett, Whit, BB23, BB30, BB33
Burnett, Whit (subject), F45
*The Burns Mantle Best Plays of 1949–1950 and the Year Book
     of the Drama in America*, B5, BB36, E19
Burton, Thomas G., E73
Busch, Frieder, J9
Butcher, Fanny, G2, G53, G248
Butler, George O., G3, G54
By and About Women, BB64
Byrne, Mary Margaret, F22–F26

C., E., G163
C., V., G164
Cabau, Jacques, J5
Cahill, Susan, BB76
Cain (subject), F71
Calder-Marshall, Arthur, G165
Calderwood, James L., BB62
Caldwell, Erskine (subject), G4
Calisher, Hortense, E15
Callaway, Joe A., H12
Calta, Louis, F28
Capes, Reggie, F30
Capital Times (Madison, Wis.), G101, G172
Capote, Truman (subject), E89, E97–E98, F169, F239, I13, I17
"CAPTAIN PENDERTON'S RIDE" (see also REFLECTIONS IN A GOLDEN
     EYE), D13
Cardwell, Guy, J6
Carey, Glenn O., BB73
Cargill, Oscar, E16
Carlson, Judith Garrett, I5
Carlton, Ann Ruth, I6
Carney, Christina F., I7
Carpenter, Frederic I., F31
Carr, Virginia Spencer, B14, E17, I8
Carroll, Mark, G166
Carson, Ada Lou, BB53, E18
Carson, Herbert, BB53, E18
Carson McCullers (Richard M. Cook), E25
Carson McCullers (Dale Edmonds), E34
Carson McCullers (Lawrence Graver), E51

Carson McCullers--Her Life and Her Work, B12, E36
"CARSON McCULLERS READS FROM *THE MEMBER OF THE WEDDING* AND
    OTHER WORKS," D11
*Carson McCullers' "The Member of the Wedding": Aspects of
    Structure and Style*, E121
Case, Elizabeth N., G4
Casey, Phil, F42
Cassill, R.V., BB83-BB84
The Catcher in the Rye (Salinger), F31
Catholic World, G5, G186, G245, H41, H76
Cestre, Charles (translator), J2
Chapin, Ruth, G168
Chapman, John, B5, BB36, E19, H13-H14, H56-H57
Charles, Timothy, G350
Charleston (S.C.) *News and Courier*, G44, G387
Charlotte *Observer*, F56-F57, F168, F212, F216, G45, G80,
    G124, G242
Chattanooga *Times*, G114, G180, G261
Cheltenham Festival of Literature, F2, F53, F220, F234
Cheney, Charlotte, G351
Cheney, Frances, G95, G249
Chicago *Daily News*, G88, G162, G359
Chicago *Daily Tribune*, G2, G53
Chicago Stagebill, F189
Chicago Sun Book Week, G131
Chicago *Sunday Tribune*, G106
Chicago Sunday Tribune Magazine of Books, G175, G248
Chicago *Sun-Times*, G297, G385
Chicago Tribune Books Today, G338
"A CHILD'S VIEW OF CHRISTMAS," A9.1-A9.2, C47
Chinoy, Helen Krich, E23
Choice, G352
Christadler, Martin, J20
Christian Century, F60, H63
Christian Science Monitor, G168, G247, G368, H8
Christie, Erling, J42
"CHRISTMAS EVE RHYME," A8.1-A8.2, C51
Chubb, Dell, G353
Cincinnati *Enquirer*, G320
Clancy, William P., G169
Clare, Tullis, G6, G55, G96
Claremont (Calif.) *Courier*, G340
Clark, Charlene, F43
Clark, Donald Lemen, BB15
Clark, George E., G354
Clark, Margaret, G56
Clayton, John L., BB80
Clearwater (Fla.) *Sun*, G374

Clemons, Walter, G355
Clerc, Charles, BB50
Cleveland, Elizabeth, G7
Cleveland *Plain Dealer*, G348
Cleveland *Press*, G328
CLOCK WITHOUT HANDS, A7.1.a-d, A7.2.a-b, A7.3, C37, C45-46,
    E3, E5, E17, E25, E34, E36, E50-E52, E70, E73, E75, E88,
    E97-E98, E106, *E113*, E118, F9, *F43*, F56, *F65*, F75, F81,
    F91, F129, F139, F173, F187, *F191*, F232, F245, J57, J70;
    Reviews: G236-G335
Clurman, Harold, E20-E23, F44, H15, H58
Clurman, Harold (subject), F103, H38
Coale, Samuel Chase, V, I9
Colby, Ethel, H16, H59
Cole, Toby, E22-E23
Coleman, Robert, H17, H60
Coleridge, Samuel Taylor (subject), F73
COLLECTED SHORT STORIES AND THE NOVEL THE BALLAD OF THE SAD
    CAFÉ, A5.6
College English, F99, F119
College English: The First Year, BB44
A College Treasury, BB13
Columbia (S.C.) *Record*, G99
Columbus (Ga.) *Enquirer*, F19, F240, G335, G382
Columbus (Ga.) *Ledger*, F23, F25-F26, F30, F90, F108-F109,
    F146, F213, F250, F252, F254
Columbus (Ga.) *Ledger-Enquirer*, C1-C2, C22, G235
Columbus (Ga.) *Sunday Ledger-Enquirer*, F22, F24, F41, F241,
    F253, G321
Columbus (Ohio) *Citizen*, G131
Columbus (Ohio) *Sunday Dispatch*, G41, G85, G122, G334, G377
Commend the Devil (Coxe), C7
Commentaries on Five Modern American Short Stories, E56
Commentary, F114
Commonweal, G103, G169, G274, H34, H66
A Concise Survey of American Literature, E124
Connolly, Cyril, G170
Contemporary American Literature--1945-1972: An Introduction,
    E61
Contemporary American Novelists, E39
Cook, Albert, E24
Cook, Richard M., E25
Cook, Sylvia Jenkins, E26
Cooke, Richard P., H18, H61
Cordell, Actor, Jr., F46
Cornwell, Dorothea, G97
"CORRESPONDENCE," A9.1-A9.2, C15, *F64*, F179
Cosmopolitan, G332

Council Bluffs (Iowa) *Nonpareil*, G123
Cournos, John, G98
"COURT IN THE WEST EIGHTIES," A9.1–A9.2, F179
Cowie, Alexander, E27
Cowley, Malcolm, E28–E29
Coxe, Howard (subject), C7
Craig, Helen Pride, G99
Crane, Milton, BB5, BB29
The Creative Present--Notes on Contemporary American Fiction,
    E98
Creekmore, Hubert, G57, G171
Crist, Judith, F48–F49
Critical Occasions, E107
Critics' Choice: New York Drama Critics' Circle Prize Plays,
    BB14
Critique, J53
Cuadernos Hispanoamericanos, J63
Cue, F123, H22, H69
Culligan, Glendy, G250
Cuniff, Robert, F50
Current Biography--Who's News and Why--1940, E6

Daily Worker (New York), G108
Dalhousie Review, F21, F94
Dalin, Ebba, D14
Dallas *Morning News*, G20, G73, G381
Danesi, Natalia, F51
Dangerfield, George, G100
Daniel, Frank, G8, G58
"THE DARK BRILLIANCE OF EDWARD ALBEE," C48
Dash, Thomas R., H19, H62
Dasher, Thomas E., E30
Davenport, Basil, G59
Davidson, Marshall B., E31
Dawkins, Cecil, G251
Dayton *News*, G219
The Death of Art: Black and White in the Recent Southern Novel,
    E118
Death of a Salesman (Miller), E86
Decision, C11, C13
Dedmond, Francis B., F52
Demonic Vision--Racial Fantasy and Southern Fiction, E93
De Mott, Benjamin, G252
Dennis, Nigel, F53
Denver *Post*, G193, G277
Derleth, August, G101, G172
Descant (Texas Christian University), F191
de Schauensee, Max, H49

Deseret News (Salt Lake City, Utah), G183
Detroit *Free Press*, G91
Detroit *News*, G325
Deutsche Rundschau, J33
"THE DEVIL'S IDLERS," C7
De Wilde, Brandon (subject), F17, F38, F184, F214, F233, H27
Diamond, David, D8
The Diary of Anaïs Nin--1939-1944, E105
Didion, Joan, G253
Diehl, Digby, F55
Dietrich, R.F., BB38
Dinesen, Isak (subject), A9.1-A9.2, C18, C49, F149
Directing the Play--A Sourcebook of Stagecraft, E23
Directions in Modern Theatre and Drama, E43
"THE DISCOVERY OF CHRISTMAS," C38
The Discovery of Fiction, BB39, E96
Doar, Harriet, F56-F57
Dodd, Wayne D., F58
"A DOMESTIC DILEMMA," A5.1.a-g, A5.2.a-b, A5.3-A5.7, B8, BB7,
    BB16, BB18, BB22, BB51, BB70, C33, E12, E24, E49-E50, *F93*,
    F173, *F176*, F179, G178
Dommergues, Pierre, J7, J43-J44
Dorfel, Hanspeter,. J8
Dorheim, Jean, G356
Dorin, Rube, F59
Dostoevsky, Feodor (subject), F174
Douglas, Marjory Stoneman, G102
Dourado, Autran (subject), F186
Dowell, Paul W., BB79
Dowling, H.M., G173
Downing, Francis, G103
Do You Sleep in the Nude?, E91
Drake, Robert, F60
Drama Critique, F62
Drinnon, Elizabeth, G357
Driver, Tom F., H63
"THE DUAL ANGEL," A9.1-A9.2, C34
Duluth *News Tribune*, G115
Dunkel, Wilbur, G104
Dunn, Douglas, G358
Durham, Frank, F61
Dusenbury, Winifred L., E33
Dwyer, Rebecca, F62

E., P., G174
Eaton, Hal, H20
Eckard, Ronald David, I10
Les Ecrivains américains d'aujourd'hui, J7

Edelstein, Arthur, I11
Edmonds, Dale, E34, F64
Educational Theatre Journal, F8
Eight Short Novels, BB40
Eisinger, Chester E., E35
Emerson, Donald, F65, G254
Empire City, BB10
An End to Innocence--Essays on Culture and Politics, E40
Engle, Paul, G106, G175
English, H43
English Journal, F31, F67, F97, F118
English Record, F187
Epoch, G289
Equchi, Yuko, J45
Erlebach, Peter, J8
Erskine, Albert, BB13
The Escape Motif in the American Novel: Mark Twain to Richard Wright, E7
Esquire, C44, F197, G299
Essays and Studies in British and American Literature, J45
Essays in Memory of Christina Burleson in Language and Literature by Former Colleagues and Students, E73
Eudora Welty, E111
Evans, Oliver, B12, BB59, E36-E37, F67-F68, F70-F71
Everett, Howard Dean, I12
Evergreen Review, F120
The Explicator, F160
Express, J37

F., C., G107
F. Jasmine Addams (Mann), D9
Fadiman, Clifton, G9, G60
Falk, Signi L., E38
Famous American Plays of the 1940s, BB17, E63
Fancher, Betsy, G255
The Faraway Country--Writers of the Modern South, E94
"FATHER, UPON THY IMAGE WE ARE SPANNED" (see also "THE DUAL ANGEL"), A9.1-A9.2, C34
Faulkner, William (subject), E3, F151, G4, G48, G72, G140, G194, I9, I24
"FAVORITE EATS," A8.1-A8.2
Fayet, Marie-Madeleine, J13
Feibleman, Peter S., F72
Feld, Rose, G10, G61
Felheim, Marvin, E39
Feminine Plural: Stories by Women About Growing Up, BB61
Ferguson, Otis, G62
A Festschrift for Professor Marguerite Roberts, on the Occasion of Her Retirement from Westhampton College, University of Richmond, Virginia, E76

Fiction: Form and Experience, BB48
Fiction: The Narrative Art, BB79
*The Fiction of Sex--Themes and Functions of Sex Difference in
    the Modern Novel*, E83
Fiction of the Forties, E35
Fiction 100, BB82
Fiedler, Leslie A., E40-E41
Field, Ben, G108
Field, Rowland, H21, H64
La Fiera Litteraria, J27
50 Best Plays of the American Theatre, BB49
55 Short Stories from "The New Yorker": 1940 to 1950, BB3
Fifty Great American Short Stories, BB29
Fifty Great Short Stories, BB5
Fifty Years of the American Novel--A Christian Appraisal, E66
*Fifty Years of the American Short Story from the O. Henry
    Awards 1919-1970*, BB52
Figaro Littéraire, J30, J56
Financial Times (London), H82
Finestone, Harry, BB59
Finger, Larry Livingston, I13
*First Printings of American Authors--Contributions Toward
    Descriptive Checklists*, E30
Firsts of the Famous, BB23
The First Time: Initial Sexual Experiences in Fiction, BB71
Fletcher, Mary Dell, F73
Flower, Dean S., BB40
"THE FLOWERING DREAM: NOTES ON WRITING," A9.1-A9.2, C44
Foley, Martha, B3, B11, BB75
Folk, Barbara Nauer, F74
Fontaine, J62
Ford, Nick Aaron, F75
Forkner, Benjamin, BB85
Form and Idea in Modern Theatre, E44
Forms of Prose Fiction, BB61
The Forties: Fiction, Poetry, Drama, E70
Fort Wayne *News Sentinel*, G204
40 Best Stories from "Mademoiselle"--1935-1960, B9, E1
Four Elements: A Creative Approach to the Short Story, BB72
Four Models: A Rhetoric of Modern Fiction, BB65
France Catholique, J58
Frank, Joseph, G110
Frank, Waldo (subject), F76
Frankie Addams, J13
Freedley, George, G152-G154, G230
Freehafer, John, G177
Freese, Peter, J8, J21
Fremont-Smith, Eliot, F78

French, Warren, E72
Freud, Sigmund (subject), E100, H28
*Freud on Broadway--A History of Psychoanalysis and the
    American Drama*, E100
Friedman, Melvin J., F79
Friend, James, G359
*From Tobacco Road to Route 66--The Southern Poor White in
    Fiction*, E26
Fuller, John, G258
Fuller, Muriel, B1-B2
Fuller, Richard, G360
Funke, Lewis, F80-F82

G., F., G178
G., M.A., G111
Gabriel, Gilbert W., H22
Gaghan, Jerry, H50
Gaillard, Dawson D., F83
Galloway, David D., G259
Gannett, Lewis, G12, G112, G179
Gardiner, Harold C., S.J., E66
Gardner, Paul, F84
Garland, Robert, H23
Garner, Maxine, G13
Gassner, John, B7, BB49, E42-E47
Gaver, Jack, BB14
Gehman, Richard, F85
Gelb, Arthur, F86-F87
*Gengo to Buntai: Higashida Chiaki Kyoju Kanreki Kinen
    Ronbunshu*, J12
Georgia Review, F7, F58, F68-F69, F74, F92, F95, F150, F157,
    F190, F194, G323
Gérard, Rolf, A8.1-A8.2
Germano-Slavica, F174
Giannetti, Louis D., F88
Gibbs, Patrick, H42
Gibbs, Wolcott, H24, H65
Gibson, Walker, G337
Gibson, Wilfred, G14
Gillespie, Sheena, I14
Ginsberg, Elaine, F89
"GIRAFFE," A8.1-A8.2
The Glass Menagerie (Williams), E86
Gloster, Hugh M., E48
Godden, Rumer, G260
Gold, Don, BB41
Gold, Herbert, BB22, E49
Gold, Robert, BB43

"THE GOLDEN EGG GOBBLER," A8.1–A8.2
Goldstein, Albert, G15, G63
Gordimer, Nadine, G361
Gordy, Mary, F90
Gossett, Louise Young, E50, I15
Gould, Ray, G113
Govan, Christine Noble, G114, G180, G261
Gower, Herschel, BB37
Gozzi, Francesco, J46
Graham, Joan, G181
Graver, Lawrence, E51–E52
Gray, James, E53, G115
Gray, Richard, E54
Great Short Stories of the World, BB30
Great Tales of City Dwellers, BB11
Green, Peter, G262
Greensboro (N.C.) *Daily News*, G3, G54, G111, G376
Greenville (Miss.) *Delta Democrat-Times*, G224, G389
Greenwood, Walter B., G263
Gregory, Sister M., O.P., G231
Gresset, Michel, J47
Griffin, Lloyd W., G264
Griffith, Albert J., F92
Grinnell, James W., F93
Gross, John, G265
The Grotesque: An American Genre and Other Essays, E87
Grumbach, Doris, G266
Guigonnat, Henri, J48
Gullason, Thomas A., G362

H., A.S., Jr., G182
H., J.A., G183
H., P., G64
Hackett, Albert (subject), F81
Hackett, Frances (subject), F81
Haddican, James, G267
Haines, Helen E., E55
Hale, Nancy (subject), E11
Hall, Barbara Hodge, G363
Hall, Ted, G268
Hamilton, Alice, F94
Hamilton, Charles, G116
Hansen, Harry, G16, G65
Harbour, Edith, G66
Hardwick, Elizabeth, G364
Hardy, John Edward, BB25, E56–E57
Harper's, F215, G19, G278
Harper's Bazaar, C4, C9, C16, C19, C21, C46, C48, F1, F63

Harrell, Don, G365
Harris, Julie (subject), F74, F87, F113, H27
Hart, Jane, F95
Harte, Barbara, E58
Hartford *Courant*, G4, G52, G89, G236
Hartford *Times*, G128, G163
Hartley, Lodwick, G366
Hartt, J.N., G269
Hassan, Ihab, E59-E61, F96-F100
Hassan, Rita, H25
"THE HAUNTED BOY," A5.6, A9.1-A9.2, C39, E50, F179
Hawkins, William, F101, H26-H27
Hawthorne, Nathaniel (subject), G79
Hayden, Robert, BB63
Hayes, Richard, H66
The Heart Is a Lonely Hunter (film), D2, F30, F46, F196, F225, F250
THE HEART IS A LONELY HUNTER (novel), A1.1.a-e, A1.2-A1.9, A5.1.a-g, B4, BB71, C41, D11, E2-E3, E5-E6, *E7*, E10, E16-E17, E25-E26, E34-E36, E41, E48, E50-E53, E64, E70, E75-*E76*, E79, E81, E83, E93, E97-E98, *E108*-E109, E115, E123, F3, F7, F12, F14, F31, F56, F60-*F61*, F63, *F69*, F78, F89, F94, F97, F99-F100, F116, *F119*, F124, F129, *F142*, F148, *F152*, F159, F168, F173, F175, F190, F194, *F202*, F208, F210, F212, *F217*, F235, G66, G70, G78, G80, G112, G226, G270, I1, I4, J66; Reviews: G1-G49
The Heath Introduction to Fiction, BB80
Heiress of All the Ages--Sex and Sentiment in the Genteel Tradition, E116
Hemingway, Ernest (subject), G3, G72
Hendrick, George, F102
Henry Bellamann Award, F132
Hermes, Liesel, J8
Herron, Ima Honaker, E62
Herself, E15
Heth, Edward Harris, G184
Hewes, Henry, BB17, E63, F103
Hicks, Granville, F104, G270
Higashida, Chiaki, J12
"HIGHWAY BRINGS WOMEN OF WEST, SOUTH GEORGIA MORE CLOSELY TOGETHER," C1
Hill, Bob, G185
Hill, George Roy (subject), F81
Hill, Gladys, D3
Hipp, Edward Sothern, H28, H67
His Eye Is on the Sparrow--An Autobiography, E117
Histoire du roman américain, J23
Histoire littéraire des États-Unis, J1

Hobby, Diana Poteat, G271
Hochman, Eleanor, E78
Hoffman, Frederick J., E64
Hogan, William, G272, G367
Holland's, G7, G176
"HOME FOR CHRISTMAS," A9.1-A9.2, C30
"A HOSPITAL CHRISTMAS EVE," A9.1-A9.2, C53
Houston Chronicle, G288, G365
Houston Post, G271
Howard, C. Jeriel, BB60
Howard, Daniel F., BB47, E65
Howe, Irving, G273
Howes, Victor, G368
"HOW HIGH IS THE SKY?," A8.1-A8.2
"HOW I BEGAN TO WRITE," A9.1-A9.2, C24
Huelsbeck, Charles, G369
Hughes, Catherine, G274
Hughes, Douglas A., BB69
Hughes, Riley, G186
The Human Commitment: An Anthology of Contemporary Short
    Fiction, BB41
Hunt, Mary Fassett, G188
Hunt, Tann H., I16
Hunter, Anna C., G117, G189, G275
"HUSH LITTLE BABY" (unpublished), C52
Huston, John, D3
Hutchens, John K., F105, G276
Hyde, Fred G., G17
"HYMEN, O HYMEN" (see also "THE DUAL ANGEL"), A9.1-A9.2, C34

"I AM OLD AND CAN REMEMBER," A8.1-A8.2
Ibert, Jean-Claude, J18
Idema, Jim, G277
Illustrated London News, H46
Imaginative Literature: Fiction, Drama, Poetry, BB45
The Impact of Fiction, BB53, E18
Impact: Short Stories for Pleasure, BB56
Inazawa, Hideo, J10
"INCANTATION TO LUCIFER" (see also "THE DUAL ANGEL"), A9.1-
    A9.2, C34
Indianapolis News, G131, G300, G346
The Inmost Leaf--A Selection of Essays, E68
In Search of Heresy--American Literature in an Age of
    Conformity, E2
Insight & Outlook--A Collection of Short Stories, BB54
"INSTANT OF THE HOUR AFTER," A9.1-A9.2, C56, F179
Intellectual America--Ideas on the March, E16
INTERVIEWS, E91, F6, F16, F27, F51, F56, F90, F105-F106,
    F124, F134, F144, F163, F200, F212, F247

Intro Bulletin, F239
"THE INVISIBLE WALL," D4
Irish Times (Dublin), F247, G107
"ISAK DINESEN: IN PRAISE OF RADIANCE," A9.1–A9.2, C49
"ISAK DINESEN: *WINTER'S TALES* (BOOK REVIEW)," A9.1–A9.2, C18
"I SOMETIMES WONDER," A8.1–A8.2, C51
*I Wish I'd Written That: Selections Chosen by Favorite
    American Authors*, BB2, E9
Izzo, Carlo, J11

Jackson, Joseph Henry, G118
Jackson, Katherine Gauss, G19, G278
Jackson (Tenn.) *Sun*, G354
Jacobs, Robert D., E37
Jacobson, Ethel, G338
Jaffe, Adrian H., BB20
Jahrbuch für Amerikastudien, F129
Jaworski, Philippe, J49
Jennings, Elizabeth, G279
"THE JOCKEY," A5.1.a–g, A5.2.a–b, A5.3–A5.7, B1, BB3, BB5,
    BB15, BB32, BB47, BB52, BB65, BB84, BB85, C12, E65, F179
John O'London's Weekly, G190
Johnson, Carlton, F118
Johnson, Constance, F109–F111
Johnson, Greer (subject), F130, F256
Johnson, James William, F112
Johnson, Pamela Hansford, G190
Johnson, Thomas Slayton, I17
Jones, Carter Brooke, G191
Jones, Dorothy, G20
Jones, William M., BB48
Joost, Nicholas, E66
Jorgensen, Paul, BB13
Journal du Dimanche, J41
Journal of Commerce (New York), H16, H59
Joyce, Edward Thomas, I18
Jubilee, G322

K., E.C., G21
Kansas City *Star*, G32, G78, G125, G315
Kapp, Isa, G119
*Katherine Anne Porter and Carson McCullers: A Reference
    Guide*, E69
Katsurada, Shigetoshi, J12
Kazin, Alfred, E67–E68, F113–F114
Kee, Robert, G192
Kelley, James E., G193
Kelley, Marion, F115
Kelly, Frank K., F116

Kemp, Robert, J50
Kennedy, John S., G280
Kentucky Review, F217
Kenyon Review, F165, G150
Kerr, Walter, H68
Kierkegaard, Soren (subject), E73
Kiernan, Robert F., E69
Kilts, Donald L., G281
King, Robin, G120
Kinney, Jeanne, G370
Kirkland, James W., BB79
Kirkus, G121, G155, G232, G282, G371
Kirvan, John J., G283
Klein, Alexander, BB10
Klein, Francis A., G284
Klein, Marcus, F117
Knowles, A.S., Jr., E70
Knoxville (Tenn.) *Journal*, G131
Kohler, Dayton, F118
Kolenich, Betty, G122
Korenman, Joan S., F119
Kostelanetz, Richard, E46, E60
Kouwenhoven, John A., BB24
Kronenberger, Louis, E71
"KROOCHEY, KAZOOCHEY, KALOOCHIE, KAZEEN," A8.1-A8.2, C51
Kusuhara, Tomoko, E72
Kwartalnik Neofilologiczny (Warsaw), F210

Lafferty, Alice P., G372
Lahr, John, F120
Lalou, René, J13
Lambert, Robert, BB58
"LANDS AFAR," A8.1-A8.2, C51
Les Langues Modernes, J43
Lantz, Robert (subject), F86
Lask, Thomas, F121-F122
Lawrence, D.H. (subject), F174, G129, G207
Laws, Frederick, G194
Lawson, Lewis A., E73
Laycock, Edward A., G285
Lee, Gypsy Rose (subject), F70
Lee, Harry, F124
Leiter, Louis, BB50
Lennertz, Franz, J15
Lenz, Siegfried, J14
Lesser, M.X., B10, E74
Let's Meet the Theatre, E21
[LETTER TO THE EDITOR], C22

Levidova, Inna, E75
Levy, Leo B., E108
Lewis, Emory, F125, H69
Lewis, Theophilus, H70
Lewiston (Me.) *Evening Journal*, G178
Lexington (Ky.) *Sunday Herald-Leader*, G343
Library Journal, G154, G230, G264, G339, G345
Lies Like Truth--Theatre Reviews and Essays, E20
Life, C23, F182, G286
"LIKE THAT," A9.1-A9.2, C54, F179
The Listener, F220, G165, G258
Literary Cavalcade, C39, F106, F148
The Literary Situation, E29
Literature & Psychology, F142
Literature/Film Quarterly, F88
*The Literature of Memory--Modern Writers of the American
    South*, E54
The Literature of the South, BB6, BB46
Littell, Robert, G22, G68
Litterair Paspoort, J72
Les Littéraires contemporaines à travers le monde, J18
"LITTLE GIRLS AT JUNIPER LAKE WRITE LETTERS ON EXPERIENCES
    DURING FRESH AIR CAMP OUTING," C2
Living with Books--The Art of Book Selection, E55
Lloyd, Pat, G373
Loewinsohn, Joseph A., G23, G69
Lombardo, Agostino, J16
London *Daily Express*, G217
London *Daily Telegraph*, H77
London *Daily Telegraph & Morning Post*, G161, G262, H42
London *Evening Standard*, H45, H79
London Magazine, F156, G293, G361
London *News Chronicle*, G194
London *Sunday Telegraph*, F53
London *Sunday Times*, G42, G82, G142, G170, G279
London *Times*, F40, G187, G296, G386, G391, H44, H80
"LONELINESS ... AN AMERICAN MALADY," A9.1-A9.2, C29
The Lonely Hunter--A Biography of Carson McCullers, B14, E17
"The Lonely Hunting," F23, F25, F110-F111
The Loners: Short Stories About the Young and Alienated,
    BB55
Long Island Daily Press (Jamaica, N.Y.), H20
"LOOK HOMEWARD, AMERICANS ...," A9.1-A9.2, C5
Loomis, Roger Sherman, BB15
Los Angeles *Daily News*, G203
Los Angeles *Times*, G25, G50
Louisville *Courier-Journal*, G77, G97, G205, G319
Louisville *Times*, G93

Love and Death in the American Novel, E41
"LOVE AND THE RIND OF TIME" (see also "THE DUAL ANGEL"),
    A9.1-A9.2, C34
"LOVE'S NOT TIME'S FOOL," C17
Lowndes, Marion, F127
Lowry, Robert, F128
Lubbers, Klaus, F129
Luso-Brazilian Review, F186
Lyon, Maclay, G125

M., T., G288
McCall's, C53
McClain, John, H71
McConkey, James, G289
McCord, Bert, F130-F131
McCullers, Carson, Interviews (see INTERVIEWS)
McCullers, J. Reeves, Jr. (subject), E95, F107, F170, F192
MacDonald, Edgar E., E76
McDonald, Edward D., G24
MacDougall, Sally, F134
Mace, Louise, H29
McGill, Ralph, F135-F139, G126
MacGregor, Martha, G196
McKenzie, Alice, G374
McNally, John, F140
McNeir, Waldo, E108
Macon (Ga.) *News*, F163-F164, G129
Macon (Ga.) *Telegraph & News*, G357
McPherson, Hugo, F141
"MADAME ZILENSKY AND THE KING OF FINLAND," A5.1.a-g, A5.2.a-b,
    A5.3-A5.7, B13, BB29, BB63, C14, E50, F179
Madden, David, E77, F142, G375
Maddocks, Melvin, F143
Mademoiselle, C17, C20, C24, C28, C30, C34, C37-C40, C42,
    F127-F128, F147, F153, F206, F222, F228, F244
La Magazine Littéraire, J28
Magny, Claude-Edmonde, E78, J17
Mahoney, W.J., Jr., G197
Malin, Irving, E79-E80
Maline, Julian L., BB42
Manchester *Guardian*, G14, G305
Mann, Elizabeth L., G376
Mann, Klaus, E81
Mann, Theodore, D9
Mansfield, Katherine (subject), F247
*Manual to Accompany "The Modern Tradition--Short Stories--
    Second Edition,"* E65
"THE MAN UPSTAIRS" (unpublished), C52

"THE MARCH," C52
Margerie, Diane de, J51
Mark Twain Journal, F238
The Marquis (Lafayette College), F144
La Marseillaise, J61
Marsh, Fred T., G70
Marshall, Margaret, H30
Martin, Jean, G290
Martin, Linton, H1
Maslin, Marsh, G233, G291
Massingham, Hugh, G198
Match, Richard, G127
Mathis, Ray, F145
Maupassant, Guy de (subject), G207
The Meaning of Fiction, E24
Mediterranean Review, G344
Meeker, Richard K., E82
Mellard, James M., BB65
The Member of the Wedding (film), D1, F88, F194
["THE MEMBER OF THE WEDDING"] (musical adaptation), D10
THE MEMBER OF THE WEDDING (novel), A3.1.a-b, A3.2-A3.3,
    A3.4.a-b, A3.5-A3.7, A5.1.a-g, A5.2.a-b, A5.5, A5.7, BB6,
    C21, D11, E2-E3, E5, E10, E17, E25, E32, E34-E36, E40-
    E41, E50-E53, E55, E64, E70, E79, E88, E97-E99, E102,
    E115, *E121*, E123, F7, F14-F16, F31, F52, F60, F79, F88-
    F89, F97, F112, F129, F173, *F180*, F208, F231, F235, F245,
    G152-G154, G192-G391, H32, I1, J30, J36, J50; Reviews:
    G87-G150
THE MEMBER OF THE WEDDING (play), A4.1.a-d, B5, B7, BB12,
    BB14, BB17, BB21, BB36, BB43, BB49, D6, E8, E17, E19-*E20*-
    E21-*E22*-*E23*, E25, *E33*-E34, E42-E47, E62-E63, E68, E72,
    E84-E86, E90, E100, E112, E117, E119, *F4*, F16-F17, F28,
    F38, F41, *F43*, F49, *F52*, F62, F66, F72, F77, F80, F82,
    F87-F88, F101, F103, F105, F114-F115, F123, F125, F130-
    F131, F146, F161-F162, F164, F182-F185, F189, F198-F201,
    F205, F214-F215, F223, F233, F242-F243, F251, H1-H48;
    Reviews: G151-G155
Memphis *Commercial Appeal*, G136, G221
Mercer, Mary (subject), F6
Merlin, Milton, G25
Mertens, Pierre, J52
Miami (Fla.) *Herald*, G195, G311
Micha, René, J53
"MICK" (see also THE HEART IS A LONELY HUNTER), C41
Middendorf, John Harlan, BB15
Miles, Rosalind, E84
Miller, Arthur (subject), E46-E47, E87
Miller, James E., Jr., BB63

Miller, Jordan Y., BB21, E85
Miller, Nolan, G199
Miller, Robert Ellis, D2
Miller, Robert Ellys, J54
Millichap, Joseph Robert, F150–F152, I19
Milwaukee *Journal*, G21, G81, G184, G251, G356
Minneapolis *Sunday Tribune*, G214, G318
Minneapolis *Tribune*, G390
Minute, J39
Missey, James, F155
Mississippi Quarterly, F83, F230
Mitchell, Julian, F156, G293
Mizuta, J., J55
Modern American Drama: Essays in Criticism, E90
Modern English Readings, BB15
Modern Fiction Studies, F94
Modern Literature and the Religious Frontier, E99
The Modern Novel in Britain and the United States, E3
Modern Short Stories: The Fiction of Experience, B10, E74
The Modern Talent: An Anthology of Short Stories, BB25, E57
The Modern Tradition, BB47
Mohrt, Michel, J18–J19, J56
Molloy, Robert, G26, G72
Monat, J67
Le Monde, J44, J65
"The Monkey" (Dinesen), F178
Montgomery, Marion, F157
Montgomery (Ala.) *Advertiser*, G113
Montgomery *Advertiser-Alabama Journal*, G197
Moody, Minnie Hite, G377
Moore, Eugene, F158
Moore, Harry T., E39, G294
Moore, Jack B., F159
Moore, Janice Townley, F160
Morehouse, Ward, F161–F162
Morgan, Nonie, F163–F164
Morris, Alton C., BB44–BB45
Morris, John N., B10, E74
Morris, Wright, F165
Morrison, Hobe, H31, H72
THE MORTGAGED HEART, A9.1–A9.2, E101, *F79*; Reviews: G342–G395
"THE MORTGAGED HEART," A9.1–A9.2, C26, C35
Mortimer, Chapman, D3
Mortimer, Penelope, G295
Morton, Tim, G378
Mt. Pleasant (Texas) *Daily Tribune*, G395
Murdock, Henry T., H2, H51–H52
Murfreesboro (Tenn.) *Daily News Journal*, G384

Murphy, Mark, BB7
Murphy, Mary Ellen, BB7
Murphy, Pat, G200
Murray, Marian, G128
Murray, Michele, G379
"THE MUTE" (see "AUTHOR'S OUTLINE OF 'THE MUTE'")
Myrick, Susan, G129

N., F.A., G130
Nance, William L., F169
Nashville *Banner*, G95, G249
Nathan, George Jean, E85-E86
Nathan, N., BB51
The Nation, F70, G36, G67, G145, G290, H30, H58
National Observer, G379
National Review, G253
Negro Voices in American Fiction, E48
Neue Zürcher Zeitung, J68
New American Gothic, E80
Newark (N.J.) *Evening News*, H21, H64
Newark (N.J.) *Star-Ledger*, H20
Newark (N.J.) *Sunday News*, G225, G268, H28, H67
New Directions, C26-C27
New Masses, G87
The New Mexican (Santa Fe), G317
New Orleans *Times-Picayune*, F33, G267
New Orleans *Times-Picayune and States*, G15, G63
New Republic, C18, E13, G48, G62, G139, G327, H15
New Statesman, G265
New Statesman and Nation, G46, G84, G120, G207, G358, H48
Newsweek, F27, F54, G287, H33
New World Writing, F71, F237
New York *Daily Compass*, F183-F185, H35
New York *Daily Mirror*, H17
New York *Daily News*, H13, H56
New York Drama Critics' Circle Award, BB14, F123, F215
New Yorker, C12, C14-C15, F229, G9, G60, G149, G201, G239,
    H24, H65
New York *Herald Tribune*, C29, E25, F17, F44, F48-F49, F130-
    F131, F229, F251, G12, G112, G179, G276, H6-H7, H68
New York Herald Tribune Book Review, F105, G211
New York Herald Tribune Books, F170, F175, G29, G61, G260
New York Herald Tribune Weekly Book Review, G127
New York *Journal-American*, H23, H71
New York *Mirror*, H60
New York *Morning Telegraph*, F59, G152-G153, H10, H55
New York *Post*, C33, F198-F201, F243, G131, G196, H39-H40, H75
New York Review of Books, F113

New York *Sun*, G26, G72, G98
New York *Sunday Compass*, F66, F77
New York *Sunday News*, H14, H57
New York *Times*, C25, F4, F6, F16, F28, F37, F39, F47, F76,
    F78, F80–F82, F84, F87, F103, F107, F121–F122, F126, F133,
    F166–F167, F195–F196, F214–F215, F245, F255–F256, G43,
    G76, G135, G206, G303, G347, H4, H54, H80
New York Times Book Review, C45, F2, F12, F34, G10, G70, G119,
    G171, G273, G337, G355
New York *World-Telegram*, F99, F134, G16, G65
New York *World-Telegram and Sun*, G240, H53
New York *World-Telegram and the Sun*, F161–F162, H26–H27
"NIGHT WATCH OVER FREEDOM," A9.1–A9.2, C6
Nin, Anaïs, E105
Norfolk *Virginian-Pilot*, F35, G35, G80, G222, G378
Norris, Hoke, G297
North, Sterling, G131
The Norton Anthology of Short Fiction, Complete Edition, BB83
The Norton Anthology of Short Fiction, Shorter Edition, BB84
Nourse, Joan, G27
Le Nouveau Roman américain, J19
Nouvelle Revue Française, J47, J49, J70
Les Nouvelles Littéraires, J31, J50, J54, J66
Le Nouvel Observateur, J29
Nyack (N.Y.) *Journal-News*, F38, F188

Oakland (Calif.) *Tribune*, G302
O'Brien, Edna, F173
O'Brien, Kate, G28
The Observer (London), G30, G83, G198, G227, G326, G388, H47,
    H78
O'Connor, Flannery (subject), E61, F79, F98, F211, G365–G366,
    G383, I9, I13, I21, I24, I28
O'Connor, Madeleine, G202
O'Connor, William Van, E87
"OCTOBER FAIR," A8.1–A8.2
O'Dell, Scott, G203
O. Henry Memorial Award Prize Stories of 1943, B2
O. Henry Memorial Award Prize Stories of 1942, B1
OEUVRES, J29, J40, J51, J54
Oklahoma City *Daily Oklahoman*, G148, G304
"OLDEN TIMES," A8.1–A8.2
Olofson, Philip H., G204
O'Mara, Roger, G234
On Contemporary Literature, E46, E60
On Directing, E22
O'Neal, Robert, BB63
O'Neill, Lois Decker, G205

"ONE WORLD," A8.1-A8.2
Onkoso, Yoshiko, E88
Onoe, Masaji, D15
On Second Thought, E53
*The Open Decision--The Contemporary American Novel and Its
    Intellectual Background*, E14
Opéra dos Martos (Dourado), F186
Oregon Journal (Portland), G212, G349
"THE ORPHANAGE," A9.1-A9.2, F179
"OUR HEADS ARE BOWED," A9.1-A9.2, C20
Our Sunday Visitor (Huntington, Ind.), G280

P., W., G133
P.-L., M., J57
PM (New York), G134
Pachmuss, Temira, F174
"PANDORA'S BOX," A8.1-A8.2, C51
Panorama de la littérature contemporaine aux États-Unis, J4
Parias, Louis-Henri, J58
Parker, Dorothy, BB32, G299
Parnasso, J60
Parshley, H.M., E32
Pasadena (Calif.) *Star-News*, G164
Paterson, Isabel M., F175
Patterns of Literature, BB42
Peden, William, E89
Penninger, Frieda Elaine, E76
Pensacola (Fla.) *News*, G373
Perrine, Laurence, BB16, F176
"THE PESTLE" (see also CLOCK WITHOUT HANDS), C37
Phelan, Kappo, H34
Philadelphia *Daily News*, H50
Philadelphia *Evening Bulletin*, H3, H49
Philadelphia Forum, G177
Philadelphia *Inquirer*, C43, F115, F249, G17, G130, G360, H1-
    H2, H51-H52
Philadelphia *Record*, G143
Philadelphia *Sunday Bulletin*, F204, G372
Phillippi, Wendell C., G300
Phillips, Louis, E90
Phillips, Robert S., F177-F181
The Phoenix (Boston), G383
Phylon, F75, F231
Pickering, James H., BB82
"PICNIC" (see also THE HEART IS A LONELY HUNTER), BB71
*Pioneers and Caretakers--A Study of 9 American Women
    Novelists*, E5
Pittsburgh *Press*, G38, G351

"THE PLACE OF DRAMA IN THE RELIGIOUS AND SPIRITUAL LIFE OF
    AMERICA," D12
Playbill (National Theatre, New York), F207, F246
Playboy, G301
Player's Magazine, H12
Play-Making--A Manual of Craftsmanship, E45
Playwright at Work, E112
A Pocket Book of Modern American Short Stories, BB7
Point of Departure, BB43
Poirier, Richard, BB31
"POLDI," A9.1-A9.2, F79
Pollock, Arthur, F183-F185, H35
Pollock-Chagas, Jeremy E., F186
Pomeranz, Regina, F187
Poore, Charles, G76, G206
Popp, Klaus-Jürgen, J20-J21
Porter, Katherine Anne (subject), F11, F169
Post, Constance, F188
Powell, Dawn, G134
Powers, Clare, F189
Powers, Dennis, G302
Le Prairie perdue--Histoire du roman américain, J5
Prescott, Orville, G135, G303
Présences contemporaines--Écrivains américains d'aujourd'hui, J3
Presley, Delma Eugene, F190-F193
Price, H. Bruce, G77
Priestley, Lee, G304
Princeton (N.J.) *Packet*, F154
Pritchett, V.S., G207
Prize of the Younger Generation, F57, F133
Prize Stories 1965: The O. Henry Awards, BB31
Prize Stories of 1951--The O. Henry Awards, B6, E11
*Prize-Winning American Drama: A Bibliographical and Descrip-
    tive Guide*, E8
Proffer, Carl R., E75
The Progressive, G254
Proletarian Writers of the Thirties, E77
Providence *Sunday Journal*, F205, G47, G64, G132, G213, G310
Pruette, Lorine, G29
Pryce-Jones, Alan, G30
Psychoanalysis and American Fiction, E79
Publishers Weekly, F172, G380
Punch, G208, G246
Purdy, James (subject), F98
Putzel, Max, G31

"'QUARRELS AND CUSSING'--PLAYWRIGHT TELLS OF PANGS," C43
Quarterly Review of Literature, G147

Quartet: A Book of Stories, Plays, Poems, and Critical Essays,
    BB66
Quest for Meaning: Modern Short Stories, BB73
Quigly, Isabel, G305
Quinn, John J., S.J., G306
Quintero, Jose (subject), F8
La Quinzaine Littéraire, J51
Le Quotidien de Paris, J48

R., B., G28, G78
Rackemann, Adelaide C., G307
Radical Innocence: Studies in the Contemporary American Novel,
    E59
Radu, Aurelia, J59
Radway, Janice Anne, I20
Ragan, Sam, G308
Raleigh *News and Observer*, F36, G13, G66, G133, G308, G366
Rantavaara, Irma, J60
"A RAT AND A RAINBOW," A8.1-A8.2, C51
Raven, Simon, G309
Rayburn, Otto Ernest, G136
Reading Literature: Stories, Plays and Poems, BB26
Reading Prose Fiction, BB27
Realismo e simbolismo, J16
Recent American Fiction, E60
Recherches Anglaises et Américaines, J64
Rechnitz, Robert Max, F194, I21
Redbook, C47, C51-C52, C54-C56, F221
Redman, Ben Ray, G33, G209
Reed, Rex, E91, F195-F197
Reflections in a Golden Eye (film), D3, F194, F225
REFLECTIONS IN A GOLDEN EYE (novel), A2.1.a-b, A2.2-A2.6,
    A5.1.a-g, A5.2.a-b, A5.5, A5.7, C4, D13-D14, E3, E5,
    E10, E17, E25, E34-E36, E50-E53, E64, E70, E79, E88, E97-
    E98, E115, E122, F3, F7, F62, F90, F94, F116, F129, *F145*,
    F165, F173, F194, F208, F235, F245, G112, G156-G157,
    G179, G192, G326, J2, J31, J62; Reviews: G50-G86
Religion in Life, F145
Remacle, Andre, J61
*Renaissance in the South--A Critical History of the
    Literature, 1920-1960*, E10
Renascence, F180
The Reporter, F117, G330
*A Requiem for the Renascence--The State of Fiction in the
    Modern South*, E106
Revue des Langues Vivantes, F79
Rexroth, Kenneth, E88
Rice, Vernon, F198-F201

Rich, Nancy B., F202
Richard, Jean-Pierre, J62
Richard Wright--A Biography, E120
Richman, Robert, E28, E92
Richmond (Va.) *Times-Dispatch*, F35, G316
Richter, Harvena, G310
Rikkyo Review, J55
Riley, Caroline, E58
"The Rime of the Ancient Mariner" (Coleridge), F73
Ríos Ruiz, Manuel, J63
Rivière, Yvette, J64
Roberts, Mary-Carter, G34, G79, G138
Robertson-Rose, Paula, BB72
Robinson, W.R., F203
Robinson, Wayne, F204
Rochester (N.Y.) *Democrat and Chronicle*, G104
*Rocking the Boat: A Political, Literary and Theatrical
    Commentary*, E113
Rockland County Journal-News (Nyack, N.Y.), F223
Rockowitz, Murray, BB54
Rodgers, Mary, D10
Rogers, Ann Tucker, I22
Rogers, W.G., G381
Rohrberger, Mary, BB86
Rolin, Gabrielle, J65
Rolo, Charles, G312
Le Roman américain au XXe siècle, J24
*Der Roman im Englischunterricht der Sekundarstufe, II: Theorie
    und Praxis*, J8
Romano, Emanuel (subject), F22
Rome (Italy) *Daily American*, F51
Rosati, Salvatore, J22
Rose, Alan Henry, E93
Rosenberger, Coleman, G211
Rosenfeld, Isaac, G139
Ross, Dorothy, F207
Rougemont, Denis de, J66
Rowe, William, G382
Roy, Emil, BB34
Rubin, Louis D., Jr., E37, E94, F208, G313
Rukeyser, Muriel, E95
Russell, Cara Green, G35, G80
"THE RUSSIAN REALISTS AND SOUTHERN LITERATURE," A9.1-A9.2, C11
Rutherford, Marjory, F209
Ryan, Michael, G383
Ryan, Thomas C., D2

S., D., G384
S., F.M., G81
Sachs, Viola, F210
Sackett, Russ, G212
Saginaw (Mich.) *News*, G281
St. Louis *Advocate*, G237
St. Louis *Globe-Democrat*, G284
St. Louis *Post-Dispatch*, G202
St. Louis *Sunday Post-Dispatch*, G353
Salomon, Louis B., G36
Samachson, Dorothy, E21
Samachson, Joseph, E21
Samuels, Charles, E117
Samway, Patrick, BB85
San Antonio *Express*, G157
Sanders, Thomas E., BB39, E96
Sandrof, Nancy, G314
San Francisco *Argonaut*, G202
San Francisco *Call-Bulletin*, G233
San Francisco *Chronicle*, G27, G118, G272, G367
San Francisco *News Call-Bulletin*, G291
Saporta, Marc, J23
"SARABAND," A9.1-A9.2, D11
Saroyan, William (subject), G179
Sarton, May, G37
Satin, Joseph, BB27, BB34
Saturday Evening Post, C50
Saturday Review, C7, C49, F13, F137, F211, F248, G33, G59,
    G100, G209, G270, G362, H11
Savage, D.S., G140
Savannah *Morning News*, G117, G189, G275
Schaefer, Ted, F211
Schäffer, Kristiane, J67
Schlueter, Paul, G385
Schmidt-von Bardeleben, Renate, J9
Schnack, Elisabeth, J68
Schneiderman, Beth K., BB64
School and Society, H9
Schorer, Mark, E97-E98
Schott, Webster, G315
Schroetter, Hilda N., G316
Schulman, Hilda N., G316
Schulman, L.M., BB55, BB70, BB81
The Scope of Fiction, BB18
The Scotsman (Edinburgh), G158, G350
Scott, Eleanor, G213, G317

Scott, Nathan A., Jr., E99
Scott, Virgil, BB20, BB57
Scruggs, Philip Lightfoot, G141
Seasons of Discontent: Dramatic Opinions 1959-1965, E13
The Second Sex, E32
Selby, John, F212
"SELECT YOUR SORROWS IF YOU CAN" (see also "SARABAND"), D11
Sellers, Tom, F213
Sensenderfer, R.E.P., H3
The Sense of Fiction, BB37
Seven Contemporary Short Novels, BB50
7 Songs by David Diamond, D8
Sewanee Review, G110, G313
Shakespeare, William (subject), G320
Shanley, J.P., F211, F215
Shapiro, Adrian Michael, E30, I23
Shaw, Joy Farmer, I24
Sheaffer, Louis, H36-H37
Sherer, Ray J., BB78
Sherman, John K., G214, G318
Sherman, Thomas B., G215
Sherrill, Anne, BB72
Sherrill, Rowland A., F217
Shorris, Earl, F218
THE SHORTER NOVELS AND STORIES OF CARSON McCULLERS, A5.7
Short Stories: An Anthology, BB51
The Short Story: An Introduction, BB77
Short Story: A Thematic Anthology, BB32
The Short Story: Fiction in Transition, B13
The Short Story and the Reader, BB19
Short Story Masterpieces, BB9
The Short Story Reader, BB67
Show, F50
Show Business (New York), H25
Shroyer, Frederick B., BB13, BB32
Shulman, Milton, H45, H79
Sibley, Celestine, F219
The Sickness Unto Death (Kierkegaard), E73
Sievers, W. David, E100
The Sign, G283, G369
Simmons, Charles, E98
Simon, Jean, J24
Simonini, R.C., Jr., E82
Simonson, Harold P., BB66
Sinclair, Andrew, F220
Singer, Isaac Bashevis (subject), E89
Skotnicki, Irene, J69
"SLUMBER PARTY," A8.1-A8.2

The Small Town in American Drama, E62
Smith, Christopher Michael, I25
Smith, Margarita G., A9.1–A9.2, B9, E1, E101, F221
Smith, Mrs. Lamar (subject), F166
Smith, Simeon Mozart, Jr., I26
Sohn, David A., BB35
Le Soir de Bruxelles, J52
"THE SOJOURNER," A5.1.a–g, A5.2.a–b, A5.3–A5.7, B6, BB9,
    BB13, BB25, BB34, BB47, BB53, BB57, BB68, BB74, BB79,
    BB81, BB85, C32, D5, E11, E18, E56–E57, E65, F179
"THE SOJOURNER" (TV script), D5
"SONG FOR A SAILOR," A8.1–A8.2, C51
The Sound and the Fury (Faulkner), F151
South Atlantic Bulletin, F52, F140, F193
South Atlantic Quarterly, F61, F236
South Bend (Ind.) *Tribune*, G137
South Central Bulletin, F73
Southern Humanities Review, F169, F203
Southern Literary Journal, F202, G375
Southern Literary Messenger, F43
Southern Quarterly, F14
Southern Writers--Appraisals in Our Time, E82
South: Modern Southern Literature in Its Cultural Setting, E37
Southwest Review, F179, F181
Soviet Criticism of American Literature in the Sixties, E75
Spain, Nancy, G217
Spearman, Walter, G218
Spécial, J26
The Spectator, F234, G28, G140, G192, G309
Spens, Willy De, J70
Spinner, Stephanie, BB61
Spokane *Chronicle*, G185
"SPORT WILLIAMS," A8.1–A8.2
Springfield (Mass.) *Sunday Republican*, H29
Springfield (Mass.) *Sunday Union and Republican*, G39, G75
THE SQUARE ROOT OF WONDERFUL, A6.1, A6.2.a–b, A6.3.a, A6.4,
    C40, C43, E17, E25, E34, E71, E90, F8, F48, F59, F86,
    F154, F204, *F208*, F249, H49–H82; Reviews: G227–G235
Stafford, Jean (subject), F236
Stanley, William T., F225
Stansbury, Donald L., BB56
Stanton, Robert, BB19
Starke, Catherine Juanita, E102
Stegner, Wallace, E103
Stein, Gertrude (subject), G140
Steinbeck, John (subject), G3
Stern, Philip Van Doren, BB7
Stevenson, David L., BB22, E49
Stewart, Randall, BB6

Stewart, Stanley, F226
Stilwell, Robert L., G319
Stone, W., BB77
"STONE IS NOT STONE," A9.1-A9.2, C13, C42, D11
Storey, Ginger (subject), F23
Storey, Mrs. Edward (subject), F111
Storia della letteratura americana, J22
Storia della letteratura Nord Americana, J11
Stories of Modern America, BB22, E49
Stories of the Modern South, BB85
Story, C3, F45
Story and Structure, BB16
Story Jubilee, BB33
Story to Anti-Story, BB86
Strasfogel, Ian, G320
Straumann, Heinrich, E104
Straus, Ralph, G42, G82, G142
Studi Americani, J46, J73
Studies in American Fiction, F89
Studies in American Literature, E108
Studies in Fiction, BB34
Studies in Short Fiction (book), BB69
Studies in Short Fiction (journal), F63, F93, F176, F178
Studies in the Humanities (Indiana University of Pennsylvania),
    F119
Studies in the Short Story, BB20, BB57
Stuhlman, Gunther, E105
Sturges-Jones, Marion, G143
Styron, William (subject), E92, I9
"SUCKER," A9.1-A9.2, B11, BB28, BB31, BB35, BB41, BB43, BB54,
    BB56, C50, F179
Sullivan, Margie [Margaret Sue], G321, I27
Sullivan, Oona, G322
Sullivan, Walter, E102, G323
Summer and Smoke (Williams), F200
Sundell, Roger H., BB38
SWEET AS A PICKLE AND CLEAN AS A PIG, A8.1-A8.2, F56; Reviews:
    G336-G341
"SWEET AS A PICKLE AND CLEAN AS A PIG," A8.1-A8.2
Swinnerton, Frank, G83
Swift, Ruth, G324
Symons, Julian, E107, F227
Syracuse 10, F15

T., C.V., G219
*Taken at the Flood--The Human Drama as Seen by Modern
    American Novelists*, B4
Tamarack Review, F141

Tampa *Tribune-Times*, G392
Taylor, Glenn, G144, G220
Taylor, Horace, E108
Taylor, J. Chesley, B13
Taylor, William E., E90
Teltscher, Herry O., F228
Ten Modern American Short Stories, BB35
"TENNESSEE WILLIAMS," C23
Tennessee Williams: Rebellious Puritan, E110
Thaddeus, Janice Farrar, BB24
Theatre Arts, C31, F85, H38, H74
*The Theatre Book of the Year 1949-1950--A Record and an
    Interpretation*, E85
The Theatre in Our Times, E47
The Theatre in the Fifties, E86
The Theme of Loneliness in Modern American Drama, E33
"THERE WAS A TIME WHEN STONE WAS STONE" (see also "THE
    TWISTED TRINITY" and "STONE IS NOT STONE"), D11
Theroux, Paul, G386
Thesmar, Sarah, G221
This Issue (McKee Publishing Co., Atlanta), F192
Thomas, Leroy, I28
Thomas, W.H.J., G387
Thompson, Ralph, G43
Thorp, Willard, F230
Time, F123, F143, F149, G11, G71, G105, G211, G292, H32, H73
Time and Tide, G6, G55, G96, G223, G295
Times Literary Supplement, F224, F227, G18, G74, G94, G167,
    G229, G257, G341
Times Weekly Review (London), G256
Timko, Michael, BB74
Tinkham, Charles B., F231
Das Tintenfass, J38
Tischler, Nancy M., E109-E110
"TO BEAR THE TRUTH ALONE" (see also CLOCK WITHOUT HANDS), C46
Tobias, Rowena W., G44
Today, F232
Toebasch, Wim, J71
Toledo *Blade*, G1, G51
Toliver, Harold E., BB62
Torrens, James, S.J., F232
Tournier, Jacques, J25
Townend, Marion, G45
Toynbee, Philip, G46, G84, G326, G388
Tracy, Honor, G327
Tracz, Richard F., BB60
Transatlantic Review, F55
A Treasury of Brooklyn, BB4

"A TREE. A ROCK. A CLOUD.," A5.1.a-g, A5.2.a-b, A5.3-A5.7, B2,
    BB7, BB11, BB19-BB20, BB24, BB26-BB27, BB37-BB39, BB44-
    BB46, BB48, BB55, BB58-BB60, BB62, BB66-BB67, BB72-BB73,
    BB77, BB80, BB82, BB86, E50, E96, F7, *F73*, *F155*, F173,
    F179
Trenton (N.J.) *Sunday Times-Advertiser*, G123
Trewin, J.C., H46
"TRICK OR TREAT," A8.1-A8.2
Trilling, Diana, G145
The Trouble Is: Stories of Social Dilemma, BB68
The Tunnel and the Light; Readings in Modern Fiction, BB58
Tunstall, Caroline Heath, G222
Tuohy, Frank, F234
Turner, Jim, G328
The Turning Point: Thirty-five Years in This Century, E81
Twelve Short Novels, BB78
Twentieth Century Literature, F18, F112, F152, F159
29 Short Stories: An Introductory Anthology, BB74
"27 LEADING WRITERS ARE OUT FOR TRUMAN," C25
"THE TWISTED TRINITY" (see also "STONE IS NOT STONE"), C13,
    C42, D11
"THE TWISTED TRINITY" (song), D8
200 Contemporary Authors, E58
200 Years of Great American Short Stories, BB75
Tyler, Betty, G329
Tynan, Kenneth, H47

Understanding Fiction, B8, E12
United States Quarterly Book List, G146
"THE UNSEEN," A8.1-A8.2, C51
"UNTITLED PIECE," A9.1-A9.2, F179
Urquhart, Fred, G223

Vaal, Hans de, J72
Valensise, Rachele, J73
Vande Kieft, Ruth M., E111
Van Druten, John, E112
Van Druten, John (subject), F80
Variety, F169, H31, H72
Vickery, John B., F235
Vickery, Olga, F236
Vidal, Gore, E113, F237, G330
Vinduet, J42
Violence in Recent Southern Fiction, E50
Virginia Quarterly Review, F98, F208, G24, G141, G331
"THE VISION SHARED," A9.1-A9.2, C31
De Vlaamse Gids, J71
Vogue, C5-C6, C8, C10, G364

"Vogue's" First Reader, BB1
Voices, C35-C36
Voss, Arthur, E114

W., C., G85
Waingrow, Hope, G340
Waldmeir, Joseph J., E60
Walker, Gerald, G332
Walker, Sue B., F238
Wallace, Henry Joseph, I29
Wall Street Journal, H18, H61
Walter, Eugene, F239
Wardle, Irving, H80-H81
Warfel, Harry R., E115
Warren, Robert Penn, B8, BB13, BB24, E12
Warren, Robert Penn (subject), E66, I28
Washington (D.C.) *Post*, F42, G29, G131, G250
Washington (D.C.) *Sunday Star*, G34, G79, G138, G191, G298
Washington (D.C.) *Times-Herald*, G102, G174
Wasserstrom, William, E116
Wasson, Ben, G224, G389
Waterlily Fire--Poems 1935-1962, E95
Waters, Ethel, E117
Waters, Ethel (subject), F49, F66, F101, F103, F198, F205, H27
Watkins, Ann, B4
Watkins, Floyd C., BB6, BB46, E118
Watson, Latimer, F240-F242, G235
Watson, Latimer (subject), F24
Watts, Richard, Jr., F243, H39-H40, H75
Weales, Gerald, E119
Webb, Constance, E120
"WE CARRIED OUR BANNERS--WE WERE PACIFISTS, TOO," A9.1-A9.2, C10
"WEDNESDAY," A8.1-A8.2, C51
Weeks, Edward, G86
Weiler, A.H., F245
Weingartner, Charles, BB71
Weiss, Renée, G147
Welch, Susan, G390
Weld, Ralph Foster, BB4
Welker, Robert L., BB37
Welles, Violet, F246
Die Welt, J34
Welty, Eudora (subject), E39, E64, E111, F11, F76, F98, F236, G139, G188, I2, I13, I21, I28
West, Mary Ellen, G148
West, Rebecca, G391
Western Mail & South Wales News (Cardiff), G173

Whaley, Russell G. , G392
"WHEN WE ARE LOST," A9.1–A9.2, C27, C36, D11
"WHEN WE ARE LOST WHAT IMAGE TELLS" (see also "WHEN WE ARE
    LOST"), D11
When Women Look at Men, BB24
White, Barbara Anne, I30
White, Terence de Vere, F247
"WHO HAS SEEN THE WIND?" (see also THE SQUARE ROOT OF
    WONDERFUL), A9.1–A9.2, B9, C40, E1, F179
Wiener, Max, G225
Wikborg, Eleanor S.M. , E121, I31
Williams, Tennessee, E122, F248
Williams, Tennessee (subject), C23, E38, E46–E47, E86, E110,
    F4, F153, F197, F200, G179, G188
Willis, Alan, G393
Willkie, Wendell (subject), F168
Wilmington (Del.) *Morning News*, G333
Wilson, Barbara L. , F249
Wilson, Edmund, G149
Wilson, W. Emerson, G333
Wilson, William E. , G47
Wilson, Zane, F250
Wilson Library Bulletin, F3
Winer, Elihu, F251
Winesburg, Ohio (Anderson), F151
Winston-Salem (N.C.) *Journal and Sentinel*, G336, G393
Winter's Tale (Dinesen), A9.1–A9.2, C18
Wisconsin Library Bulletin, G226, G238
Wisconsin Studies in Contemporary Literature, F65, F235
Witham, W. Tasker, E123
Wolfe, Ann F. , G334
Wolfe, Thomas (subject), G3, G172, I28
A Woman's Place, BB70
Women and Fiction, BB76
Women's Wear Daily, H19, H62
Wood, Audrey (subject), F85, F201
Woodall, W.C. , F252–F254
Woods, Eugene J. , BB2, E9
Woolf, Virginia (subject), G129
Worcester (Mass.) *Sunday Telegram*, G116, G182, G314
The World of the Short Story: Archetypes in Action, BB59
The World We Imagine: Selected Essays, E97
Worsley, T.C. , H48
Wright, Richard, G48
Wright, Richard (subject), E120, F70
The Writer, G394
The Writer in America, E103

"WUNDERKIND," A5.1.a-g, A5.2.b, A5.3–A5.7, A9.1–A9.2, B10,
    BB23, BB30, BB33, BB46, BB61, BB64, BB76, C3, E74, F179
Wyatt, Euphemia Van Rensselaer, H41, H76
Wykes, Alan, E124

Yale Review, G22, G68, G269
Young, B.A., H82
Young, Marguerite, G150
Young, Thomas Daniel, BB6, BB46

Die Zeit, J35
Zeitschrift für Anglistik und Amerikanistik, J69
The Zephyr Book of American Prose, D13
Zinnemann, Fred, D1
Zolotow, Sam, F256
The Zoo Story (Albee), F155
Zulch, Betty, G395
Zyskind, Irvin, G335